DIALOGUE

Also by Robert McKee

Film Works (BBC Press)

Story: Substance, Structure, Style and
the Principles of Screenwriting

DIALOGUE

The Art of Verbal Action for Page,
Stage, Screen

ROBERT McKEE

TWELVE

NEW YORK · BOSTON

Twelve

Hachette Book Group

1290 Avenue of the Americas

New York, NY 10104

twelvebooks.com

twitter.com/twelvebooks

First Edition: July 2016

Twelve is an imprint of Grand Central Publishing.

The Twelve name and logo are trademarks of Hachette Book Group, Inc.

The publisher is not responsible for websites (or their content) that are not owned by the publisher.

The Hachette Speakers Bureau provides a wide range of authors for speaking events. To find out more, go to www.hachettespeakersbureau.com or call (866) 376-6591.

Library of Congress Cataloging-in-Publication Data

Names: McKee, Robert, 1941- author.

Title: Dialogue : the art of verbal action for page, stage, screen / Robert McKee.

Description: First edition. | New York : Twelve, 2016. | Includes bibliographical references and index.

Identifiers: LCCN 2016001679| ISBN 9781455591916 (hardcover) | ISBN 9781478907435 (audio download) | ISBN 9781478938422 (audio cd) | ISBN 9781455591923 (ebook)

Subjects: LCSH: Dialogue. | Playwriting. | Fiction—Technique. | Motion picture authorship. | Television plays—Technique.

Classification: LCC PN1551 .M46 2016 | DDC 809/.926—dc23 LC record available at http://lccn.loc.gov/2016001679

Printed in the United States of America

RRD-C

10 9 8 7 6 5 4 3 2 1

For Mia
When she speaks, my heart listens.

ACKNOWLEDGMENTS

Every writer needs a circle of the trusted who will read rough drafts, take insightful notes, and never let friendship blunt criticism. I am indebted to Carol Tambor, Bassim El-Wakil, James McCabe, Joel Bernstein, Paul McKee, Mia Kim, Marcia Friedman, Steven Pressfield, and Patrick McGrath.

CONTENTS

PART TWO:
FLAWS AND FIXES

PART THREE:
CREATING DIALOGUE

PART FOUR:
DIALOGUE DESIGN

PREFACE:
IN PRAISE OF DIALOGUE

We talk.

Talk, more than any other trait, expresses our humanity. We whisper to lovers, curse enemies, argue with plumbers, praise the dog, swear on our mother's grave. Human relationships are in essence long, long talks into, around, through, and out of the entanglements that stress or bless our days. Face-to-face talk between family and friends may go on for decades, while self-to-self talk never ends: A guilt-ridden conscience scolds unconscionable desires, ignorance ridicules wisdom, hope consoles despair, impulse mocks caution, and wit laughs at it all as the inner voices of our best and worst selves argue to our last breath.

Over decades, this downpour of talk can drain words of their meaning, and when meaning erodes, our days shallow out. But what time dilutes, story condenses.

Authors concentrate meaning by first eliminating the banalities, minutia, and repetitious chatter of daily life. They then build their tellings to a crisis of complex, conflicting desires. Under pressure, words fill with connotation and nuance. What a character says in the face of conflict radiates the meanings hidden beneath her words. Expressive dialogue becomes a translucency through which readers and audiences perceive thoughts and feelings shadowed in the silence behind a character's eyes.

Fine writing turns audiences and readers into virtual psychics.

Dramatized dialogue has the power to unite two unspoken realms: the inner life of a character and the inner life of the reader/audience. Like radio transmitters, one subconscious tunes to another as our instincts sense the churnings within characters. As Kenneth Burke put it, stories equip us to live in the world, in intimacy with others, and, most importantly, in intimacy with ourselves.

Authors give us this power through a series of steps: First, they create those metaphors for human nature we call characters. Next, they dig into the characters' psychologies to unearth conscious wishes and subconscious desires, those longings that impel inner and outer selves. With this insight in hand, writers clash the characters' most compelling desires into flashpoints of conflict. Scene after scene, they interlace their characters' actions and reactions around turning points of change. In a last step, authors let their characters speak, but not in the repetitious monotones of the everyday, rather in the demi-poetry known as dialogue. Like an alchemist, a writer mixes and molds concoctions of character, conflict, and change, and then gilds them with dialogue, transforming the base metal of existence into the burnished gold of story.

Once spoken, dialogue carries us on waves of sensation and substance that reverberate through the said to the unsaid and the unsayable. **The said** are those ideas and emotions a character chooses to express to others; **the unsaid** are those thoughts and feelings a character expresses in an inner voice but only to himself; **the unsayable** are those subconscious urges and desires a character cannot express in words, even to himself, because they are mute and beyond awareness.

No matter how lavish a play's production, how vivid a novel's descriptions, how lush a film's photography, character talk shapes the deepest complexities, ironies, and innerness of story. Without expressive dialogue, events lack depth, characters lose dimension, and story flattens. More than any other technique of characterization (gender, age, dress, class, casting), dialogue has the power to pull a story up through life's multilayered strata, thus lifting a merely complicated telling into the full array of complexity.

Do you, like me, memorize favorite lines? I think we learn dialogue passages by heart because reciting them again and again not only re-inspires the vivid word-pictures they paint, but in the echoes of the character's thoughts we hear our own:

> Tomorrow and tomorrow and tomorrow,
> Creeps in this petty pace from day to day,
> To the last syllable of recorded time,
> And all our yesterdays have lighted fools
> The way to dusty death.
>
> —Macbeth in *The Tragedy of Macbeth*

> Of all the gin joints in all the towns in all the world she walks into mine.
>
> —Rick in CASABLANCA

> Towards thee I roll, thou all-destroying but unconquering whale; to the last I grapple with thee; from hell's heart I stab at thee; for hate's sake I spit my last breath at thee.
>
> —Ahab in *Moby Dick*

> Not that there's anything wrong with that.
>
> —Jerry in SEINFELD

Like these four characters, each of us has suffered the scald of irony, that flash of insight into what the world has done to us, or worst yet, what we have done to ourselves, that double-edged moment when life's joke is on us and we don't know whether to grin or groan. But without writers to marinate these ironies in words, how could we savor their delicious distaste? Without the mnemonics of dialogue, how could we hold these paradoxes in memory?

I love the art of dialogue in all its variety. Moved by that amity, I have written *Dialogue: The Art of Verbal Action on Page, Stage, Screen* to explore the crowning act of story-making: giving voice to your characters.

INTRODUCTION

Part One: The Art of Dialogue radically expands the definition of dialogue and multiplies its usage. Chapters Two through Five look at the functions, contents, forms, and techniques of character talk across the four major storytelling media.

Part Two: Flaws and Fixes pinpoints maladies from incredibility and clichés to writing on-the-nose and repetitiousness, seeks their causes, then prescribes cures. To illustrate the varied techniques of crafting dialogue, I cite examples from novels, plays, films, and television.

Part Three: Creating Dialogue examines the writer's final step—finding the words that create the text. When we say an author has an "ear for dialogue," we mean he writes character-specific talk. Each of his characters speaks with a syntax, rhythm, tonality, and, most importantly, word choices that no one but that character would use. Ideally, every character is a walking dictionary of his or her unique collection of words. Dialogue originality, therefore, begins with vocabulary.

To illustrate the power of character-specific dialogue, we will look at scenes from Shakespeare's play *The Tragedy of Julius Caesar*, Elmore Leonard's novel *Out of Sight*, Tina Fey's television series 30 ROCK, and Alexander Payne and Jim Taylor's film SIDEWAYS.

Part Four: Dialogue Design opens with a study of the components of story and scene design. Chapter Twelve shows how these forms determine what characters say. Six case studies follow using scenes of balanced conflict from the cable series THE SOPRANOS, comic conflict from the network series FRASIER, asymmetric conflict from the play *A Raisin in the Sun*, indirect conflict from the novel *The Great Gatsby*, reflexive conflict from the novels *Fräulein Else* and *The Museum of Innocence*, and implied conflict from the film LOST IN TRANSLATION.

In these scansions, we look at the two primary principles of effective dialogue: First, each exchange of dialogue creates an action/reaction that progresses the scene. Second, although these actions find expression in the outer behavior of talk, the wellspring of character action flows invisibly from the subtext.

Like a GPS for writers, *Dialogue: The Art of Verbal Action* offers guidance to the aspirant and redirection to the perplexed. If you recently ventured into this art and find yourself backed into a creative cul-de-sac, *Dialogue* will put you on the path to excellence; if you write for a living but have lost your bearings, this book will guide you home.

DIALOGUE

PART I

THE ART OF DIALOGUE

1

THE FULL DEFINITION
OF DIALOGUE

Dialogue: Any words said by any character to anyone.

Tradition defines dialogue as talk between characters. I believe, however, that an all-encompassing, in-depth study of dialogue begins by stepping back to the widest possible view of storytelling. From that angle, the first thing I notice is that character talk runs along three distinctly different tracks: said to others, said to oneself, and said to the reader or audience.

I place these three modes of talk under the term "dialogue" for two reasons: First, no matter when, where, and to whom a character speaks, the writer must personalize the role with a unique, character-specific voice worded in the text. Second, whether mental or vocal, whether thought inside the mind or said out into the world, all speech is an outward execution of an inner action. All talk responds to a need, engages a purpose, and performs an action. No matter how seemingly vague and airy a speech may be, no character ever talks to anyone, even to himself, for no reason, to do nothing. Therefore, beneath every line of character talk, the writer must create a desire, intent, and action. That action then becomes the verbal tactic we call dialogue.

Let's survey the three tracks of dialogue:

One, talk to others. The accurate term for two-way talk is **duo-logue**. Three characters in conversation would generate a **trialogue**. A family of a dozen souls gathered for Thanksgiving Day dinner might be called a multilogue, if such a term existed.

Two, talk within oneself. Screenwriters seldom ask characters to talk to themselves; playwrights, on the other hand, often do. As for prose writers, mental talk is the stuff and substance of their art. Prose has the power to invade a character's mind and project inner conflict across the landscape of thought. Whenever an author tells his story in a first-person or second-person voice, that voice belongs to a character. Prose, therefore, often fills with reflexive, self-to-self dialogue that the reader, as it were, overhears.

Three, talk to readers and audiences. In the theatre, the conventions of soliloquy and aside allow characters to turn directly to the audience and talk in confidence. In television and film, this convention usually puts the character offscreen to talk voice-over, but occasionally calls for the character to turn to the camera in direct address. In prose, this is the essence of first-person prose—the character tells his tale to the reader.

The etymology of the word "dialogue" traces back to two Greek terms: *dia-*, meaning "through," and *legein*, referring to "speech." These two terms translated directly into English become the compound noun "through-speech"—an action taken through words as opposed to deeds. Every line a character speaks, whether spoken aloud to others or silently in the mind, is, in J. L. Austin's term, a performative: words that perform a task.[1]

To say something is to do something, and for that reason, I have expanded my redefinition of dialogue to name any and all words said by a character to herself, to others, or to the reader/audience as an action taken to satisfy a need or desire. In all three cases, when a character speaks, she acts verbally as opposed to physically, and each of her through-speech actions moves the scene she's in from one beat to the next, while at the same time, it dynamically propels her closer to (positive) or further from (negative) the satisfaction of her core desire. Dialogue-as-action is the foundation principle of this book.

Dialogue carries out its actions in one of two ways: dramatized or narratized.

DRAMATIZED DIALOGUE

Dramatized means acted out in scenes. Whether the tone is comic or tragic, dramatized dialogue sends lines back and forth between characters in conflict. Each line contains an action with a specific intention and causes a reaction somewhere within the scene.

This is true even in one-character scenes. When someone says, "I'm mad at myself," who is mad at whom? Just as you see your image in a mirror, you can see yourself in your imagination. To argue within yourself, your mind creates a second self and talks to it as if it were another person. A character's inner dialogue becomes a dynamically dramatized scene between two conflicted selves of the same person, one of which may or may not win the argument. Therefore, strictly defined, all monologues are in fact dialogues. Whenever a character talks, she is always talking to someone, even if it's her other side.

NARRATIZED DIALOGUE

Narratized means spoken outside the scene. In these cases, the so-called fourth wall of realism vanishes, and a character steps out of the story's dramatizations. Once again, strictly speaking, narratized speeches are not monologues but dialogues in which the character takes vocal action to talk directly to the reader, audience, or self.

In terms of desire, a first-person narrator in prose or a character narrating from the stage or screen may simply want to bring the reader/audience up to date on past events and arouse their curiosity about future events. She may use narratized dialogue to act out this straightforward ambition and no more.

In more complex situations, however, she might, for example, use words to arm-twist the reader/audience into forgiving her past misdeeds while prejudicing them to see her enemies from her biased point of view. From story to story, the possible desires that might move a character to action and the tactics she uses while talking to the reader/audience seem unlimited.

The same applies to a character who turns inside her mind to talk to herself. She may be pursuing any purpose: rerunning a memory for pleasure, puzzling out whether or not she can trust her lover's love, building her hopes by fantasizing about life to come, and so on, as her thoughts roam the past, present, and possible futures, real and imagined.

To demonstrate how the same content could be expressed in the three different modes of dialogue, I'll work with a passage from the novel *Doctor Glas*, written in 1905 by the Swedish author Hjalmar Söderberg.

The book takes the form of a diary kept by the eponymous protagonist. A real-life diary records the closet conversations of a diarist talking to himself; a fictional diary, therefore, must be written so the reader feels that he somehow overhears these secret inner dialogues.

In Söderberg's novel, Dr. Glas wants to save one of his patients (a woman he secretly loves) from her sexually abusive husband. Day after day his mind wages moral arguments for and against killing the man; in nightmare after nightmare he commits the murder. (Later in the book he in fact poisons the husband.) In an entry dated August 7, a nightmare wakes him in a cold sweat. Listen in on his rambling narratized dialogue as Glas tries to convince himself that his horrid dream is not a prophecy:

"Dreams run like streams." Hoary proverbial wisdom, I know you well. And in reality most of what one dreams is not worth a second thought—loose fragments of experience, often the silliest and most indifferent fragments of those things consciousness has judged unworthy of preservation but which, even so, go on living a shadow life of their own in the attics and box-rooms of the mind. But there are other dreams. As a lad I remember sitting a whole afternoon pondering a geometrical problem, and in the end having to go to bed with it still unresolved: asleep, my brain went on working of its own accord and a dream gave me the solution. And it was correct. Dreams there are, too, like bubbles from the depths. And now I come to think of it more clearly—many a time has a dream taught me something about myself, often revealed to me wishes I did not wish to wish, desires of which I did not wish to take daylight cognizance. These wishes, these dreams, I've afterward weighed and tested in bright sunlight. But rarely have they stood up to daylight, and more often than not I've flung them back into the foul depths where they belong. In the night they might assail me anew, but I recognized them and, even in dreams, laughed them to scorn, until they relinquished all claim to arise and live in reality and the light of day.[2]

In the first line, Glas speaks to a proverb floating in his mind as if the idea had a mind of its own. Then he turns to argue with his silent, dark immoral side, a self that roils with murderous desire. By the last sentence, Glas thinks his better self has won the argument...at least for the moment. Notice how the sentences roll out in the lengthy, cumulative shapes of rumination.

Now suppose Söderberg had written this passage as narratized dialogue said by Dr. Glas directly to the reader. To write in a voice Glas might use when talking to another person, Söderberg might give Glas that authoritative voice that doctors often use when prescribing to a patient. The sentences might shorten and turn into imperatives. Do's, don'ts, and buts might be added to give ideas a sharp twist:

"Dreams run like streams." A proverb I know you've heard. Don't believe it. Most of what we dream isn't worth a second thought. These fragments of experience are the silly, indifferent things our consciousness judges unworthy. Even so, in the attic of your mind they go on living a shadow life. That's unhealthy. But some dreams are useful. When I was a boy, I sat a whole afternoon pondering a geometrical problem. I went to bed with it unresolved. But in sleep, my brain went on working and a dream gave me the solution. Then there are dangerous dreams that rise like bubbles from the depths. If you dare think about them, they seem to teach you something about yourself—a wish you didn't think you wished, a desire you didn't dare say out loud. Don't believe them. When weighed and tested, these dreams do not stand up to bright daylight. So do what a healthy person would do. Fling them back into the foul depths where they belong. If at night they assail you anew, laugh at them until they relinquish all claim on your reality.

As a third choice, Söderberg, who also wrote plays, may have chosen to dramatize these ideas onstage. He could have split the doctor into two characters: Glas and Markel. In the novel, the journalist Markel is Glas's best friend. In a play, Markel might personify the morally righteous side of Glas, while Glas could play the tormented side that's tempted toward murder.

In the subtext of the scene below, Glas seeks Markel's help to cure his troubling dreams. Sensing this, Markel makes positive moral statements in answer to the doctor's questions. The text retains the novel's imagery (the theatre in fact encourages figurative language), but it changes line design from cumulative to periodic to aid the actors' cueing. (See Chapter Five for studies in line design.)

```
Glas and Markel sit in a café.
As dusk turns to night, they sip
after-dinner brandies.

GLAS: Do you know the proverb "Dreams
run like streams"?

MARKEL: Yes, my grandmother always
said that, but in reality, most
```

dreams are just fragments of the day,
not worth keeping.

GLAS: Worthless as they are, they
live shadow lives in the attic of the
mind.

MARKEL: In your mind, Doctor, not
mine.

GLAS: But don't you think dreams give
us insights?

MARKEL: At times. When I was a lad,
I spent a whole afternoon pondering a geometrical problem and went
to bed with it unsolved. But my brain
went on working and a dream gave me a
solution. Next morning I checked and
damned if it wasn't correct.

GLAS: No, I mean something hidden,
insights into oneself, bubbles of
truth from the depths, those dark
desires one wouldn't dare admit over
breakfast.

MARKEL: If I ever had such, and I'm
not saying I ever have, I'd fling them
back into the foul depths where they
belong.

GLAS: And what if these desires came
back, night after night?

MARKEL: Then I'd dream a dream of
ridicule and laugh them out of my
thoughts.

These three versions contain the same essential content, but when what's said changes direction from told to self, to told to the reader, to told to another character, language radically changes shape, diction, tonality, and texture. The three fundamental dialogue modes require three sharply contrasted writing styles.

DIALOGUE AND THE MAJOR MEDIA

All dialogue, dramatized and narratized, performs in the grand symphony of story, but from stage to screen to page, its instruments and arrangements vary considerably. For that reason, a writer's choice of medium greatly influences the composition of dialogue—its quantities and qualities.

The theatre, for example, is primarily an auditory medium. It prompts audience members to listen more intently than they watch. As a result, the stage favors voice over image.

Cinema reverses that. Film is primarily a visual medium. It prompts the audience to watch more intently than it listens. For that reason, screenplays favor image over voice.

The aesthetics of television float between the theatre and cinema. Teleplays tend to balance voice and image, inviting us to look and listen more or less equally.

Prose is a mental medium. Whereas stories performed onstage and onscreen strike the audience's ears and eyes directly, literature takes an indirect path through the reader's mind. The reader must first interpret the language, then imagine the sights and sounds it describes (every reader's imaginings are her own), and, finally, allow herself to react to what she envisions. What's more, because literary characters are actorless, their author is free to use as much or as little dialogue, as dramatized or narratized, as he sees fit.

So let's look at how a story's medium shapes its dialogue.

DIALOGUE ONSTAGE

Dramatized Dialogue

The scene is the basic unit of story structure in all four major story media. In the theatre, the majority of talk plays out as dramatized dialogue, performed by characters in scenes with other characters.

The one-character play is no exception. When a lone character paces the stage, he creates scenes of inner dramatized dialogue by splitting himself in two, as it were, and pitting his warring selves against each other. If the character sits back to air his thoughts, these memories, fantasies, and philosophies play best as inner actions, motivated by a desire and taken with a purpose. No matter how passive and aimless such musings may seem on the surface, they are in fact dramatized dialogue, said within a scene by a conflicted character struggling within himself to understand himself or forget the past or sell himself on a lie—or any other inner action a playwright might invent. Samuel Beckett's *Krapp's Last Tape* stands as a brilliant example of dramatized dialogue in the one-character play.

Narratized Dialogue

In keeping with the theatre's ancient conventions, a playwright may employ narratized dialogue by stepping his character out of the flux of scenes and turning him to the audience to speak in soliloquy, or if very brief, in an aside.[3] What's revealed is often a confession, a secret, or a revelation of what a character genuinely thinks, feels, or wants to do but could never say aloud to another character. For example, the painful contritions of Tom Wingfield in Tennessee Williams's *The Glass Menagerie*.

In one-person performances like *The Year of Magical Thinking*, *Mark Twain Tonight*, and *I Am My Own Wife*, the soliloquy becomes an entire play. These works often stage adaptations of biographies or autobiographies, and so the actor plays a well-known contemporary

(Joan Didion) or a personage from the past (Mark Twain). In the course of the evening, the actor may use all three forms of character talk. For the most part, however, he will confess his story to the audience in narratized dialogue. Now and then, he might impersonate other characters and act out scenes from the past in dramatized dialogue.

Modern stand-up comedy came of age when comics moved from joke telling to narratized dialogue. A stand-up comedian must either invent a character to play (Stephen Colbert) or perform a selected, characterized version of himself (Louis C.K.) for this reason: No one can step onstage as the exact same self that got out of bed that morning. It takes a persona to perform.

Onstage, the line between dramatized and narratized dialogue can shift, depending on the actor's interpretation. When Hamlet, for example, questions his continued existence, does he aim the phrase "To be or not to be" at the audience or at himself? It's the actor's choice.

Narration

On those occasions when a play's story encompasses a large cast over decades of time, a playwright may stand a narrator at the side of the stage. These non-characters perform any number of tasks: They relate historical exposition, introduce characters, or counterpoint the action with ideas or interpretations that could not be directly dramatized in scenes.

Examples: In Donald Hall's *An Evening's Frost* (an enactment of the life of poet Robert Frost) and Erwin Piscator's epic theatre adaptation of Tolstoy's *War and Peace*, onstage narrators bring a godlike knowledge of history and personae to the audience, but they have no personal desires. They stand above the drama, facilitating the storytelling. By contrast, in *Our Town*, playwright Thornton Wilder's narrator, known as the Stage Manager, mixes functions. He narrates exposition, guides the audience's attitudes, but from time to time, he steps into dramatized scenes to play some small parts.

DIALOGUE ONSCREEN

Dramatized Dialogue

Like the theatre, the majority of onscreen talk is dramatized dialogue, spoken in-character on-camera in live action or voiced off-camera in animation.

Narratized Dialogue

Screen characters narratize dialogue in one of two modes: either off-camera voice-over over the images, or direct to camera in cinematic soliloquy.

Off-camera, self-narrating characters have been a staple since movies began to talk. Sometimes they speak in calm, logical, and reliable voices (HOW I MET YOUR MOTHER); sometimes they rant in hysterical, irrational, and unreliable outbursts (PI). Sometimes they make sense out of bewildering events (MEMENTO); sometimes they counterpoint events (THE BIG LEBOWSKI). Some characters expose painfully honest thoughts in dramatized dialogues with their inner selves (ADAPTATION); some hide their secret self behind excuses and rationalizations (A CLOCKWORK ORANGE); some comment on their predicaments with wit (MY NAME IS EARL).

When characters look down the camera lens and whisper something secret and personal, it's usually a self-serving tactic to win us to their side (HOUSE OF CARDS). Since Bob Hope, comedians have tossed lines and looks to camera to punch jokes (IT'S GARRY SHANDLING'S SHOW). And the greatest of all, Woody Allen, uses narratized dialogue both off-camera and to-camera to charm our empathy and sting gags (ANNIE HALL).

In Ingmar Bergman's WINTER LIGHT, a woman (played by Ingrid Thulin) sends her ex-lover (Gunnar Bjornstrand) a letter describing his cowardly failure to love her. As he picks it up to read, Bergman cuts to her face in close-up as she speaks the letter, eyes direct to camera, for six uninterrupted minutes. Bergman's subjective camera transports us into the ex-lover's imagination, so that as he envisions her speaking, we identify with him and his suffering, while Ingrid Thulin's work to camera ignites their intimacy.

Narration

In films such as BARRY LYNDON, AMÉLIE, and Y TU MAMÁ TAMBIÉN, non-character, offscreen narrators with resonant, articulate voices (Sir Michael Hordern, André Dussollier, Daniel Giménez Cacho, respectively) link episodes, fill in exposition, and counterpoint the telling.

Counterpoint narration imports ideas and insights from outside the story's world to add dimension and depth to the telling. A narrator, for example, might lade comedy with drama or leaven drama with comedy; he might punctuate delusion with reality or reality with fantasy; his comments might play the political world off against the private realm or the reverse. As often as not, the ironic observations of this non-character rescues a film from sentimentality by undercutting the emotional indulgences of its characters. For example, TOM JONES.

DIALOGUE ON PAGE

Stories performed onstage and onscreen move through the physical media of air and light, and then enter the mind through the senses of sound and sight. Stories performed in prose move through the mental medium of language to find life in the reader's imagination. Because the imagination is far more complex, multifaceted, and multileveled than the senses, literature offers a greater variety and flexibility of dialogue techniques than the theatre, television, or cinema.

Stories in prose can be told from either inside the story's world by a character or from outside the story's world by a narrator. This simple division, however, becomes further complicated by literature's three point-of-view choices: **first**, **second**, and **third person**.

First person. In a first-person telling, a character who refers to herself with the pronouns "I" or "me" speaks to the reader about events as she remembers them. She may describe these events or present them dramatically as scenes in which she and other characters talk directly among themselves. She may also turn inward and talk to herself. If so, the reader comes along with her to overhear, as it were, her self-to-self conversations.

Because the first-person narrator is a character involved in the story, she is an imperfect witness to the life around her, unable to comprehend events in their entirety, often less than objective as she pursues her unspoken or subconscious desires. For this reason, the reliability of first-person narrators spans a wide spectrum from trustworthy to deceitful.

What's more, the first-person narrator is often more focused on herself than others, so her inner actions, self-observations, and ruminations tend to fill the page. The inner life of other characters, therefore, can only be known by the first-person narrator's speculations or implications the reader draws from between the lines.

An omniscient first-person narrator with preternatural insight into the thoughts and feelings of other characters is a rare device. This conceit needs an exceptional explanation. In *The Lovely Bones* by Alice Sebold, for example, the first-person narrator is the spirit of a murdered girl who looks down from her otherworldly vantage and sees into the hearts of her family as they struggle with her disappearance.

A first-person narrator could be the story's protagonist (Brother William of Baskerville in *The Name of the Rose* by Umberto Eco), a confidant to the protagonist (Dr. Watson to Sherlock Holmes), a group speaking in the first person plural (*The Virgin Suicides* by Jeffrey Eugenides), or a distant observer (Joseph Conrad's unnamed narrator in *Heart of Darkness*).

Third person. In a third-person telling, a narrating intelligence guides the reader through the story's events. This intelligence often has deep insight into the thoughts and feelings of all characters. Even though this awareness is not a character, it may have strong opinions, moral and otherwise, about the fictional world and its society. Yet, by convention, it maintains a distance by referring to the cast with the pronouns "her," "he," and "they."

Because this third-person intelligence is not a character, its narration is not dialogue. Nor is it the transcribed voice of the writer. No one, not even the most eloquent talk show guest on NPR, goes through life talking in a third-person voice.

This non-character may be more or less compassionate than its author, more or less political, more or less observant, more or less moral. Whatever the case, in the same fashion the prose writer creates a voice for each of her characters, she invents a linguistic manner for narration, knowing that in the same way that audiences put themselves in the hands of onstage and offscreen narrators, the reader accepts narration as a storytelling convention, characterless and dialogueless.

The language used by this intelligence may be profoundly expressive, and the reader may listen to it in her imagination as if it were someone's voice, but it is not. Only characters have true voices. What we call a third-person narrator's "voice" is simply the author's literary style. That is why the reader feels neither empathy for this voice nor curiosity about the fate of the consciousness behind it.

The reader knows via conventions older than Homer that the author invented this non-character for the sole purpose of putting the telling into language that the reader can follow. If, on the other hand, this intelligence should suddenly refer to itself as "I," a non-character would become a character, and the telling would shift into first person.

The breadth of knowledge in third-person narrators ranges from omniscient to limited; their judgment from morally neutral to morally critical; their presence in the mind of the reader from overt to covert; their reliability from truthful to (in very rare cases) deceitful. As the prose writer plays with these dimensions, he can shade his third-person narrators with degrees of objectivity/subjectivity, ranging from ironically detached to deeply invested.

The **third-person objective** (a.k.a. covert or dramatic) mode shows far more than it tells. It observes but never interprets. This awareness sits back like a patron in the theatre of life, never entering the inner realms, never describing the thoughts and feelings of any character. Famous examples: Ernest Hemingway's short stories such as "Hills Like White Elephants" and "The Snows of Kilimanjaro." In the mid-twentieth century, the French nouveau roman took this technique to its absolute limit in works such as *Jealousy* by Alain Robbe-Grillet.

The **third-person subjective** mode penetrates the inner life and may switch between the thoughts and feelings of more than one character. More often than not, however, the author restricts access to the inner life of the story's protagonist only. This mode may feel something like first person but keeps its distance by using the impersonal pronouns "he" and "she" rather than "I."

In George R. R. Martin's A Song of Ice and Fire series, for example, each chapter takes up a separate storyline, each restricted to the point of view of that tale's protagonist.

This technique of subjective exploration, in both its limited and omniscient variants, became the most popular narrative perspective in twentieth-century prose. A subjective narrator may come with a touch of personality and overt opinions (see the passage from *The Corrections* quoted below), but no matter how playful or sarcastic, how familiar or personal a third-person narrator may be, this voice is the author's creature, a special dimension of himself that he invents to convey his story from outside its events.

An author may even choose to let his narrator break the bond of trust that millennia of poetry and prose has built between writers and their readers. In rare tellings, writers have given this voice character-like traits of confusion or duplicity. But, once again, no matter how manipulative, unreliable, or uncertain a third-person narrator may become, its language is not dialogue. This is an author speaking from behind a mask. Third-person narration requires unique strategies and techniques that are outside the focus of this book.

Second person. The second-person mode is a disguise for either the first person or third person. In this mode, the storytelling voice eliminates the pronouns "I/me" of first person and the "she/he/they" of third person to address someone as "you." This "you" could be the protagonist himself. When, for example, a person berates himself with the thought "you idiot," one aspect of the self criticizes another aspect. A second-person voice, therefore, could be analyzing or encouraging or reminiscing with himself (*Second Thoughts* by Michel Butor). Or "you" could be a silent, unnamed other character, thus turning the telling into a one-sided dramatized dialogue (*A Song of Stone* by Iain Banks). Or in the third possibility, "you" could be the reader. In Jay McInerney's novel *Bright Lights, Big City*, an ineffable awareness takes the reader through the story in the present tense until the reader feels as if he's acting out the events himself:

> You're not sure exactly where you are going. You don't feel you have the strength to walk home. You walk faster. If the sunlight catches you on the streets, you will undergo some terrible chemical change.
>
> After a few minutes you notice the blood on your fingers. You hold your hand up to your face. There is blood on your shirt, too. You find a Kleenex in your jacket pocket and hold it up to your nose. You advance with your head tilted back against your shoulders.[4]

If this passage were rewritten into the past tense with "you" switched to "I," it would become a conventional first-person novel; if "you" were changed to "he," it would become a conventional third-person telling. The second-person present tense makes this tale ambiguously both, and moves through a filmic atmosphere akin to subjective camera.

To help clarify this complexity, let's compare the conventions of prose to their equivalent onstage and onscreen.

Dramatized Dialogue

Dramatized scenes in prose can be written from any of the three points of view—first, second, or third person. In all three voices, scenes take place in their temporal and spatial settings, the characters and their behaviors are described, and their talk is quoted verbatim.

Conceivably, such scenes could be lifted off the page and transported, more or less intact, to a theatre or sound stage to be performed by actors.

Narratized Dialogue

Everything said outside of dramatized scenes in a first- or second-person voice is, by my definition, narratized dialogue. These passages are spoken in-character with a story-driven purpose and affect the reader much like an onstage soliloquy or a direct-to-camera address. When narratized dialogue modulates into stream of consciousness (see below), the pages read like an inner monologue in a play or a protagonist's voice-over in films like MEMENTO and PI. In all instances, the author writes in-character.

INDIRECT DIALOGUE

All four major media offer the writer the choice to either recall scenes from the past and describe them, or to put them in front of the reader/audience and act them out. If he chooses description, what could have been a scene of dramatized dialogue turns into **indirect dialogue**.

Should the writer use a character to describe a prior scene, then her immediate dialogue paraphrases another character's previous dialogue. For example, in this passage from Bruce Norris's play *Clybourne Park*, Bev complains about her husband.

BEV

—the way he sits up all night long.
Last night he was just sitting
there at three o'clock in the morning and I say to him, "Say, don't you
feel sleepy? Do you want to take a
Sominex, or play some cards maybe?"
and he says, "I don't see the point of

> it," as if there has to be some grand
> justification for every single thing
> that a person does.[5]

The audience can only guess at the accuracy of her paraphrases, but in this context, exactly what was said is not important. Norris uses indirect dialogue so that the audience hears what is important: Bev's interpretation of her husband's behavior in her own words.

When third-person narration paraphrases dialogue, once again the reader must interpret how it sounded when spoken. This scene, for example, between a husband and wife from Jonathan Franzen's novel *The Corrections*:

> Made happy by pregnancy, she got sloppy and talked about the wrong thing to Alfred. Not, needless to say, about sex or fulfillment or fairness. But there were other topics scarcely less forbidden, and Enid in her giddiness one morning overstepped. She suggested he buy shares in a certain stock. Alfred said the stock market was a lot of dangerous nonsense best left to wealthy men and idle speculators. Enid suggested he nonetheless buy shares of a certain stock. Alfred said he remembered Black Tuesday as if it were yesterday. Enid suggested he nonetheless buy shares of a certain stock. Alfred said it would be highly improper to buy that stock. Enid suggested he nonetheless buy it. Alfred said they had no money to spare and now a third child coming. Enid suggested that the money could be borrowed. Alfred said no. He said no in a much louder voice and stood up from the breakfast table. He said no so loudly that a decorative copper-plate bowl on the kitchen wall briefly hummed, and without kissing her goodbye he left the house for eleven days and ten nights.[6]

By repeating the word "suggested" five times, Franzen pushes Enid's nagging and Alfred's rage to the edge of farce. The phrase "eleven days and ten nights" presages their holiday cruise, and the image of a bowl humming on the wall pushes the scene beyond farce to absurdity.

Because indirect dialogue invites the reader to imagine the scene, the heated, possibly melodramatic language of direct dialogue becomes a more personalized, believable version invented by the reader.

THE THREE FUNCTIONS OF DIALOGUE

Dialogue, dramatized and narratized, performs three essential functions: exposition, characterization, action.

EXPOSITION

Exposition is a term of art that names the fictional facts of setting, history, and character that readers and audiences need to absorb at some point so they can follow the story and involve themselves in its outcome. A writer can embed exposition in the telling in only one of two ways: description or dialogue.

Onstage and onscreen, directors and their designers interpret the writer's descriptions into every expressive element that isn't dialogue: settings, costumes, lighting, props, sound effects, and the like. Comic book artists and graphic novelists illustrate their stories as they tell them. Prose authors compose literary descriptions that project word-images into the reader's imagination.

Dialogue can do the same work. For example, picture this: a gilt-gleaming, marbled lobby with business-dressed, fair-haired visitors signing in at a security desk manned by uniformed guards, while in the background busy elevators open and close. The moment we glimpse this image, it instantly denotes a number of expositional facts: Place—an office building in a major city somewhere in the Northern Hemisphere. Time—a weekday between eight a.m. and six p.m. Society—the professional class of Western culture that hires armed guards to protect the executives on the upper floors from the poverty class on the streets. What's more, the subtext of this image connotes a commercial, competitive, white-male-dominated world, questing for wealth and power, always on the verge of corruption.

Now picture a high-energy investment broker lunching with a potential client. Listen for the implications beneath his glib double entendre: "Come on up, meet my young hawks. We roost on the seventy-seventh floor and prey on Wall Street." In fewer graphemes than a tweet, word-pictures can express more dimensions than a camera can see.

Virtually anything expressed in images or explained in narration can be implied in dialogue. Therefore, the first function of dialogue is to pass exposition to the eavesdropping reader/audience. The following precepts guide this difficult work:

Pacing and Timing

Pacing means the rate or frequency with which exposition is spliced into the telling. Timing means choosing the precise scene and the exact line within that scene to reveal a specific fact.

The risks governing the pacing and timing of exposition are these: Give the story-goer too little exposition and he will disengage in confusion. On the other hand, big helpings of static exposition choke interest: The reader puts down the book; audiences shift in their seats, wishing they had bought more popcorn. Therefore, you must pace and time the placement of exposition with care and skill.

To keep interest moving, fine writers parse exposition out, detail by detail, passing on only what the audience member or reader needs to know when she absolutely needs and wants to know it. Not a moment before. They give only the minimal exposition necessary to maintain the flow of curiosity and empathy.

If you give the modern, story-savvy reader/audience too much exposition too soon, not only does their stride shuffle to a crawl, but they also foresee your turning points, including your ending, long before they happen. Annoyed and disappointed, they sit in front of your work thinking, "I saw it coming." As the nineteenth-century novelist Charles Reade advised: "Make 'em laugh, make 'em cry, make 'em wait."

Lastly, not all expositional facts are of equal value to the telling, and therefore do not deserve equal emphasis. In a separate file, list every fact in your story, and then rank them in order of importance to the reader/audience. As you rewrite and polish your work, you may realize that certain facts need to be stressed and repeated in more than one scene to guarantee that the reader/audience remembers them at a critical future turning point. Other less important facts need only a single hint or gesture.

Showing versus Telling

The axiom "Show, don't tell" warns against dialogue that substitutes passive explanations for dynamic dramatization. "To show" means to present a scene in an authentic setting, populated with believable characters, struggling toward their desires, taking true-to-the-moment actions while speaking plausible dialogue. "To tell" means to force characters to halt their pursuits and talk instead and at length about their life histories or their thoughts and feelings, or their loves and hates, past and present, for no reason intrinsic to the scene or its characters. Stories are metaphors for life, not theses on psychology, environmental crises, social injustice, or any cause extraneous to the characters' lives.

Too often, recitations of this kind simply serve the writer's extrinsic need to opine into the ear of the captive reader/audience, rather than a character's intrinsic need to take action. What's worse, telling erases subtext. As a character copes with antagonisms and pursues desires, her vocal reactions and tactics invite readers and audiences to seek her unspoken thoughts and feelings. But when a writer forces unmotivated exposition into a character's mouth, these opaque lines block the story-goer's access to the speaker's inner life. And as the character flattens into a spokesperson for its author's ideas, interest fades.

Finally, showing speeds involvement and pace; telling discourages curiosity and halts pace. Showing treats readers and audiences like adults, inviting them into the story, encouraging them to open their emotions to the writer's vision, to look into the heart of things and then forward to future events. Telling treats them like a child who a parent sits on a knee to explain the obvious.

This speech, for example, is telling: As Harry and Charlie unlock the door to their dry-cleaning business, Charlie says:

> CHARLIE
> Oh, Harry, how long have we known
> each other now? What, twenty years,
> maybe even more, ever since we were
> in school together. It's been a long
> time, hasn't it, old friend? Well, how
> are you this fine morning?

That dialogue has no purpose except to tell the reader/audience that Charlie and Harry have been friends for over twenty years, went to school together, and the day is just beginning.

This speech, on the other hand, shows:

As Charlie unlocks the door to the dry cleaners, an unshaven Harry, dressed in a T-shirt, leans against the jamb, toking on a joint and giggling uncontrollably. Charlie looks over at him and shakes his head.

> CHARLIE
> Harry, when in hell are you going to
> grow up? Look at you and your stu-
> pid tie-dyed shirts. You're the same
> immature ass you were twenty years
> ago in school and you haven't changed
> since. Sober up, Harry, and smell the
> shit you're in.

The reader's imagination or the audience's eye glances to Harry to capture his reaction to that insult, and invisibly, as it were, they happened to have learned "twenty years" and "school."

At some point, every vital fictional fact must find its way into the story, timed to arrive at the most effective moment, loaded to deliver a critical insight. These details, and the perceptions they inspire, must pass into the reader/audience's awareness without distracting them from the flow of events. Somehow the writer must send the reader/audience's attention in one direction while he smuggles a fact in from another.

This sleight of hand calls upon one of two techniques or both: **Narrative drive** and **exposition as ammunition**. The former skill draws on intellectual curiosity, the latter emotional empathy.

Narrative Drive

Narrative drive is a side effect of the mind's engagement with story. Change and revelations incite the story-goer to wonder, "What's going to happen next? What's going to happen after that? How will this turn out?" As pieces of exposition slip out of dialogue and into the background awareness of the reader or audience member, her curiosity reaches ahead with both hands to grab fistfuls of the future to pull her through the telling. She learns what she needs to know when she needs to know it, but she's never consciously aware of being told anything, because what she learns compels her to look ahead.

Witness, for example, the power of exposition to compel narrative drive in a novel titled after a piece of exposition: *Catch-22*. The author, Joseph Heller, invented the term to name bureaucratic traps that cage their victims in a vicious circle of logic.

The story takes place on an air force base in the Mediterranean during World War II. In Chapter Five, Captain John Yossarian, the novel's protagonist, asks Dr. Dan Daneeka, the base physician, about a pilot named Orr:

"Is Orr crazy?"

"He sure is," Doc Daneeka said.

"Can you ground him?"

"I sure can. But first he has to ask me to. That's part of the rule."

"Then why doesn't he ask you to?"

"Because he's crazy," Doc Daneeka said. "He has to be crazy to keep flying combat missions after all the close calls he's had. Sure, I can ground Orr. But first he has to ask me to."

"That's all he has to do to be grounded?"

"That's all. Let him ask me."

"And then you can ground him?" Yossarian asked.

"No. Then I can't ground him."

"You mean there's a catch?"

"Sure there's a catch," Doc Daneeka replied. "Catch-22. Anyone who wants to get out of combat duty isn't really crazy."

There was only one catch and that was Catch-22, which specified that a concern for one's own safety in the face of dangers that were real and immediate was the process of a rational mind. Orr was crazy and could be grounded. All he had to do was ask; and as soon as he did, he would no longer be crazy and would have to fly more missions. Orr would be crazy to fly more missions and sane if he didn't, but if he was sane he had to fly them. If he flew them he was crazy and didn't have to; but if he didn't want to he was sane and had to. Yossarian was moved very deeply by the absolute simplicity of this clause of Catch-22 and let out a respectful whistle.

"That's some catch, that Catch-22," he observed.

"It's the best there is," Doc Daneeka agreed.

Notice how Heller inserted a passage of indirect dialogue into a scene of dramatized dialogue. The prose paragraph's summary tells us what Daneeka said to Yossarian and how Yossarian whistled in reaction to it. Even though it's in a third-person voice that adds a touch of authorial commentary, this is showing and not telling for these reasons: 1) It happens within the scene. 2) It furthers the dynamic actions of the scene: Daneeka wants Yossarian to stop pestering him with excuses to get out of combat, and Yossarian suddenly realizes the futility of claiming to be crazy. Daneeka's revelation becomes a turning point that moves the Yossarian plot to the negative.

In terms of narrative drive, the instant the reader grasps the inescapable logic of Catch-22, her expectations leap ahead. How, if possible, she wonders, will Yossarian, or any of the other characters, escape the vise grip of this absurd military rule? The reader/audience's constant search for answers to questions aroused by revelations of exposition propels narrative drive.

Exposition as Ammunition

The second technique for passing exposition unnoticed to the reader/audience relies on the story-goer's emotional involvement. Empathy begins with this thought: "That character is a human being like me. Therefore, I want that character to get whatever the character wants because if I were that character, I'd want the same thing for myself." The moment a story-goer recognizes a shared humanity between herself and your characters, she not only identifies with them but also transfers her real-life desires onto their fictional desires.

Once this empathetic connection hooks involvement, the technique of exposition as ammunition operates in this way: Your cast has the knowledge of the past, present, themselves, and each other that your readers or audience members will need to know in order to follow events. Therefore, at pivotal moments, let your characters use what they know as ammunition in their struggles to get what they want. These revelations will deliver the pleasure of discovery to the emotionally invested reader/audience as the fact quickly vanishes into the story-goer's background awareness.

Consider, for example, the original Star Wars trilogy. All three films hinge on one story-fact: Darth Vader is Luke Skywalker's father.

The storytelling problem for George Lucas was when and how to deliver that piece of exposition. He could have revealed it at any point in the first film by having C-3PO whisper to R2-D2, "Don't tell Luke, he'd really be upset to hear this, but Darth's his dad." The fact would have reached the audience but with minimum, almost laughable effect. Instead, he employed exposition as ammunition to turn the trilogy's most famous scene.

At the story climax of the second film, THE EMPIRE STRIKES BACK, Luke Skywalker makes a hero's choice to fight Darth Vader. As lightsabers clash, the arch-villain takes command and the underdog struggles. Empathy for Luke and anxiety about outcome lock the audience into the moment.

In the conventional action climax, the hero finds an unforeseen way to turn the tables on the villain. Instead, in the midst of the duel, George Lucas puts in play a motivation he has hidden in the subtext: Darth Vader wants his estranged son to join him on the infamous dark side, but faces a lesser-of-two-evils dilemma: Kill his own child, or be killed by him. To escape this dilemma, Vader uses one of the most famous pieces of exposition in film history as ammunition to disarm his son: "I am your father." But, instead of saving his son with his revelation, he drives Luke to attempt suicide.

Suddenly, the truth hidden behind the first two films shocks and moves the audience to compassion for Luke and fear for his future. This biographical fact used as ammunition delivers massive retrospective insight into deep character and past events, floods the audience with feeling, and sets up the trilogy's final episode.

Revelations

In almost every story told, comedy or drama, the most important expositional facts are secrets, dark truths that characters hide from the world, even from themselves.

And when do secrets come out in life? When a person faces a lesser-of-two-evils dilemma: "If I reveal my secret, I risk losing the respect of those I love" versus "But if I do not reveal my secret, something even worse will happen." The pressure of this dilemma pries secrets loose, and as they come to light, their impact spins powerful turning points. And where do secrets come from?

Backstory: Past events that propel future events

Backstory is an often misunderstood term, misused to mean "life history." A character's biography contains a lifelong interaction of genes and experience. Backstory is a subset of this totality—an excerption of past, usually secret, events that the writer exposes at key moments to propel his story to climax. Because revelations from the backstory often inflict more impact than straightforward actions, they are reserved for major turning points. Below is a famous example of this technique.

Who's Afraid of Virginia Woolf?

In this play written by Edward Albee in 1962, George and Martha, a middle-aged couple, endure a conflict-filled marriage. For two decades they have fought constantly over every minute aspect of the raising of their son, Jim. After an exhausting, raucous, drink-filled, insult-filled, adulterous party, topped off with a vicious argument about their son in front of their guests, George turns to Martha and says:

>   GEORGE. We got a little surprise for
>   you, baby. It's about sunny-Jim.
>
>   MARTHA. No more, George....
>
>   GEORGE. YES!...Sweetheart, I'm
>   afraid I've got some bad news for
>   you...for us, of course. Some rather
>   sad news.
>
>   MARTHA. (afraid, suspicious) What is
>   this?
>
>   GEORGE. (oh, so patiently) Well,
>   Martha, while you were out of the

room...well, the doorbell chimed...
and...well, it's hard to tell you,
Martha...

MARTHA. (a strange throaty voice)
Tell me.

GEORGE....and...what it was...it
was good old Western Union, some little boy about seventy.

MARTHA. (involved) Crazy Billy?

GEORGE. Yes, Martha, that's right...
Crazy Billy...and he had a telegram,
and it was for us, and I have to tell
you about it.

MARTHA. (as if from a distance)
Why didn't they phone it? Why did
they bring it; why didn't they
telephone it?

GEORGE. Some telegrams you have to
deliver, Martha, some telegrams you
can't phone.

MARTHA. (rising) What do you mean?

GEORGE. Martha...I can hardly bring
myself to say it...(sighing heav-
ily) Well, Martha...I'm afraid
our boy isn't coming home for his
birthday.

MARTHA. Of course he is.

GEORGE. No, Martha.

MARTHA. Of course he is. I say he is!

GEORGE. He . . . can't.

MARTHA. He is! I say so!

GEORGE. Martha . . . (long pause) . . . our son is . . . dead. (silence) He was . . . killed . . . late in the afternoon . . . (a tiny chuckle) . . . on a country road, his learner's permit in his pocket, he swerved, to avoid a porcupine, and drove straight into a . . .

MARTHA. (rigid fury) YOU . . . CAN'T . . . DO . . . THAT!

GEORGE. . . . . large tree.

MARTHA. YOU CANNOT DO THAT.

GEORGE. (quietly, dispassionately) I thought you should know.

MARTHA. (quivering with rage and loss) NO! NO! YOU CANNOT DO THAT! YOU CAN'T DECIDE THAT FOR YOURSELF! I WILL NOT LET YOU DO THAT!

GEORGE. We'll have to leave around noon, I suppose . . .

MARTHA. I WILL NOT LET YOU DECIDE THESE THINGS!

GEORGE: . . . because there's matters of identifications, naturally, and arrangements to be made . . .

MARTHA. (leaping at him, but ineffectual) YOU CAN'T DO THIS! I WILL NOT LET YOU DO THIS!

GEORGE. You do not seem to understand, Martha; I haven't done anything. Now pull yourself together. Our son is DEAD! Can you get that into your head?

MARTHA. YOU CAN'T DECIDE THESE THINGS!

GEORGE. Now listen, Martha; listen carefully. We got a telegram; there was a car accident; and he's dead. POUF! Just like that! Now, how do you like it?

MARTHA. (a howl that weakens into a moan) NOOOOOOoooooo . . . (pathetic) No; no, he is not dead; he is not dead.

GEORGE. He is dead. Kyrie, eleison. Christie, eleison. Kyrie, eleison.

MARTHA. You cannot. You may not decide these things.

GEORGE. That's right, Martha; I'm not God. I don't have power over life and death, do I?

MARTHA. YOU CAN'T KILL HIM! YOU CAN'T HAVE HIM DIE!

GEORGE. There was a telegram, Martha.

MARTHA. (up, facing him) Show it to me! Show me the telegram!

GEORGE. (long pause; then, with a straight face) I ate it.

> MARTHA. (a pause; then with the greatest disbelief possible, tinged with hysteria) What did you just say to me?
>
> GEORGE. (barely able to stop exploding with laughter) I...ate...it. (Martha stares at him for a long time, then spits in his face) Good for you, Martha.

The climax of *Who's Afraid of Virginia Woolf?* turns on the revelation of George and Martha's backstory secret: Jim, their contentious son, is imaginary. They made him up to fill their empty marriage. The use of backstory to turn story is the single most powerful technique in the execution of exposition.

Direct Telling

The admonition to show rather than tell only applies to dramatized dialogue in acted scenes. Skillful, straightforward telling, whether on page, stage, or screen, whether in narratized dialogue or third-person narration, has two vital virtues: speed and counterpoint.

1) **Speed.** Narration can pack a lot of exposition into a few fast words, plant understanding in the reader/audience, and move on. Inner monologues have the power to turn subtext into text in a blink. A character's conversations with herself can leap randomly from memory to memory in free association, or flash with images that bob up from her subconscious. Such passages, beautifully written, can move emotion within a sentence. For example, from the Gabriel García Márquez novel *One Hundred Years of Solitude*: "Many years later, as he faced the firing squad, Colonel Aureliano Buendía was to remember that distant afternoon when his father took him to discover ice." This is swift, vivid telling—a complex, concentrated image in a single sentence.

However, all too often, filmic narration becomes a device to pump out bland exposition in the format of "and then...and then... and then." This practice substitutes the easy work of telling for the arduous task of showing. Dialogue scenes on film and television that dramatize complex characters demand talent, knowledge, and imagination; word-thick narrations need only a keyboard.

To turn narratized exposition into a dramatized scene, call upon one of two techniques:

One, interpolate a scene. Convert the "and then...and then... and then" of telling into a narrated scene of dramatized "I said/(s)he said." Narrators (whether first person in prose, onstage, or voice-over onscreen) can either act out a scene's dialogue verbatim from memory or use indirect dialogue to suggest it.

The Netflix series HOUSE OF CARDS, for example, often interpolates scenes of indirect dialogue. Kevin Spacey's Frank Underwood frequently turns to the camera and talks to us as if he were a professor and we his students in a course on political tradecraft. In the aside below, Underwood dramatizes exposition by giving us insights into himself as well as a character named Donald. Underwood acts out Donald's character flaw in this vivid, two-sentence metaphorical scene:

What a martyr craves more than anything is a sword to fall on.
So you sharpen the blade, hold it at the right angle, and then 3, 2, 1...

In the next beat, just as Professor Frank predicted, Donald takes the fall for Underwood's misdeeds.

Two, generate inner conflict. Stage a self-to-self duel in which one side of a narrating character argues with another. Two film examples: Frank Pierce (Nicolas Cage) in Martin Scorsese's BRINGING OUT THE DEAD, or the adult Ralphie Parker (Jean Shepherd) in Bob Clark's A CHRISTMAS STORY.

2) **Counterpoint.** In my experience, the narration technique that most enriches a story is counterpoint. Rather than using a narrator to tell the tale, some writers fully dramatize their story, then appoint a

narrator to contradict or ironize its themes. They may use wit to ridicule the dramatic, or the dramatic to deepen the satire. They may counterpoint the personal with the social, or the social with the personal.

Take, for example, John Fowles's postmodern, historical, antinovel novel, *The French Lieutenant's Woman*. Half the pages dramatize the story of Charles Smithson, a Victorian gentleman, and his involvement with Sarah Woodruff, a disgraced governess. Interlaced with this tale, however, a narrator with modern knowledge of nineteenth-century culture and class conflicts undercuts the Charles and Sarah romance. Counterpoint after counterpoint, the narrator argues that the nineteenth century offered women without means far more misery than romance.

Other examples: In Y TU MAMÁ TAMBIÉN the voice-over narrator frequently reminds the audience of Mexico's social suffering as a counterpoint to the coming-of-age drama. Woody Allen's witty voice-over in ANNIE HALL counterpoints his protagonist's self-inquisition. In Samuel Beckett's play *Play*, a trio of characters, buried to the neck in urns, stare out over the audience and narrate their seemingly random thoughts in a three-way system of counterpoint.

Prose is the natural medium for direct telling. The novelist and short-story writer can foreground exposition as nakedly as they wish, and draw it out for as many pages as they wish, so long as their language captivates and satisfies. Charles Dickens, for example, opens *A Tale of Two Cities* with a burst of counterpointing exposition that hooks the reader's curiosity:

> It was the best of times, it was the worst of times, it was the age of wisdom, it was the age of foolishness, it was the epoch of belief, it was the epoch of incredulity, it was the season of Light, it was the season of Darkness, it was the spring of hope, it was the winter of despair, we had everything before us, we had nothing before us, we were all going direct to Heaven, we were all going direct the other way . . .

Notice how Dickens's omniscient third-person narration uses "we" to put an arm around the reader's shoulder and draw him into the telling. Compare that to the confrontational first-person, fast-paced voice of "I" that opens Ralph Ellison's *Invisible Man*:

> I am an invisible man. No, I am not a spook like those who haunted Edgar Allan Poe; nor am I one of your Hollywood-movie ectoplasms. I am a man of substance, of flesh and bone, fiber and liquids—and I might even be said to possess a mind. I am invisible, understand, simply because people refuse to see me. Like the bodiless heads you see sometimes in circus sideshows, it is as though I have been surrounded by mirrors of hard, distorting glass. When they approach me they see only my surroundings, themselves, or figments of their imagination—indeed, everything and anything except me.

In later chapters, both Dickens and Ellison dramatize scenes, but some prose writers never do. Instead, they pave page after page with direct telling narration, never acting out a single event.

Try to imagine how you might dramatize the exposition in the two passages above into scenes of actable dialogue. In theory it could be done. Shakespeare could have managed it, but with what difficulty? When writing for readers, telling works wonders. When writing for actors, the reverse is true.

Ideally, in the performance arts of stage and screen, exposition flows to the audience unnoticed within the spoken words. As we've seen, the craft of rendering exposition invisible takes patience, talent, and technique. Lacking those three qualities, impatient and uninspired screenwriters force exposition on the audience and hope to be forgiven.

Forced Exposition

Since the dawn of cinema, filmmakers have inserted shots of newspapers with foot-high headlines announcing events such as "War!" They have walked characters past televisions or radios conveniently tuned to a news broadcast of exactly what the audience needs to know precisely when it needs to know it. Rapidly edited montages and split-screen collages have packed screens with as much information as possible in the briefest possible time. Filmmakers rationalize these devices with the notion that if exposition comes fast and flashy, it won't bore the audience. They would be wrong.

Similar thinking governs opening films with a title roll, as did STAR WARS (which delivered rapid-fire exposition and a tone of grandiosity), or closing with one, as did A FISH CALLED WANDA (which got laughs and a touch more closure). When thrillers race against time, hopscotching from place to place, they often superimpose location names and dates over establishing shots. In such cases, a little telling goes a long way. With a brief halt for a cogent image or a quick-printed fact, the story stubs its toe but then strides on, and the audience shrugs it off.

But audiences will not forgive a deluge of facts artlessly shoehorned into dialogue for no reason intrinsic to the characters or the scene. When inept writing forces characters to tell each other facts they already know, the pace trips over a high hurdle, falls face-first in the cinders, and may never get up.

For example:

```
INT. LUXURIOUS GREAT ROOM—DAY

John and Jane sit on a silk-tasseled
sofa, sipping martinis.


              JOHN
Oh my goodness, darling, how long
have we known and loved each other
now? Why, it's over twenty years,
isn't it?


              JANE
Yes, ever since we were at the uni-
versity together, and your frater-
```

nity threw a mixer and invited the
Women's Socialist Club. Your house
was so rich, we poor girls called
Beta Tau Zeta Billions, Trillions,
and Zillions.

                    JOHN
(gazing around their magnificent home)

Yes, and then I lost my inheritance.
But we both worked very hard over the
years to make our dreams come true.
And they did, didn't they, my little
Trotskyite?

This exchange tells the audience seven fictional facts: This couple is rich, they are in their forties, they met within the elite of their university, he was born to a wealthy family, she came up from poverty, they once had opposite political views but no longer, and over the years they've developed a banter that's so sweet it hurts your teeth.

The scene is false and its dialogue tinny because the writing is dishonest. The characters are not doing what they seem to be doing. They seem to be reminiscing, but in fact they're mouthing exposition so the eavesdropping audience can overhear it.

As mentioned above, prose writers can avoid these fake scenes by sketching a brief marital history that strings facts together with a pleasing style. If they wish, prose writers can, within limits, simply tell their readers what they need to know. Some playwrights and screenwriters ape novelists by resorting to narration, but with rare exceptions, direct address onstage and voice-over onscreen cannot mete out exposition with the intellectual power and emotional impact of fully dramatized dialogue.

To make this point for yourself, do an exercise in exposition as ammunition. Rewrite the scene above so that the two characters use their expositional facts as weapons during a fight in which one character forces the other to do something that he or she does not want to do.

Now do it again. But this time, put the same facts into a seduction scene in which one character uses what he or she knows as ammunition to subtly manipulate the other into doing something the other does not wish to do.

Write the scene so that the exposition becomes invisible and the characters' behaviors credible. In other words, write it so that the conflict or seduction fascinates the reader/audience, and the exposition they need to know slips unawares, invisibly, as it were, into their minds.

CHARACTERIZATION

The second function of dialogue is the creation and expression of a distinctive characterization for each character in the cast.

Human nature can be usefully divided into two grand aspects: appearance (who the person seems to be) versus reality (who the person actually is). Writers, therefore, design characters around two corresponding parts known as true character and characterization.

True character, as the term implies, names a character's profound psychological and moral being, a truth that can only be revealed when life backs the character into a pressure-filled corner and forces him to make choices and take actions. The Principle of Choice is foundational to all storytelling, fictional and nonfictional: to wit, a character's true self can only be expressed through risk-filled choices of action in the pursuit of desire.

Characterization denotes a character's total appearance, the sum of all surface traits and behaviors. It performs three functions: to intrigue, to individualize, to convince.

1) **To intrigue.** The reader/audience knows that a character's appearance is not her reality, that her characterization is a persona, a mask of personality suspended between the world and the true character behind it. When the reader/audience encounters a one-of-a-kind

personality, they listen to the character's words and naturally wonder: "That's who she seems to be, but who is she really? Is she actually honest or a liar? Loving or cruel? Wise or foolish? Cool or rash? Strong or weak? Good or evil? What is the core identity behind her intriguing characterization? What is her true character?"

Having hooked the reader/audience's curiosity, the story becomes a series of surprising revelations that answer these questions.

2) **To convince.** A well-imagined, well-designed characterization assembles capacities (mental, physical) and behaviors (emotional, verbal) that encourage the reader/audience to believe in a fictional character as if she were factual. As the poet Samuel Taylor Coleridge noted two centuries ago, the reader/audience knows that stories and characters are not actual. But they also know that to involve themselves in the telling, they must temporarily believe, or more precisely, they must willingly suspend their disbelief and accept the character's actions and reactions without doubt, without argument.

If your reader/audience thinks the thought, "I don't believe a word she says" because they sense your character is a liar, that could be a revelation of true character. But if they think the same thought because they don't simply believe in your character, then it's time for a rewrite.

3) **To individualize.** A well-imagined, well-researched characterization creates a unique combination of biology, upbringing, physicality, mentality, emotionality, education, experience, attitudes, values, tastes, and every possible nuance of cultural influence that has given the character her individuality. Moving through her days, pursuing career, relationships, sexuality, health, happiness, and the like, she gathers behaviors into a one-of-a-kind personality.

And the most important trait of all: talk. She speaks like no one we have ever met before. Her language style not only sets her apart from all other cast members but also, if the writing is masterful, from all other fictional characters. A recent example: Jeanette "Jasmine" Francis (Cate Blanchett) in Woody Allen's BLUE JASMINE. (Dialogue to characterize will be fully explored in Chapters Ten and Eleven.)

ACTION

Dialogue's third essential function is to equip characters with the means for action. Stories contain three kinds of action: mental, physical, and verbal.

Mental Action: Words and images compose thoughts, but a thought does not become a mental action until it causes change within a character—change in attitude, belief, expectation, understanding, and the like. A mental action may or may not translate into outer behavior, but even if it stays secret and unexpressed, the character who took the mental action is not quite the same person afterward as she was before. Character change through mental action impels much of modern storytelling.

Physical Action: Physical action comes in two fundamental kinds: gestures and tasks.

By gestures, I mean all varieties of body language: facial expression, hand movements, posture, touch, proxemics, vocalics, kinesics, and the like. These behaviors either modify spoken language or substitute for it, expressing feelings words cannot.[1]

By tasks, I mean activities that get something done: working, playing, traveling, sleeping, lovemaking, fighting, daydreaming, reading, admiring a sunset, and the like—all those actions that do not require talk.

Verbal Action: As novelist Elizabeth Bowen put it, "Dialogue is what characters do to each other."[2]

On the level of outer behavior, a character's dialogue style melds with his other traits to create his surface characterization, but at the inner level of true character, the actions he takes into the world reveal his humanity or lack of it. What's more, the greater the pressure in the scene (the more he stands to lose or gain in that moment), the more his actions tell us who he really is.

What a character says, however, only moves the reader/audience if the actions he takes beneath his lines ring true to that specific character in that specific moment. Therefore, before writing a line, ask these questions: What does my character want out of this situation? At this precise moment, what action would he take in an effort to reach that desire? What exact words would he use to carry out that action?

Spoken words suggest what a character thinks and feels; the action he takes beneath his words expresses his identity. To uncover a character's inner life, seek the subtextual action and label it with an active gerund ("-ing") phrase. Below are the four dialogue quotes from the preface. Look into the subtext of each, and name the character's action with a gerund. When done, compare your interpretations to mine.

Tomorrow and tomorrow and tomorrow,
Creeps in this petty pace from day to day,
To the last syllable of recorded time,
And all our yesterdays have lighted fools
The way to dusty death.
                    —Macbeth in *The Tragedy of Macbeth*

"Of all the gin joints in all the towns in all the world she walks into mine."
                    —Rick in CASABLANCA

"Towards thee I roll, thou all-destroying but unconquering whale; to the last I grapple with thee; from hell's heart I stab at thee; for hate's sake I spit my last breath at thee."
                    —Ahab in *Moby Dick*

"Not that there's anything wrong with that."
                    —Jerry in SEINFELD

All four quotes above imply disgust, but Macbeth, Rick Blaine, Ahab, and Jerry Seinfeld express their disdain in such radically different speech styles that their personalities could not be more unalike. (Dialogue style as the door to characterization will be the focus of Part Three.)

My sense of the deep character under the four speeches suggests these subtextual actions: Macbeth—denouncing existence; Rick Blaine—lamenting lost love; Ahab—blaspheming God's power; Jerry Seinfeld—ridiculing the political correctness that protects asinine behavior from ridicule. Your interpretations of implied action may differ from mine (not that there's anything wrong with that), but the purpose of this exercise is to reveal the difference between the activity of talk and the taking of action.

Part Four will further demonstrate this technique by parsing seven scenes beat by beat to separate their outer language from their inner actions and trace how these dynamic designs motivate what's said as they arc scenes around their turning points.

3

EXPRESSIVITY I: CONTENT

As You Like It, Act 2, Scene 7

Jaques
(to Duke Senior)
All the world's a stage,

And all the men and women merely
players:

They have their exits and their
entrances;

And one man in his time plays many
parts...

Jaques believes that in the theatre of life, everyone acts out his own cast of characters decade after decade from infant to adult to geezer. Jaques steps back to survey this pattern from a philosophical, objective, long-term, outside-in, public point of view. But in order to create Jaques's dark doctrine, Shakespeare worked (my guess) from the reverse perspective—psychological, subjective, here and now, inside-out, and profoundly private.

As you compose dialogue, I think it's useful to imagine character design as three concentric spheres, one inside the other—a self
within a self within a self. This three-tiered complex fills dialogue
with content of thought and feeling while shaping expression in
gesture and word. The innermost sphere churns with the unsayable; the middle sphere restrains the unsaid; the outer sphere releases
the said.

THE SAID

The surface level of things said supports the more or less solid meanings that words, spoken or written, directly express with both denota-
tions and connotations. "Snake," for example, literally means "a legless
reptile," but in Western culture it also symbolizes treachery and evil.
The word "house" connotes more than domicile. It carries overtones
of home, hearth, and family, plus undertones of shack, crash pad, and
flophouse.

This is why quotable dialogue such as "Get busy livin' or get busy
dyin'" (Ellis Boyd "Red" Redding in THE SHAWSHANK REDEMP-
TION) and "I'm just one stomach flu away from my goal weight"
(Emily Charlton in THE DEVIL WEARS PRADA) outlive their stories and their characters. These sentences express their meaning no
matter who says it or when.

Word choices (busy dyin', stomach flu) naturally enrich the lines
with connotations from the culture outside their fictional setting. But
because a specific character in a specific situation speaks the lines with
a specific purpose, a wholly new and deeper realm comes into play:
the character's intelligence, imagination, and other genetic givens.

By creating an original dialogue style of vocabulary, diction, syntax, grammar, tone, tropes, and accent, the writer characterizes a role.
Verbal choices express the character's education or lack of it, wit or
lack of it, his outlook on life, the range of his emotional behavior—all
the observable traits that jigsaw into a personality.

THE UNSAID

A second sphere, the unsaid, revolves within a character. From this inner space the self gazes out at the world. As thoughts and feelings form at this level, the self deliberately withholds them. Nonetheless, once the character speaks (text), readers and audiences instinctively look past the words to intuit the unsaid, to glimpse what the character actually thinks and feels (subtext) but chooses not to put into words. The writer, therefore, must hone dialogue so that this is possible, so that the unsaid can be sensed by implication.[1]

When Emily Charlton (Emily Blunt) says to Andy Sachs (Anne Hathaway) "I'm just one stomach flu away from my goal weight," what she does not say, but we know she is thinking, might go something like this: "The fashion world forces me to live an anorexic life, but I want my career more than my health. Perpetual hunger is a price I'm happy to pay. If you value your job future, you will do the same."

Novels thrive at the level of the unsaid. In Chapter One of Ian McEwan's *Enduring Love*, a violent accident kills a man. In the next chapter, as Joe Rose stands among the other survivors, surveying the aftermath, he confides to the reader:

Clarissa came up behind me and looped her arms around my waist and pressed her face into my back. What surprised me was she was already crying (I could feel the wetness on my shirt) whereas to me, sorrow seemed a long way off. Like a self in a dream I was both first and third persons. I acted, and saw myself act. I had my thoughts, and I saw them drift across a screen. As in a dream, my emotional responses were nonexistent or inappropriate. Clarissa's tears were no more than a fact, but I was pleased by the way my feet were anchored to the ground and set well apart, and the way my arms were folded across my chest. I looked out across the fields and the thought scrolled across: *That man is dead.* I felt a warmth spreading through me, a kind of self-love, and my folded arms hugged me tight. The corollary seemed to be *And I am alive.* It was a random matter, who was alive or dead at any given time. I happened to be alive.

THE UNSAYABLE

Deepest yet, concealed beneath the unsaid, the sphere of the unsayable roils with subconscious drives and needs that incite a character's choices and actions.

A character's truest nature can only be expressed when, under the pressures of life, he chooses to act in pursuit of a life-defining desire. As antagonistic pressures build greater and greater power, the character's choices of action reveal his hidden self, until a final choice under the maximum pressure of life exposes the character's primal, irreducible self. How deliberate versus instinctive the motivations are that propel human choice of action has been debated for centuries. But whatever the case, choices begin in this innermost sphere.

Language, therefore, cannot express who a character actually is, only who he seems to be. As the Bible teaches, a person is known not by his words but his deeds. The truth comes full circle, however, once the writer realizes that words are deeds.

Talk is the foremost vehicle for human action. When a character says something, he is, in fact, doing something. By speaking, he could be comforting a loved one, bribing an enemy, begging for help, refusing to help, obeying authority, defying authority, paying the price, remembering the day, and so on down the limitless list of human actions. Dialogue expresses far more than the meanings of its words. As language, dialogue conveys characterization, but as action, dialogue expresses true character.

Moment by moment, your character struggles in pursuit of her desires; she takes actions and uses her spoken words to carry them out.

At the same time, however, her language choices convey her inner life, conscious and subconscious, without announcing it. Whether read or acted, fine dialogue creates a transparency that allows the reader/audience to gaze through the text of talk. This phenomenon turns the story-goer into a mind reader.

When you read a page of expressive dialogue or watch a fine actor perform a complex scene, your sixth sense invades the character. You become a telepathist, often better aware of what's going on inside her than she knows herself. Your story-trained sonar traces vibrations down through the character's subconscious currents, until the actions she takes in the subtext of her lines enunciate her identity and you discover her profound personal dimensions.

If, as some people believe, anything and everything can be expressed in words, we should stop telling stories and write essays instead. But we don't, because at the rock bottom of being, the unsayable energies in the subconscious mind are real and demand expression.

Dialogue unites these realms because the spoken word resonates through all three spheres. Dialogue wields the double power to express the effable (characterization) while it illumines the ineffable (true character)—what can be put into words versus what can only be put into action. Dialogue, therefore, is the writer's foremost vehicle for character content.

ACTION VERSUS ACTIVITY

The axiom "nothing is what it seems" expresses the primal duality of life: *What seems* is the surface of life, the activity we see and hear, the outer behavior of what a character says and how she behaves. *What is* is the substance of life, the action the character takes below the surface of activity.

Outer goings-on such as playing cards, working out, sipping wine, and, most of all, talking are simply activities. These textual behaviors mask the truth of what the character is actually doing. For even though an activity like chatting with a stranger at a bus stop may seem without purpose, it never is. Therefore, no line of dialogue is finished until you've answered this question: In the subtext of my character's verbal activity, what action is he in fact taking?

Consider ice cream. We never eat ice cream simply because we're hungry. Like all behaviors, a conscious or subconscious action underlies this activity. What is the ice cream eater really doing? Perhaps he's drowning his sorrows in something sweet or rebelling against doctor's orders or rewarding himself for sticking to his diet. Those actions—drowning sorrows, rebelling, or rewarding—find expression in the activity of eating ice cream.

The same of talk. As Character A and Character B converse, what are they doing? Are the words Character A uses consoling Character B or ridiculing her? When B reacts, does her dialogue suggest that she is submitting to A or dominating him? Is A feigning interest or falling in love? Is B deceiving A or confessing to him? And on the questioning goes. Behind the textual activities of the characters, what subtextual actions actually drive the scene?

An activity, therefore, is simply the surface manifestation of an action; it's the way a character carries out an action. Action is foundational to storytelling, and every activity contains one.

"Drama" is the ancient Greek word for action, derived from the verb *draō*, meaning "to do" or "to act." The audiences of classical Greece knew that no matter what was happening on the surface of a play, an inner action drives all outer activity. Extending this principle to the writing of a scene, we realize that even silence has underlying action. Not speaking when a situation calls for talk is an action, perhaps a cruel one, aimed at another person. When a character speaks, he is doing something: helping or hurting, begging or bribing, persuading or dissuading, explaining or misleading, attacking or defending, complimenting or insulting, complaining or thanking, and so on down an endless list of actions. Even pauses play into a beat of action/reaction: When a character pauses, she's either reacting to the scene's previous action or preparing her next move.

The term "dialogue" is often contrasted with "monologue," as if dialogue were always a two-way process. But that's misleading. As I mentioned in Chapter One, dialogue is a contraction of two Greek terms (*dia* and *legein*) meaning "through" and "speak." "Dialogue" connotes actions taken through talk. Therefore, when a character talks to herself, she takes action within herself. "Monologue" connotes someone talking to no one or nothing, but in reality, that's impossible. Someone, something, or some aspect of the self is on the receiving end of every word ever spoken or thought.

TEXT AND SUBTEXT

Activity and action run parallel to another pair of terms: text and subtext.

Text means the surface of a work of art and its execution in its medium: paint on canvas, chords from a piano, steps by a dancer. In the art of story, text names the words on the page of a novel, or the outer life of character behavior in performance—what the reader imagines, what an audience sees and hears. In the creation of dialogue, text becomes the said, the words the characters actually speak.

Subtext names the inner substance of a work of art—the meanings and feelings that flow below the surface. In life, people "speak" to each other, as it were, from beneath their words. A silent language flows below conscious awareness. In story, subtextual levels enclose the hidden life of characters' thoughts and feelings, desires and actions, both conscious and subconscious—the unsaid and unsayable.

Skillful dialogue creates a kind of transparency. The text of a character's spoken words conceals her inner life from other characters, while at the same time allowing the reader/audience to see through the surface of her behavior. Adept dialogue delivers the sensation of insight, the sense of reading a character's mind and knowing what she is really thinking, really feeling, really doing to the point of understanding her inner life better than the character herself.

We who live in the word-centric culture of European heritage tend to believe that language sets the limits of experience. While there can be no doubt that language molds thinking in subtle ways, a writer must come to grips with how other modes of expression—the paralanguage of gesture and facial expression, along with tone of voice, dress, movement, and the like—influence a character's experience of his inner self and outer life, and most importantly, how he expresses himself with or without words.

When, for example, Character A says to Character B: "Hi, how ya doing? Oh look, you've lost weight!" On the text, Character A's actions greet and compliment Character B. But depending on the nature and history of their relationship, in the subtext Character A could be doing anything from encouraging to seducing to taunting to insulting Character B. The possible subtextual actions under the most seemingly neutral expressions are as varied as the beings who take them.

Human nature constantly combines an outer behavior (text) with subterranean selves (subtext). Those rare and rather strange people who put their unsaid directly into their said seem mechanical, unreal, inhuman, disconnected, even insane. Hitler, for example, had no subtext. *Mein Kampf* was not a metaphor; it was a timetable for the holocaust. He stated his full intentions in the text, but because his visions were too horrible to believe, allied politicians spent the 1930s searching for consolation in a nonexistent subtext.

4

EXPRESSIVITY II: FORM

The qualities and quantities of dialogue vary with the levels of conflict used in the storytelling.

THE CONFLICT COMPLEX

Conflict disrupts our lives from any one of four levels: the physical (time, space, and everything in it), the social (institutions and the individuals in them), the personal (relationships of intimacy—friends, family, lovers), and the private (conscious and subconscious thoughts and feelings). The difference between a complicated story and a complex story, between a story with minimum dialogue versus maximum dialogue, hinges on the layers of conflict the writer chooses to dramatize.

The action genres put their protagonists up against physical conflict almost exclusively. For example, J. C. Chandor's film ALL IS LOST. On the other hand, the novelistic technique of stream of consciousness submerges the telling entirely at the layer of inner conflict. There, it churns crosscurrents of dream and memory, of regret and yearning that flood the protagonist's mind. For example, Virginia Woolf's *Mrs. Dalloway*.

Filmmakers like Chandor, who strive for a purity of objectivity, or authors like Woolf, who seek a purity of subjectivity, complicate their works at the extreme of only one level of conflict. As a result, their genius crafts a compelling story with little or no need for spoken dialogue. Stories told with highly kinetic concentration at just one level of life are complicated, often dazzlingly so, but, in my definition, not complex.

Complex stories embrace two, three, or even all four levels of human conflict. Authors with worldviews both wide and deep often bracket their tellings with inner conflict at one level, physical strife at another, and then concentrate on the middle ranges of social and personal conflicts—the two venues of talk.

Personal conflicts embroil friends, family, and lovers. Intimacy, by its nature, begins in talk, then builds, changes, and ends in talk. Personal conflicts, therefore, roil with multilayered, multi-meaning dialogue.

For example, this exchange between Walter White and his wife, Skyler, in Season 4, Episode 6 of BREAKING BAD. From the first season's first episode on, Walter White's characterization portrays a nervous, insecure, defensive man. But by the end of this scene we glimpse his true character.

        INT. BEDROOM—DAY.
        Husband and wife sit on the bed.

                    SKYLER
            I said before, if you are in danger,
            we go to the police.

                    WALTER
            No, I don't want to hear about the
            police.

                    SKYLER
            I do not say that lightly. I know
            what it could do to this family, but

if it is the only real choice we
have, if it's either that or you getting shot when you open your front
door—

> WALTER

—I don't want to hear about the
police.

> SKYLER

You're not some hardened criminal,
Walt. You are in over your head.
That's what we tell them, that's the
truth.

> WALTER

That's not the truth.

> SKYLER

Of course it is. A schoolteacher,
cancer, desperate for money—

> WALTER
>
> (getting up)

—We're done.

> SKYLER

—roped into working, unable to quit.
You told me that yourself, Walt.
Jesus, what was I thinking?
> (pause)

Walt, please, let's both of us stop
trying to justify this whole thing,
and admit you're in danger.

Walter slowly turns to her.

> WALTER
> Who are you talking to right now? Who
> is it you think you see?
> (pause)
> Do you know how much I make a year?
> Even if I told you, you wouldn't
> believe it. Do you know what would
> happen if I suddenly decided to stop
> going to work? A business big enough
> that it could be listed on the NASDAQ
> goes belly up. Disappears. It ceases
> to exist without me.
> (pause)
> No, you clearly don't know who you're
> talking to, so let me clue you in.
> I am not in danger, Skyler. I am the
> danger. A guy opens a door and gets
> shot. You think that's me? No, I am
> the one who knocks.

He walks out of the bedroom; Skyler stares
after him.

Walter is describing his new, other self, the doppelgänger we come
to know as Heisenberg. Skyler, dumbfounded by her husband's words,
can only grasp for the meaning.

Social conflicts surge through institutions of public purpose: medical, educational, military, religious, governmental, corporate—all
societal enterprises, legal and criminal. As people move from personal
to social relationships, they often speak with less sincerity and greater
formality. When public conflicts peak, characters break into speeches.

Consider this example from HOUSE OF CARDS. A political

operative rejects a proposal from Frank Underwood. As the operative walks off, Frank turns to camera with this aside:

```
                    FRANK
          Such a waste of talent. He chose
          money over power. In this town a mis-
          take nearly everyone makes. Money is
          the McMansion in Sarasota that starts
          falling apart after ten years; power
          is the old stone building that stands
          for centuries. I cannot respect some-
          one who does not see the difference.
```

To generalize: The more physical and social a story's conflicts, the less the dialogue; the more personal and private the conflicts, the more the dialogue.

Therefore, to create a complex story, the writer must master the double dimension of dialogue—the outer aspect of what is said versus the inner truth of what is thought and felt. When first spoken, a line of dialogue conveys a surface meaning, the meaning the speaker hopes other characters will believe in and act on. This first meaning seems logical in its context, conveys a sense of character purpose and tactic, and arouses curiosity as we glance across the scene to see its effect. The language itself may also delight us with tropes or wordplay, especially when written for the stage. In the next moment, however, this solid speech seems to dissolve, and we sense a second, deeper meaning hidden behind the words.

Thanks to our powers of intuition and perception, character-specific dialogue inspires a sudden insight into the character's ineffable inner self, his unseen needs and desires. True-to-character talk lets us read past conscious thoughts and sense unspoken feelings down to a character's subconscious urges. This effect is so powerful that the fullness and depth of insight we have into fictional characters often surpasses what we glimpse in the living people around us.

Dialogue, at its best, hangs suspended between a character's public face and her secret self. Like multifaceted crystals, her spoken words refract and reflect aspects of her inner and outer lives. Because personal and social lives begin, evolve, and end through talk, the complex relationships and conflicts between human beings cannot be fully dramatized without expressive, character-specific dialogue.

Inept dialogue, on the other hand, not only rings false, but also shallows out the characters who speak it. Weak dialogue suffers from many faults such as poor word choices, but the root cause runs much deeper:

Dialogue problems are story problems.

With almost algebraic symmetry, the worse the storytelling, the worse the dialogue. And because stories are so often hackneyed, we suffer dissonant dialogue in countless films and plays and on hundreds of TV channels. The same is true of the novel. Although modern prose often speeds the read with page after page of dialogue, when was the last time you were deeply moved by a chapter of talk? The majority of dialogue published or performed is serviceable at best and instantly forgotten.

We're drawn to stories not only because they reflect the life around us, but also because they illuminate the life within. One of the great pleasures of story is staring, self-absorbed, into the mirror of fiction. Dialogue shows us how we lie to others, how we lie to ourselves, how we love, how we beg, how we fight, how we see the world. Dialogue teaches us what could or should be said in life's harshest or most rapturous moments.

DIALOGUE ONSTAGE

The stage is a symbolic space. From that moment untold millennia ago when the first actor stood up to perform a story for his tribe, audiences have instinctively understood that what is said and done in that precious space means far more than words and gestures.[1]

The stage puts the artificiality of art on open display. In the ritual of theatre, actors act out fictional people in the living presence of other people, everyone breathing the same air, all the while pretending that this unreality is, for the moment, real. By taking her seat, the theatergoer signs an implicit contract with the playwright: He may turn the onstage space into any world he imagines, symbolic of whatever meaning he wishes to express; she in turn will suspend her disbelief and react to his characters as if they were living their lives in front of her.

Are there limits to the "as if" convention? Apparently not. Since the advent of Dada over a century ago, audiences have signed on for the wildest rides, embracing surrealist plays such as André Breton's *If You Please* (1920), Theatre of the Absurd pieces such as Eugène Ionesco's anti-play *The Bald Soprano* (1950), the fragmentations of the Furth and Sondheim concept musical *Company* (1970), and the literally hundreds of avant-garde plays performed at the Edinburgh Festival Fringe every August.

The "as if" conspiracy between author and audience licenses playwrights to write dialogue at heights and depths of sublimity no human being has ever actually spoken. From the master dramatists of classical Greece, through Shakespeare, Ibsen, and O'Neill, to contemporaries like Jez Butterworth, Mark O'Rowe, and Richard Marsh, playwrights have used imagistic language and verse rhythms to intensify dialogue with poetic force. And the audience listens because in the theatre we want to hear first, see second.

What's more, the stage inspires the constant exploration and reinvention of language. When Shakespeare couldn't find the word he wanted, he made one up: barefaced, obscene, eyeball, lonely, zany, gloomy, gnarled, bump, elbow, amazement, torture, and over 1,700 other words are Shakespeare's invention.

From the naturalistic barroom grit of Eugene O'Neill's *The Iceman Cometh* to the poetic elegance of T. S. Eliot's *Murder in the Cathedral*, the spectrum of language in the theatre is unmatched in the other media of story.

For example, consider the coffee table talk in Yasmina Reza's play *God of Carnage* as translated by Christopher Hampton. Two couples begin the evening discussing a playground fight between their children. Their civilized conversation, lubricated with alcohol, descends into ugly truths about their marriages. In the dialogue below, both wives use sharp "as if" similes to belittle their husbands.

MICHAEL: Drinking always makes you unhappy.

VERONICA: Michael, every word that comes out of your mouth is destroying me. I don't drink. I drank a mouthful of this shitty rum you're waving about as if you were showing the congregation the Shroud of Turin. I don't drink and I bitterly regret it. It'd be a relief to be able to take refuge in a little drop at every minor setback.

ANNETTE: My husband's unhappy as well. Look at him. Slumped. He looks as if someone left him by the side of the road. I think it's the unhappiest day of his life.[2]

Now compare the phlegmatic ridicule of these two wives to this vibrant speech from *Blood Wedding* (1933) by Federico García Lorca, translated by Fernanda Diaz. As a servant sets the table for a wedding, she warns the bride of a coming tragedy, spinning trope upon trope:

SERVANT:
For the wedding night
let the warping moon
part the black leaves
and gaze down

from her white window.
For the wedding night
let the frost burn,
let the acid almond
turn sweet as honey.
O exquisite woman
your wedding night nears.
Tighten your gown, hide
beneath your husband's wing.
He is a dove
with a breast of fire.
Never leave the house.
The fields wait for the cry
of eloping blood.

To the ancient "as if" convention of the legit theatre, the musical theatre adds yet another glaze, transfiguring the poetics of spoken lines into lyrics and arias that heighten emotion the way dance enhances gesture. Indeed, all the principles and techniques of dialogue discussed in this book apply to musical theatre. From the recitativo of opera to the sung-through scenes of the modern musical, characters who sing and dance vocalize dialogue into music. Songs are simply another form of in-character talk.

Theatre audiences hold to their belief in the "as if" so long as the play creates an internally consistent setting in which characters talk (or sing) in a manner that seems true to their world and to themselves; in other words, as long as dialogue stays in-character. For without credibility, stories risk billowing into meaningless, emotionless spectacles.

DIALOGUE IN FILM

A camera can fly through 360 degrees of global reality, devouring every object, shape, and color in its path. Anything a writer can dream,

CGIs can duplicate beyond his dreams. Because the big screen foregrounds images and backgrounds sounds, film audiences instinctively absorb the story through their eyes, while they half listen to the score, sound effects, and dialogue.

In fact, for some cinema purists, the ideal film would be wordless. I appreciate their aesthetic, but while it's true that moving moments in film are often mute, when I compare the best silent films with the finest sound films, for me, stories told with audible dialogue win hands down. The image of Thelma and Louise driving over a cliff into the Grand Canyon shines vividly in my memory, but as I recall, they were shouting a joyful "Keep going!" as they did. Without that line, the impact of their suicide would have been halved.

Although storytelling on the big screen clearly favors image over language, the balance varies greatly from genre to genre. An Action/Adventure film, such as ALL IS LOST, is told with no dialogue, whereas an education plot, such as MY DINNER WITH ANDRE, is told in all dialogue.

The greatest difference between the screen versus stage and page, therefore, is not the quantity of dialogue but the quality. The camera and microphone so magnify and amplify behavior, that every phony glance, every false gesture, every affected line looks and sounds more amateur than the worst dinner party charade. Screen acting calls for a naturalistic, believable, and seemingly offhanded technique. To make this possible, screen dialogue must feel spontaneous. When forced to deliver ornamented dialogue, even the finest actors sound ludicrous, cueing the audience to react with "People don't talk like that." This holds true in all genres, realistic and nonrealistic, in television and film.

There are, of course, exceptions.

One: Stylized Realism

Realism bends with a certain elasticity. Setting a story in an unfamiliar world allows the writer to enhance dialogue with greater figurative language than a commonplace location, but the talk must still stay within the realm of believability that the story's world sets for itself. A film or television series in a foreign setting (THE GRAND BUDAPEST HOTEL and HOMELAND), a criminal society (PULP FICTION and DEADWOOD), a regional culture (BEASTS OF THE SOUTHERN WILD and JUSTIFIED), or the distant past (SPARTA-CUS and VIKINGS) can take dialogue well beyond the everyday, so long as it maintains credibility within its self-imposed limits.

In these exotic cases consistency becomes a problem. The writer must be able to sustain an eccentric yet believable style over a full-length film or even long-form television series such as THE WIRE. No easy task.

Two: Nonrealism

Genres of nonrealism (science fiction, musical, animation, fantasy, horror, and farce) tend to tell allegorical stories, acted out by archetypal or symbolic characters. In these genres, audiences not only accept but also enjoy highly stylized dialogue. Think of THE MATRIX, 300, CORPSE BRIDE, THE LORD OF THE RINGS, DR. SEUSS' THE CAT IN THE HAT, GAME OF THRONES, or GLEE.

Three: Extreme Characters

In life, some people outfeel, outthink, and outtalk the people around them. Such characters deserve and should get imaginative, one-of-a-kind dialogue.

Suppose you were writing for extreme characters such as Walter White (Bryan Cranston) in BREAKING BAD; Captain Jack Sparrow (Johnny Depp) in PIRATES OF THE CARIBBEAN; Melvin Udall in AS GOOD AS IT GETS, Jimmy Hoffa in HOFFA, or Frank Costello in THE DEPARTED (all played by Jack Nicholson); or Sophie Zawistowski in SOPHIE'S CHOICE, Suzanne Vale in POSTCARDS FROM THE EDGE, or Margaret Thatcher in THE IRON LADY (all played by Meryl Streep). Excellent writers gave these bigger-than-life characters image-rich language that attracted actors who knew what to do with it.

Consider these two characters: Philip Marlowe (Humphrey Bogart) and Vivian Rutledge (Lauren Bacall) from THE BIG SLEEP (1946). William Faulkner, Leigh Brackett, and Jules Furthman adapted the film from Raymond Chandler's novel. In Hollywood jargon, the film is a crimedy, the merger of two genres: crime story and romantic comedy. Repartee and mimicry leaven the intrigue and gunplay. In one sequence, for example, Marlowe, a private detective, pretends to be a gay rare book collector.

In the scene below, Marlowe meets his client's daughter, Vivian. The two use racehorses as metaphors for themselves, and horse racing as a metaphor for sex. Their flirtation characterizes them as quick-witted, worldly-wise, self-assured, amusing, and mutually attracted. (To "rate" a Thoroughbred means to restrain the horse early in a race in order to conserve its energy for the finish.)

> VIVIAN
> Speaking of horses, I like to play
> them myself. But I like to see them
> work out a little first to see if
> they're front-runners or come from
> behind, find out what their hole card
> is, what makes them run.

> MARLOWE
> Find out mine?

> VIVIAN
> I think so. I'd say you don't like
> to be rated, you like to get out in
> front, open up a lead, take a little
> breather in the backstretch, then
> come home free.

> MARLOWE
> You don't like to be rated yourself.

> VIVIAN
>
> I haven't met anyone yet who could do
> it. Any suggestions?

> MARLOWE
>
> Well, I can't tell till I've seen you
> over a distance of ground. You got
> a touch of class but...I don't know
> how far you can go.

> VIVIAN
>
> That depends on who's in the saddle.

> MARLOWE
>
> There's one thing I still can't figure
> out.

> VIVIAN
>
> What makes me run?

> MARLOWE
>
> Uh-huh.

> VIVIAN
>
> I'll give you a little hint. Sugar
> won't work. It's been tried.

When writing for the screen, even within the most fantasied genres, always write for the actor. Language knows no limits, but acting does. Once your work is in production, an actor will have to act your lines with clarity and conviction. Therefore, what's said must be kept within the realm of what's actable. This demand leads to a major difference between dialogue for the stage versus the screen: improvisation.

In the theatre, the playwright owns the play's copyright. As a result, actors may not improvise or paraphrase dialogue without the author's permission. In film and television, however, the writer assigns copyright to the production company, so that when the need arises, directors, editors, and actors can cut, change, or add dialogue. The professional reality of writing for the screen is that the script you write may not be performed verbatim as you wrote it. As a result, sadly, an actor's improvisations may diminish your work.

Inept improvisations are easy to spot. When spontaneity blears and actors lose track, they often buy time by repeating each other's cues until the scene sounds like an echo chamber:

                        ACTOR A
        I think it's time for you to leave.

                        ACTOR B
        So you want me to leave, huh? Well,
        I'm not going anywhere until you lis-
        ten to what I have to say.

                        ACTOR A
        I've listened to everything you have
        to say and none of it makes sense.

                        ACTOR B
        Sense? Sense? You want me to make
        sense? What did I say that didn't
        make sense?

And on they ramble.

In rare cases, however, such as Robert DeNiro's "You talkin' to me?" riff in TAXI DRIVER, an actor's improvisation eclipses the script. In FORREST GUMP, for example, Forrest (Tom Hanks) joins the army and befriends fellow enlistee Bubba Blue (Mykelti Williamson). During a montage of their boot-camp labors, Williamson improvises this passage as transcribed from the screen:

Bubba Blue: Anyway, like I was sayin', shrimp is the fruit of the sea. You can barbecue it, boil it, broil it, bake it, sauté it. Dey's uh, shrimp kabobs, shrimp creole, shrimp gumbo. Pan-fried, deep-fried, stir-fried. There's pineapple shrimp, lemon shrimp, coconut shrimp, pepper shrimp, cave shrimp, shrimp stew, shrimp salad, shrimp and potatoes, shrimp burger, cave shrimp. That– that's about it."

Notice that Williamson used "cave shrimp," a colorless crustacean found in the subterranean streams of Alabama and Kentucky, twice. Even the best of improvisations are prone to accidental repetition.

DIALOGUE ON TELEVISION

Comparing film to television, film (with exceptions) likes to take the camera out-of-doors onto the streets and into nature; television (with exceptions) gravitates toward indoor stories of families, friends, lovers, and coworkers. For that reason, television tends to write more face-to-face scenes, leaning the balance of dialogue versus image toward talk for three reasons:

1) **The small screen.** Facial expressions are hard to read in full-length shots. This motivates the television camera to close in on a character's face, and when it does, that face talks.

2) **Genre.** Television favors genres such as family comedy, family drama, the love story, the buddy story, and professional dramas of all kinds (cops, criminals, lawyers, doctors, psychologists, etc.). These series frame personal relationships in homes and workplaces where intimacy begins, changes, and ends first and foremost through talk.

3) **Small budgets.** Image costs money, resulting in high film budgets. Because dialogue is relatively inexpensive to stage and shoot, television's limited budgets encourage talk.

Looking toward the future, if wall-mounted screens continue to grow in size and popularity, TV budgets will also rise, causing a spike in subscription fees. In time, large home screens will merge film and television into one grand medium—the screen. On the other hand, when not at home, people will consume stories on their iPads and iPhones, thus keeping dialogue critical to the tellings. In either case, however, movie theatres will close.

DIALOGUE IN PROSE

Prose translates conflicts from the private, personal, social, and physical realms into word-pictures, often colored by the inner lives of characters, before projecting them onto the reader's imagination. Consequently, prose writers pour their most vivid, high-intensity language into first- or third-person narration rather than exchanges of dialogue. Indeed, free indirect dialogue turns speech itself into narration. When prose writers do use direct dialogue in dramatized scenes, they often restrict themselves to very naturalist language in order to contrast the plainness of talk with the figurative potency of their narration. With exceptions, such as Stephen King's *Dolores Claiborne*, many novelists and short-story writers use quoted dialogue as a technique to simply change pace or break up blocks of prose.

The stage and screen confine dialogue to acted scenes and occasional direct address that soliloquizes or narrates. Both media rely on actors to enrich their characters with subtext and the paralanguages of tonality, gesture, and facial expression. For that reason, an author's expressivity in the theatre or on film and television has to work within the possibilities of the actor's art. But because prose performs in the reader's imagination, it offers the writer the widest spectrum of dialogue styles.

At one end of the continuum, prose creates conventional scenes that could be transplanted directly to the stage or screen without changing a word. In the middle ranges, the first-person voice becomes a novel-length, uninterrupted speech composed of tens of thousands of words, all spoken to the reader. Some authors turn away from the reader, as it were, and distill thought into inner dialogues—secret conversations argued between the many voices of a multifaceted self.

Finally, at the far opposite edge of the spectrum, third-person prose often eliminates quotation marks and characterized voices altogether to subsume character talk into free indirect dialogue.

Chapter One looked at the three categories of point of view in prose and how they affect the qualities and quantities of dialogue. Now, let's take those distinctions into more depth and detail by grouping the many varieties of prose dialogue into two grand modes: in-character versus non-character.

Non-Character Narration

The non-character side of prose tells its stories through a third-person narrator, an intelligence that is neither a character nor the real-life voice of the author, but a guiding awareness a writer invents and then endows with varying degrees of omniscience and objectivity to describe characters and events as well as provide commentary in various kinds of discourse.

A non-character narrator can present dialogue explicitly in dramatized scenes or implicitly via narratized indirect dialogue. Consider this from the short story "The Widow Predicament" by David Means:

> They sat across from each other at the Hudson House and conversed. His skin was weathered and he talked about Iceland most of the time until rising naturally out of his talk was the suggestion that perhaps she might want to see the country someday; nothing about dancing on the lip of volcanoes, or throwing themselves into one sacrificially, but a hint of it.[3]

Indirect dialogue in non-character narration gives the writer the usual assets of direct dialogue. It channels exposition when the reader needs to know that the talk took place and the upshot of what was said. It characterizes the speaker in terms of what the character talks about, although not how he says it. And as in the example above, the narration that surrounds indirect dialogue can express its subtext.

Note how Means describes subtext as something "rising naturally out of his talk," and uses the words "suggestion" and "hint" to convey a sense of ineffability.

The two chief benefits of indirect dialogue in non-character narration are 1) acceleration of pace, and 2) protection against banality. The dinner table talk about Iceland that Means summarized in a phrase could have gone on for an hour. He saved us from that. And unless his character could describe with a Hemingwayesque eye, Means knew best to leave landscape adjectives off-page.

The characterless voice of a third-person narration can be quite distant, observant, and objective.

For example, a Joseph Conrad narrator describes a tropical dawn:

> The smooth darkness grew paler and became blotchy with ill-defined shapes, as if a new universe were being evolved out of somber chaos. Then outlines came out, defining forms without any details, indicating here a tree, there a bush; a black belt of forest far off. The day came rapidly, dismal and oppressed by the fog of the river and the heavy vapors of the sky—a day without color and without sunshine: incomplete, disappointing, sad.

When non-character awareness moves in the opposite direction and becomes intimate, imitative, and subjective, it adopts a stream of consciousness mode to invade the unsaid and unsayable realms and mirror a character's inner life. This technique mixes the third-person narrator's composure with the character's emotional energies and word choices, melding into the role, replicating her thought processes, generating the impression of inner dialogue but without crossing the line to an in-character voice.

Consider, for example, this passage from Virginia Woolf's novel *Mrs. Dalloway*. Woolf's non-character narrator uses words plucked from Clarissa Dalloway's vocabulary ("lark," "plunge," "something awful") to emulate the flow of memory:

What a lark! What a plunge! For so it always seemed to her when, with a little squeak of the hinges, which she can hear now, she burst open the French windows and plunged into the open air. How fresh, how calm, stiller than this of course, the air was in the early morning; like the flap of a wave; the kiss of a wave; chill and sharp and yet (for a girl of eighteen as she then was) solemn, feeling as she did, standing there at the open window, that something awful was about to happen...

Not all stream of consciousness "streams" with Virginia Woolf's breathless fluidity. Some interiorized passages zigzag or circle or pulse (see the Ken Kesey and David Means examples below). For that reason, some schools of writing use "stream of consciousness" and "inner dialogue" interchangeably as if the terms were synonyms. But for the purposes of this book, I give them distinct definitions. I draw the line with the answer to this question: Who is talking to whom? Stream of consciousness uses a third-person non-character voice to talk to the reader (as in the Woolf example above); inner dialogue uses a character's voice in first or second person to talk to himself (as in the Nabokov example below).

The In-Character Voice

The in-character side of prose speaks with character-specific voices. Dialogue, as I previously defined the term, includes all purposeful character talk, whether spoken in duologues with other characters, said to the reader, or by the character talking to herself. As we noted in Chapter One, because prose does its acting in the reader's imagination, it offers a far greater range of in-character techniques than stage or screen. In-character prose employs six tactics: 1) dramatized dialogue, 2) first-person direct address, 3) indirect dialogue, 4) inner dialogue, 5) paralanguage, and 6) mixed techniques (see Chapter Five for the last two tactics).

Dramatized Dialogue

In the novel, dramatized dialogue rarely reaches the intensity of a verse play. Nonetheless, within the limits of genre and characterizations set by the author, figurative language may enhance scenes, just as it does onstage and onscreen. First-person narrators often enact "I said"/"she said"/"he said" scenes, purely dramatized and without commentary.

Robert Penn Warren's *All the King's Men* is narrated by Jack Burden, an aide to a ruthless politician and the novel's central character, Willie Stark, a.k.a. the Boss. Stark needs a secret piece of dirt to smear the reputation of a political foe, Judge Irwin. Note how Stark uses the decades that span from diapers to the coffin as a metaphor for life:

> It all began, as I have said, when the Boss, sitting in the black Cadillac which sped through the night, said to me... "There is always something."
>
> And I said, "Maybe not on the Judge."
>
> And he said, "Man is conceived in sin and born in corruption and he passeth from the stink of the didie to the stench of the shroud. There is always something."[4]

Direct Address

First-person narration is first cousin to soliloquys onstage and in-character voice-overs onscreen. In all three cases a character speaks directly to the person consuming the story. More often than not, the protagonist narrates his or her story, but occasionally a supporting character does the talking. Direct address can be more or less emotional, more or less objective, the specific tone dependent on the personality of the narrator.

Here, a Rudyard Kipling protagonist recalls looking out to sea and describes the wide, calm, objective pleasure of his experience to the reader:

I remember the windjammer as she sailed toward me. The setting sun ablaze astern. Out flung water at her feet, her shadow slashed rope furled sails bulging sideways like insolent cheeks of angels.

Or, a first-person narrator's view may contract, blinded by strong emotions or lesser degrees of sanity. In Ken Kesey's *One Flew Over the Cuckoo's Nest*, a patient in a mental hospital, "Chief" Bromden, begins the novel with:

They're out there. Black boys in white suits up before me to commit sex acts in the hall and get it mopped up before I can catch them. They're mopping when I come out of the dorm, all three of them sulky and hating everything, the time of day, the place they're at here, the people they got to work around. When they hate like this, better if they don't see me. I creep along the wall quiet as dust in my canvas shoes, but they got special sensitive equipment to detect my fear and they all look up, all three at once, eyes glittering out of the black faces like the hard glitter of radio tubes out of the back of an old radio.[5]

Bromden's imaginings of unseen orgies and fear-detecting technology, enriched with his metaphors (quiet as dust) and similes (faces like the hard glitter of radio tubes) express his paranoid inner life, but at the same time, give the impression that despite the Chief's constricted, insane thoughts, he is knowingly talking to us, the reader.

Indirect Dialogue

When a non-character third-person narrator uses indirect dialogue, subtext often becomes text. For example, in the David Means scene above, his third-person narrator tells the reader what was not said:

"...nothing about dancing on the lip of volcanoes, or throwing them-selves into one sacrificially, but a hint of it."

When in-character first- or second-person prose relates indirect dialogue, subtext can only be implied because a first-person narrator doesn't have access to his own subconscious. For example, this scene from *The Sense of an Ending* by Julian Barnes: Webster, the protagonist, wants to take action against an ex-lover because she won't give him a letter he believes is rightfully his, so he consults a lawyer:

> Mr. Gunnell is a calm, gaunt man who doesn't mind silence. After all, it costs his clients just as much as speech.
>
> "Mr. Webster."
>
> "Mr. Gunnell."
>
> And so we mistered one another for the next forty-five minutes, in which he gave me the professional advice I was paying for. He told me that going to the police and trying to persuade them to lay a charge of theft against a woman of mature years who had recently lost her mother would, in his view, be foolish. I liked that. Not the advice, but the way he expressed it. "Foolish": much better than "inadvisable" or "inappropriate."[6]

The reader senses that beneath his glib approval of Gunnell's choice of words, Webster rages.

Inner Dialogue

Onstage and onscreen, the actor brings the unsaid to life within her performance, where it stays mute in the subtext. But when novelists and short-story writers wish, they can turn subtext into text and con-vert the unsaid directly into literature. The chief difference, therefore, between in-character direct address and inner dialogue is who's listen-ing. A first-person voice narrates to the reader; an inner dialogist talks to himself.

Lolita, for example, begins with Vladimir Nabokov's protagonist, Humbert Humbert, in self-celebration:

Lolita, light of my life, fire of my loins. My sin, my soul. Lo-lee-ta: the tip of the tongue taking a trip of three steps down the palate to tap, at three, on the teeth. Lo. Lee. Ta.

Humbert is not talking to us. Rather, we sit outside, listening as his inward-facing mind revels in memories. To capture this self-absorbed admixture of sex and worship, Nabokov opens with metaphors for passion as prayer, then focuses on Humbert's tongue as it pounds "t" sounds in alliteration.

Compare Humbert's masturbatory fantasy with a passage from "The Knocking," a short story by David Means. Means's protagonist talks directly to us as he reclines in his New York apartment, listening to the tenant above him hang pictures or do repairs. His in-character voice guides us through his hopscotching thoughts as they leap from now to then and back to now.

A piercingly sharp metallic tap, not too loud and not too soft, coming out from under the casual noise of summer afternoon—the roar of traffic on Fifth combined with high heel taps, taxi horns, and the murmur of voices—again, many of these knockings come late in the day when he knows, because he knows, that I'm in my deepest state of reverie, trying to ponder—what else can one do!—the nature of my sadness in relation to my past actions, throwing out, silently, wordlessly, my theorems: Love is a blank senseless vibration that, when picked up by another soul, brings form to something that feels eternal (like our marriage) and then tapers and thins and becomes wispy, barely audible (the final days in the house along the Hudson) and then, finally, nothing but air unable to move anything (the deep persistent silence of loss).

Inner dialogue mimics free association to leapfrog through a character's mind. When we glance in the cracks between the images, we glimpse the unsayable.

To sum up: from stage to screen to page, the nature, need, and expressivity of dialogue vary considerably. Stage dialogue is the most embellished, screen dialogue the most concise, and prose dialogue the most mutable.

5

EXPRESSIVITY III: TECHNIQUE

FIGURATIVE LANGUAGE

Figurative devices range from metaphor, simile, synecdoche, and metonymy to alliteration, assonance, oxymoron, personification, and beyond. In fact, the list of all linguistic tropes and ploys numbers in the hundreds. These turns of phrase not only enrich what's said, but also send connotations of meaning resonating into the subtexts of the unsaid and unsayable as well.

For example: In Scene Six of Tennessee Williams's play *A Streetcar Named Desire*, Blanche DuBois, a desperately vulnerable, aging Southern belle on the edge of mental and emotional collapse, meets Mitch, a lonely, sensitive, working-class bachelor who lives with his dying mother. After an evening out, they confess to very different but equally pain-filled lives. Their attraction builds to this moment:

> MITCH: (drawing Blanche slowly into his arms) You need somebody. And I need somebody, too. Could it be you and me, Blanche?

> She stares at him vacantly for a moment,
> then with a soft cry huddles in his
> embrace. She makes a sobbing effort to
> speak but the words won't come. He kisses
> her forehead and her eyes and finally her
> lips. Her breath is drawn and released in
> long, grateful sobs.

> BLANCHE: Sometimes—there's God—so
> quickly.

These five words condense tremendous meaning and emotion. The phrase "there's God" is not a metaphor comparing Mitch to a deity, but rather hyperbole to express Blanche's sense of an overwhelming, heaven-like salvation. We suspect, however, that this epiphany is not her first.

The words "Sometimes" and "so quickly" suggest that Blanche has been rescued by men many times in the past. But the men who suddenly saved her must have abandoned her just as fast because here she is, still desperately alone, clinging to yet another stranger. In five words the audience instantly glimpses the implied pattern: When Blanche meets men, she plays the victim and inspires their inner white knight. They rescue her, but then, for reasons we are yet to discover, desert her. Will Mitch be any different?

In one ear-catching trope, Tennessee Williams exposes the tragic cadence of Blanche's life and raises a dread-filled question in the audience's mind.

Language composed into dialogue offers a spectrum that runs from mental meanings at one end to sensual experiences at the other. For example, a character might call a singer's voice either "lousy" or "sour." Both terms make sense, but "lousy" is a dead metaphor that once meant "covered with lice." "Sour" still has life. The moment the audience hears "sour," their lips start to pucker. Which line stirs the most inner feeling: "She walks like a model" or "She moves like a slow, hot song"? Dialogue can express the same idea in countless ways, but, in general, the more sensory the trope, the deeper and more memorable its effect.[1]

Tropes work within a single sentence, but because dialogue dramatizes conflict-filled talk speech after speech, temporal and counter-punctual techniques also come into play: rapid rhythms versus silent pauses, run-on sentences versus fragments, repartee versus argument, literate versus illiterate grammars, monosyllabic versus polysyllabic vocabularies, politeness versus profanity, verisimilitude versus verse, understatement versus overstatement, and countless other examples of stylistics and wordplay. Dialogue can dance to as many different tunes as life can sing.

I have emphasized the infinite array of creative possibilities that face the writer a few times already and will again. I repeat this point because I want writers to understand that **form does not limit expression; it inspires it**. This book explores the forms that underlie dialogue but never proposes formulae for writing it. Creativity is choice-making.

PARALANGUAGE

Actors provide their audiences with all forms of paralanguage, those nonlexical nuances of voice and body language that enhance the meanings and feelings of words—facial expression; gestures; posture; rate of words; pitch, volume, rhythm, intonation, stress; and even proxemics, the distances characters keep between themselves and others. An actor's paralanguage speaks a gesticulate dialogue. The eye of the audience reads these microexpressions at up to one twenty-fifth of a second.[2] On page, however, paralanguage calls for description enhanced with figurative language.

In this example from "Railroad Incident, August 1995," a short story by David Means, four homeless men sit around a fire at night when a half-dressed man comes out of the shadows.

What they saw emerge was a man softening into middle age. In his limp was a slight residue of dignity and formality, the way he lifted his feet as if they were still shod and weighted by the expensive shoes; or maybe all of that wasn't noticed until, coming up to them, he opened his mouth and spoke, saying hello softly, the vowels widening, the cup of his mouth over those words like an expensive shell . . .[3]

(David Means writes short stories, I suspect, because his arsenal of prose techniques is so diverse, he needs hundreds of tellings to explore them all.)

MIXED TECHNIQUES

Prose techniques can be used singularly or in concert. In this exchange from *An American Dream*, Norman Mailer weaves three: direct dialogue, first-person direct address, and paralanguage, both literal and figurative.

"You want a divorce?" I said.

"I think so."

"Like that?"

"Not like that, darling. After all that." She yawned prettily and looked for a moment like a fifteen-year-old Irish maid. "When you didn't come by today to say goodbye to Deirdre—"

"—I didn't know she was leaving."

"Of course you didn't know. How could you know? You've been nuzzling and nipping with your little girls." She did not know that at the moment I had no girl.

"They're not so little any more." A fire had begun to spread in me. It was burning now in my stomach and my lungs were dry as old leaves, my heart had a herded pressure which gave promise to explode.

"Give us a bit of the rum," I said.[4]

A quick point about adaptation from medium to medium: If you wish to adapt a prose story to the screen, recognize that novelists and short-story writers tend to concentrate their finest language in the voices of their narrators and not in the dialogue of their dramatized scenes—just as Mailer did above.

Literature resists filmic adaptation for the obvious reason: The camera cannot photograph thought. Inner dialogues of concentrated prose cannot shift sideways from page to screen. Therefore, to adapt you must reinvent. You must re-envision the novel's storytelling from the inside out, and transform its novelistic narratized dialogue into filmic dramatized dialogue. No small task.

LINE DESIGN

A line's design pivots around its key term—the word or phrase essential to its meaning. An author can place that key term first, last, or anywhere in the middle. That choice results in one of three fundamental line designs: suspenseful, cumulative, balanced.

The Suspense Sentence

Curiosity drives the thirst for knowledge—our intellectual need to solve puzzles and answer questions. Empathy drives the hunger for connection—our emotional need to identify with others and root for their well-being. When the rational and emotional sides of life merge, they generate the phenomenon of suspense. Suspense, simply put, is curiosity charged with empathy.

Suspense focuses the reader/audience by flooding the mind with emotionally tinged questions that hook and hold attention: "What's going to happen next?" "What'll happen after that?" "What will the protagonist do? Feel?" And the major dramatic question (MDQ) that hangs suspended over the entire telling: "How will this turn out?" These powerful questions so grip our concentration that time vanishes. As events build to story climax, suspense intensifies and peaks at the final and irreversible turning point that answers the MDQ and ends the telling.

This combination of curiosity and concern arcs the story's overall suspense, but when we zoom in for a close-up, we see that inquisitive emotions permeate every story component, no matter its size. Each scene dramatizes a suspense-filled turning point; each speech within the scene grips interest from first line to last; even the smallest element of all, the line of dialogue, shapes itself into a miniature unit of suspense. A superbly told story holds unbroken intellectual and emotional involvement scene by scene, speech by speech, line by line. The reader never pauses and the audience never looks away, not for a moment.

The key to composing dialogue that holds the eye to page and the ear to the stage and screen is the **periodic sentence**. A periodic sentence withholds its core idea until the final word. By front-loading the sentence with modifiers or subordinate ideas and thus delaying the meaning to last, the periodic sentence compels uninterrupted interest.

For example: "If you didn't want me to do it, why did you give me that_____?" What word would give that line its specific meaning? "Look?" "Gun?" "Kiss?" "Nod?" "Photo?" "Money?" "Report?" "Smile?" "E-mail?" "Ice cream sundae?" Almost any noun imaginable could nail the meaning. To inspire intrigue, the periodic design makes meaning wait, and thus compels the reader/audience to listen in wonder from the first word to the last.

In other words, the periodic sentence is the suspense sentence.

For example, the opening scene from *Art*, a play by Yasmina Reza, translated by Christopher Hampton. I have put the core word or phrase in each sentence in bold.

```
Marc, alone onstage.
```

```
Marc: My friend Serge has bought
a painting. It's a canvas about
five-foot by four: white. The
```

background is **white.** If you screw up
your eyes, you can make out some **fine
white diagonal lines.**

Serge is one of my oldest **friends.**
He's done very well for himself, he's
a dermatologist and he's keen on **art.**

On Monday, I went to see the
painting; Serge actually got hold
of it on the Saturday, but he's
been lusting after it for **several
months.** This **white painting with
white lines.**

At Serge's.

At floor level, a white canvas with fine
white diagonal scars. Serge looks at his
painting, thrilled. Marc looks at the
painting. Serge looks at Marc looking at
the painting.

Long silence: from both of them, a whole
range of **wordless emotions.**

Marc: Expensive?

Serge: Two hundred thousand.

Marc: Two hundred thousand?

Serge: Huntington would take it off my
hands for **two hundred and twenty.**

Marc: **Who's** that?

Serge: Huntington?

Marc: **Never heard** of him.

Serge: Huntington! The Huntington Gallery!

Marc: The Huntington Gallery would take it off your hands for two hundred **and twenty**?

Serge: No, not **the Gallery. Him.** Huntington himself. For his **own collection.**

Marc: Then why didn't Huntington **buy it**?

Serge: It's important for them to sell to **private clients.** That's how the market **circulates.**

Marc: Mm hm...

Serge: Well?

Marc: ...

Serge: You're not in the **right place.** Look at it from this **angle.** Can you see **the lines**?

Marc: What's the **name** of the...?

Serge: Painter. **Antrios.**

Marc: Well-known?

Serge: **Very.** Very.

Pause.

Marc: Serge, you haven't bought this painting for **two hundred thousand Euros**?

> Serge: You don't understand, that's what it **costs**. In an **Antrios**.
>
> Marc: You haven't bought this painting for **two hundred thousand Euros**?
>
> Serge: I might have known you'd **miss the point**.
>
> Marc: You paid two hundred thousand Euros for **this shit**?

Serge, as if alone.

> Serge: My friend Marc's an **intelligent** enough fellow, I've always **valued** our relationship, he has a **good job**, he's an aeronautical engineer, but he's one of those **new-style intellectuals**, who are not only **enemies of modernism**, but seem to take some sort of incomprehensible pride in **running it down**...[5]

Of the forty-five ideas expressed in these two soliloquies of narratized dialogue and the scene of dramatized dialogue they bracket, forty are shaped for suspense. Even the brief description of paralanguage (the nonverbal facial expressions on Marc and Serge) delays its point until the phrase "wordless emotions."

The suspense sentence is not only the most dramatic design but the most comic as well. Almost all verbal jokes trigger laughter by ending on a suspense sentence that suddenly severs its rising tension with a final punch word. By saving the core word for last, Reza and Hampton energize their lines, hold the audience's interest, and concentrate impact into a single, final, often comic punch.

The Cumulative Sentence

How old is the cumulative technique? Aristotle advocated it over 2,300 years ago. In Book Three, Part Nine of *On Rhetoric*, he examined the differences between the tight, periodic suspense sentence and the loose, free-running cumulative sentence. The two designs reverse mirror each other: the suspense structure puts subordinate phrases first and ends on its core word; the **cumulative design** puts its core word up front, then follows with subordinate phrases that develop or modify the point.

Consider the line design of Character B's dialogue:

Character A

Remember Jack?

Character B
(nodding)
Smoke circling his head like an angry
halo, cigarette butt burning his lip,
wrestling the spare, cursing the
jack, trying to fix a flat...

(with a sense of loss)
...last time I ever saw him.

When we reverse the design, this suspense sentence turns into a cumulative sentence:

Character A

Remember Jack?

Character B
(with a sense of loss)
I saw him, last time ever, trying to
fix a flat, cursing the jack, wrestling

```
with the spare, cigarette butt burn-
ing his lip, smoke circling his head
like an angry halo.
```

Although the free-running cumulative style may be less dramatic than a suspense sentence, it is not slapdash. When well crafted, it paints an ever-growing, more detailed picture of its subject. This snowballing quality gives dialogue a conversational spontaneity while its phrases roll out with a pleasing rhythm.

The suspense design offers many advantages but drawbacks as well. First, the meaning, constantly delayed, risks sounding contrived. Second, a long suspense sentence may force the reader/audience to remember too many pieces of a complex idea while waiting for the ending to pull the thoughts together. If overwritten, a suspense sentence takes on the same tedious feebleness of a badly built cumulative sentence.

The suspense and cumulative designs sit at opposite ends of the spectrum. Between opening a line with its core word versus closing with it run countless variations.

Parallel designs, for example, link phrases of similar length, meaning, and design for contrast and emphasis:

When I walked into that **church**, I walked into a **new life**.

The Balanced Sentence

The **balanced sentence** puts its core word(s) somewhere in the middle with subordinate phrases on either side:

Jack's sex and gambling obsessions are high risk enough, but I think the guy must be an **adrenaline junkie** when I add his rock climbing and skydiving.

The suspense sentence, straight or in parallel, is dialogue's most compelling and dramatic design. So for tension, emphasis, flourish, and laughs, delay the core word. On the other hand, cumulative and balanced sentences are the most conversational and free-running designs. But the constant use of any single technique becomes as repetitious as wallpaper and artificial as a robot. Therefore, to compel involvement and build tension, while at the same time expressing a sense of characters living in the moment and making up whatever they say, dialogue calls for a mixture of designs.

Mixed Designs

In Season 1, Episode 3 of TRUE DETECTIVE, the co-protagonist, Rustin Cohle, relates his worldview to Detectives Gilbough and Papania. Once again, I bolded the core words. Note where each is located within its sentence. (DB is cop-talk for dead body.)

> RUSTIN COHLE
> This . . . **This** is what I'm talking
> about. This is what I mean when I'm
> talkin' about **time** and **death** and
> **futility.** All right there are broader
> ideas at work, mainly what is owed
> between us as a society for our
> **mutual illusions.** Fourteen straight
> hours of staring at **DB's,** these are
> the things **ya think of.** You ever
> done **that**? You look in their **eyes,**
> even in a picture, doesn't matter if
> they're dead or alive, you can still
> **read 'em.** You know what you **see**? They
> **welcomed** it . . . not at first, but . . .
> right there in the last instant. It's
> an unmistakable **relief.** See, 'cause
> they were afraid, and now they saw
> for the very first time how easy it
> was to just . . . **let go.** Yeah, they saw,

in that last nanosecond, they saw...
what they were. You, yourself, this
whole big drama, it was never more
than a jerry rig of **presumption and
dumb will,** and you could just **let
go.** To finally know that you didn't
have to hold on so tight. To realize
that all your life, all your love,
all your hate, all your memories, all
your pain, it was all the **same thing.**
It was all the same *dream*, a dream
you had inside a locked room, a dream
about being a **person.** And like a lot
of dreams, there's a **monster** at the
end of it.

Of the twenty-plus ideas Rust expresses, a dozen use suspense sentences, and the rest are a mix of balanced, parallel, and cumulative structures. As a result, this long passage hooks, builds, and pays off interest, yet seems spontaneous, almost wandering. Note also how series creator and writer Nic Pizzolatto caps Rust's speech with a metaphor: Life is a dream. Like a grace note that enhances a passage of music, a trope tagged on a suspense sentence can add a mind-catching ornament.

ECONOMY

One final but critical quality of expressive dialogue is economy—saying the maximum in the fewest possible words. All fine writing, especially of dialogue, follows the principle of economy as laid down by William Strunk Jr. and E. B. White in *The Elements of Style*: "Vigorous writing is concise. A sentence should contain no unnecessary words, a paragraph no unnecessary sentences, for the same reason that a drawing should have no unnecessary lines and a machine no unnecessary parts. This requires not that the writer make all his sentences short, or that he avoid all detail and treat his subjects only in outline, but that he make every word tell."[6]

Not vacuity, but economy.

This principle became the Strunk and White imperative: "Omit needless words." Do your writing a favor and tape that dictate to your computer screen, then do it. No speech, no matter its length, should ask the reader/audience to absorb one more word than necessary. Extraneous language annoys us. Omit it.

(The dialogue in Sofia Coppola's film LOST IN TRANSLATION executes the principle of economy with perfection. See Chapter Eighteen.)

THE PAUSE

Inside the give-and-take of dialogue, the pause serves many uses. When used prior to a turning point, a moment of wordless hesitation tightens tension in the reader/audience, focuses their attention on what will happen next, and emphasizes the gravity of the event. A pause after a turning point allows the reader/audience time to absorb the meaning of the change and savor its aftermath.

A pre-crisis pause dams emotion momentum. In a well-written scene, curiosity and concern flow toward the moment of critical change. The reader/audience asks itself, "What's going to happen next? What's she going to do when it does? How will this turn out?" As this impetus peaks, a pause holds it in check and compresses its power. When the turning point pivots, all that pent-up energy explodes into the scene's climactic beat.

Overused, however, the pause—like talk—can wear out its welcome. The principle of economy applies as much to this tactic as any other. If dialogue halts again and again and again to signal emphasis, emphasis, emphasis, nothing gets emphasis. Like "The Boy Who Cried Wolf," the more often an author repeats a technique, the less effect it has. Then when the scene arrives in which she wants the tactic to deliver its effect in full, she discovers that repetition has blunted its edge.

Be judicious in the placement of pauses. Shape the rhythm of scenes without undo hesitation, so that when you put on the brakes, the standstill moment grips attention. There are no free rests: A pause must be earned.

THE CASE FOR SILENCE

Lean, pacey dialogue, more implicit than explicit, keeps readers and audiences hungry for more; stuffed, sluggish speeches, more explicit than implicit, discourage interest. As overwritten dialogue wears on and on, the reader skims, the audience stops listening. So, in the same way that tragic scenes often call for comic relief, surplus talk may call for silence.

From story to story, scene to scene, how much is too much is impossible to say. Your taste and judgment must guide that decision. But if you feel that your pages overtalk their scenes, switch gears and write for the eye rather than the ear, make image substitute for language.

Challenge yourself with this question: How could I write this scene in a purely visual way, doing all that needs to be done for character and story without resorting to a single line of dialogue? You can call upon the power of images in one of two ways:

One, paralanguage. Gestures and facial expressions are not, strictly speaking, linguistic. Nonetheless, they can speak with all the overtones and undertones of words. So rather than cluttering scenes with verbalized affirmations or disaffirmations such as "yes/no," "I agree/I disagree," or "I think you're right/I think you're wrong," carry the moment with a nod, a glance, a wave of the hand.

This is especially true when writing for television and film. Whenever possible, leave room for the screen actor's creativity. Because the camera can magnify a face many times larger than life, thoughts and emotions seem to flow behind the eyes and under the skin like swells across a sea. Silence invites the camera in. Use it.

Two, physical action. At every opportunity ask yourself this question: What physical, rather than verbal, behavior would execute my characters' actions and reactions? Let your imagination paint word-pictures of doing rather than saying.

Consider, for example, a scene from a film by Ingmar Bergman with an apt title in this context, THE SILENCE. In it, a woman in a hotel restaurant allows herself to be seduced by a waiter. How to write that?

Does the waiter offer her the menu, listing the specials of the day? Does he recommend his favorite dishes? Does he compliment her on how she's dressed? Does he ask her if she's staying at the hotel? Traveling far? Does he ask if she knows the city? Does he mention he's getting off work in an hour and would love to show her the sights? Talk, talk, talk?

Here's how Bergman played it: The waiter, accidently on purpose, drops a napkin on the floor next to her chair. As he slowly stoops and kneels to pick it up, he sniffs and smells the woman from head to crotch to foot. She, in reaction, inhales a deep, pleasure-filled sigh. Bergman then cuts to a hotel room where the customer and waiter writhe in passion. Their intensely erotic, visual, physical, wordless seduction in the restaurant executes its turning point on her inhale.

Silence is the ultimate economy of language.

PART 2

FLAWS AND FIXES

SIX DIALOGUE TASKS

Effective dialogue executes six tasks simultaneously:

1. Each verbal expression takes an inner action.
2. Each beat of action/reaction intensifies the scene, building to and around its turning point.
3. Statements and allusions within the lines convey exposition.
4. A unique verbal style characterizes each role.
5. The flow of progressive beats captivates the reader/audience, carrying them on a wave of narrative drive, unaware of the passage of time.
6. The language strikes the reader/audience as authentic in its setting and true to character, thus maintaining belief in the story's fictional reality.

Fine dialogue harmonizes all six of these objectives at once, so let's look at the various faults that break the flow and cause discord.

6

CREDIBILITY FLAWS

INCREDIBILITY

The standards of credibility we set for the physical behaviors of characters apply equally to what they say. Dialogue written for television, stage, or film must inspire believable performances in its actors. Scenes written for a novel or short story must inspire the reader to imagine credible behaviors in literary characters. So, no matter how complex and compelling the psychology of your characters, no matter how emotional and meaningful your story design, if your characters do not talk in a manner true to their natures, true to the setting and genre, the reader/audience loses faith. Unconvincing dialogue destroys interest faster than sour notes destroy a recital.

Hollow, phony dialogue cannot be cured with naturalism. If you eavesdrop on the conversations of your fellow passengers on planes, trains, and buses, you realize in a flash that you would never put those gossipy bull sessions on stage, page, or screen. Actual chatter repeats like a dribbling basketball. Everyday talk lacks vividness, resonance, expressivity, and, most critically, significance. Business meetings, for example, often roll on and on, hour after hour, without metaphor, simile, trope, or imagery of the least expressivity.

The crucial difference between conversation and dialogue is not the number, choice, or arrangement of words. The difference is content. Dialogue concentrates meaning; conversation dilutes it. Therefore, even in the most realistic settings and genres, credible dialogue does not imitate actuality.

In fact, credibility has no necessary relationship to actuality whatsoever. Characters who live in impossible worlds, such as Alice's Wonderland, deliver lines that would never be said by a living person but are true to themselves and true to the settings.

In all settings from the most down-to-earth to the most magical, in all genres from war stories to musicals, in all styles of speech from inarticulate monosyllables to lyrical verse, dialogue should sound like the spontaneous talk of its characters. For that reason, we gauge dialogue against a standard of fictional authenticity, not factual accuracy. A character's word choices and syntax should not be so true to life that they imitate the redundant banalities of the everyday. Rather, they must strike us as plausible and vernacular within the context of the story's world and genre(s).

The reader/audience wants to believe that characters speak offstage, off-page, or offscreen exactly as they speak onstage, on the page, or onscreen, no matter how fantasized the story's setting. Even in worlds as fantastic as Guillermo del Toro's film PAN'S LABYRINTH, as absurd as Eugène Ionesco's play *Exit the King*, as poetic as T. S. Eliot's play *Murder in the Cathedral,* or as archaic as Robert Graves's novel, *I, Claudius,* the cast's talk need not be factual, but it must seem credible.

On the other hand, anyone might say anything at any time. So, how do we judge dialogue credibility? How do we know when a line is true to its character and true to the moment, or false on both counts?

Aesthetic judgment will never be a science. It is, by nature, as feeling as it is thoughtful. Instead, you must rely on skilled intuition, on your sense of rightness based on knowledge, experience, and inborn taste. Learn to judge your dialogue by listening past the words and sensing the harmony or disharmony between cause and effect. Dialogue rings true when a character's verbal actions resonate with his motivations, when his inner desires and outer tactics seem to complement each other.

Exactly how you will master judgment in your own work is yours to discover, but to help guide you in that goal, below is a short list of faults that damage credibility: empty talk, overly emoted talk, overly knowing talk, overly perceptive talk, and excuses substituting for motivation.

EMPTY TALK

When a character speaks, the reader/audience looks into the subtext for a motivation to make sense out of the lines, a cause to explain the effect. If they find none, the dialogue sounds phony and the scene with it. The most commonplace example: one character telling another character something they both already know to satisfy the author's expositional exigencies.

OVERLY EMOTIVE TALK

When a character uses language that seems far more emotional than his actual feelings, again the reader/audience wonders why and checks the subtext for an explanation. If they find none, they may assume that either this hyper-dramatic character is a hysteric or that the author is desperately trying to make too much out of too little. At some social/psychological level, emotive dialogue and its context should complement each other.

OVERLY KNOWING TALK

Know what your characters know. Characters are an author's creatures, born of exhaustive research into the story's setting and cast, countless observations of human behavior, and ruthless self-awareness. A bold line, therefore, runs between creator and created. Or should. But if a writer crosses that line and injects his author's knowledge into his character's awareness, we sense a cheat. When a character onscreen or onstage talks about current events with a breadth and depth of understanding only his author could have, or when a novel's first-person protagonist looks back on past events with factuality and clarity of insight beyond his experience, again, the reader may sense that the author is whispering into his character's ear.

OVERLY PERCEPTIVE TALK

Similarly, beware characters who know themselves better than you know yourself. When a character describes himself with a depth of insight more profound than Freud, Jung, and Socrates combined, readers and audiences not only recoil at the implausibility; they lose faith in the writer. Authors set traps for themselves when they create characters with excessive, unconvincing self-awareness.

It happens like this: Hardworking writers fill notebooks and files with character biographies and psychologies, generating ten or twenty times more material than they would directly use in the writing. They do this, as they must, to give themselves a surfeit of material in order to win the war on clichés with original, unexpected choices. Having amassed this knowledge, the desire to get all they know out into the world can become an irresistible temptation. Unwittingly, the author crosses the line between writer and character, turning his creation into a mouthpiece for his research.

EXCUSES MISTAKEN FOR MOTIVATION

Create honest motivation for behavior. In an effort to match a character's over-the-top action with a cause, writers often backtrack to the character's childhood, insert a trauma, and pass it off as motivation. Over recent decades, episodes of sexual abuse became an overused, all-purpose, mono-explanation for virtually any extreme behavior. Writers who resort to this kind of psychological shorthand do not understand the difference between excuse and motivation.

Motivations (hunger, sleep, sex, power, shelter, love, self-love, etc.) are needs that drive human nature and compel behavior.[1] More often than not, these subconscious drives go unrecognized, and as often as not, cause more trouble than they cure. Unwilling to face the truth of why they do what they do, human beings invent excuses.

Suppose you were writing a pivotal scene for a political drama in which a national leader explains to his cabinet why he is taking the country to war. Throughout history, two primary motivations have driven one people to war against another. First, the drive for power abroad. Land, slaves, and wealth seized from the defeated empowers the victor. Second, the drive for power at home. When rulers fear losing strength, they provoke war to distract their citizens and regrip domestic power. (George Orwell dramatized both motivations in his masterpiece, *1984*.)

These two motivations compel the reality of war, but no ruler who declares war thinks like that. Or if he does, he would never say it. So, to write your scene, you would have to bury motivation in the subtext, create a leader with just the right quality of self-deception, and then write his dialogue to frame an excuse other characters believe and follow.

Some of the excuses warring peoples have used throughout history include: "Saving souls for God" (Christian Crusades, Spanish Empire, Ottoman Empire), "Shining the light of civilization into the darkness of savagery" (British Empire), "Manifest Destiny" (genocide of Native Americans), "Purifying the race" (the holocaust), and "Transforming capitalist tyranny into Communist equality" (the Russian and Chinese revolutions).[2]

For an example of an excuse masquerading as motivation, consider Shakespeare's *The Tragedy of Richard III*. In Act 1, Scene 1, Richard, the hunchbacked Duke of Gloucester, says that because his deformity is repellent, he "cannot prove a lover." So, instead he will "prove a villain" and murder everyone between himself and the throne.

Then, in the very next scene, Richard meets Anne, the beautiful widow of a rival he recently assassinated. She hates Richard and curses him, calling him the devil. Nonetheless, Richard, ugly as he is, guilty as he is, mounts a campaign of brilliant psychological seduction. He claims that because Anne is so breathtakingly beautiful and he is so desperately in love with her, he had to kill her husband in the hopes of having her. He then kneels down and offers her his sword so she can kill him, if she wishes. She declines and by the end of the scene this blend of flattery and self-pity wins her heart.

With that seduction, Richard reveals himself as a masterful lover. So why does he say he is not? Because he needs an excuse to mask his lust for power.

To write intriguing, layered, credible dialogue, first study the difference between the two motors for human action—motivation and justification. Then see if masking your characters' subconscious drives with their conscious efforts to excuse, or to at least make sense out of their unexplainable behaviors, adds depth to their words.

In most cases, false dialogue is not the signature of an overly confident, overly knowledgeable writer, but the opposite: a nervous, unschooled writer. Anxiety is the natural by-product of ignorance. If you don't know your character beyond his name, if you cannot imagine how he reacts, if you cannot hear his voice, if you write in bewilderment, your hand will scratch out nothing but bogus dialogue. In the fog of not knowing, you have no other choice.

Therefore, do the hard work. Surround your character with all the knowledge and imagining you can. Test his traits against the people around him and, most importantly, yourself. For at the end of the day, you are the touchstone of truth. Ask yourself: "If I were my character in this situation, what would I say?" Then listen with your most truth-sensitive ear for the honest, credible answer.

MELODRAMA

The adjective "melodramatic" indicts writing for excessiveness—shrill voices, lurid violence, tear-stained sentimentality, or sex scenes one shadow this side of pornography. On the other hand, Shakespeare's *The Tragedy of Othello* rages with murderous jealousy; Sam Peckinpah's

THE WILD BUNCH turns violence into cinematic poetry; Stephen Sondheim's *A Little Night Music* explores deep, painful sentiments; and Nagisa Oshima's masterpiece IN THE REALM OF THE SENSES indulges explicit sex; and none of them is melodrama.

Long before Oedipus gouged out his eyes, great storytellers have sought the limits of human experience. Twenty-first-century artists continue this quest because they sense that the depths and breadths of human nature know no limits. Anything you can picture your characters doing, believe me, human beings have already done it and in ways beyond imagining.

The problem of melodrama, therefore, is not over-expression but under-motivation.

When a writer scores a scene with ping-ponging histrionics, trying to make a snit seem lethal; when he cascades tears down a character's face, hoping to make a setback seem tragic; or when he forces behavior to exceed what's actually at stake in a character's life, we dismiss his work as melodrama.

Melodramatic dialogue, therefore, is not a matter of word choices. Human beings are capable of doing anything and saying anything while they do it. If you can imagine your character talking in a passionate, pleading, profane, or even violent way, then lift his motivation to match his action. Once you have behavior balanced with desire, take it a step further and ask yourself: "Would my character state or understate his action?"

Compare two versions of a "Cut off his head!" scene: Suppose GAME OF THRONES were to develop a plotline in which two kings fight each other in a long war to a blood-soaked end. Then comes the climax: The victorious king sprawls on his throne; his defeated enemy kneels at his feet, awaiting sentencing. A courtier asks the king, "What are your wishes, sire?" and the king screams his answer: "Smash every bone in his body! Burn his skin black, peel it off, and feed it to him! Rip his eyes from his head and his head from his neck."

Or, the courtier asks the king's wishes, and as the victor examines his manicure, he whispers, "Crucify him."

The subtext under "Crucify him" implies a death as hideous as the screamed answer, but which answer conveys greater personal power? The lurid, harsh, overstated rant, or the simple, understated "Crucify him"?

Either answer could be perfectly in-character, but what kind of character? The first answer implies a weak king at the mercy of his emotions; the second suggests a powerful king in command of his emotions. In the matter of melodrama, motivation and character are never separate. What would drive one character over a cliff wouldn't get another character off his sofa. Therefore, the balance of motivation versus action is unique to every role and has to be struck inside a character who first feels it and then does it.

7

LANGUAGE FLAWS

CLICHÉS

Clichés are scenes we've seen too many times before, acted with predictable behaviors, mouthed in dialogue we can recite before the actor says a word.

Like the weeds of repetition, clichés grow in the barren mind of the lazy writer. Many wannabes assume that writing is easy, or it should be, so they try to make it easy by rummaging through the trash of old stories, and pulling out the same tired phrases we've heard or read a hundred times in the same tired scenes we've heard or read a thousand times.

Why lazy writers lack originality is no mystery, but why do diligent, professional authors, who should know better, also resort to clichés? Because they work. Once upon a time, today's hackneyed expressions were inspired creative choices.

In CASABLANCA (1942), Captain Renault's gem-quality imperative "Round up the usual suspects" encapsulated political corruption in five smart words. Since then, the phrase "the usual suspects" has topped the list of the usual clichéd suspects in dozens of dictionaries devoted to clichés.[1]

Somewhere in humanity's past, a cave-dwelling storyteller first described a teardrop in a character's eye to express sorrow, and everyone around the fire felt a wave of sadness. Once upon a time, a king's raconteur first compared an enemy's military trap to a spider's web, and the whole palace felt a rush of fear. Although time has dulled the cliché's edge, the original invention was so sharp it still cuts a sliver of truth.

Here, for example, is a short list of clichés that frequently find their way into modern dialogue (to set a limit, I restricted the slate to phrases that begin with the letters "ba"): backseat driver, back to basics, back to square one, back to the drawing board, bad hair day, bag of tricks, ballpark figure, ball's in your court, bang your head against a brick wall, barking up the wrong tree, battle royal…and the list goes on.

Familiarity breeds comfort. People, on occasion, enjoy a cliché because it signals cultural continuity. The past is still present. What people loved in their childhood, they still love today. For that reason, clichés infect their everyday talk. People use them because, trite or not, they make immediate sense. As a result, the infrequent cliché adds verisimilitude.

Just remember this: Sooner or later, every cliché reaches its use-by date and becomes so odorous the world finally turns away in disgust.

To create fresh, original dialogue, set high standards and never settle for the obvious choice. Indeed, never settle for the first choice. Just write it down, then improvise, experiment, go a little crazy, pour out as many choices as your talent can create. Let your character say any off-the-wall thing that comes into her head. By playing with every wild thing you can imagine, you might discover that one of your lunatic choices is crazy but brilliant.

At the end of the day make your best choice, then cut the rest. No one has to see your weak choices…unless you're foolish enough to leave them on the page.

CHARACTER-NEUTRAL LANGUAGE

Character-neutral dialogue substitutes generality for specificity.

When writers use the stale language of everyday talk, they defend their vapidities, once again, with appeals to verisimilitude. And again, they would be correct. For when you turn an objective ear to the talk around you, banalities and clichés do indeed echo and re-echo down the caverns of conversation. In states of surprise, for instance, people call upon their deities. "Oh my God!" naturally pops out of the startled. As dialogue, however, this ready-made phrase robs the actor of a chance to create a revealing, character-specific moment.

What to do?

Ask yourself this question: If my character, in a state of shock, were to call upon God, how would she and she alone do it? If she were from Alabama, would she say, "Sweet, bleeding Jesus"? If she were from Detroit, would she look up to the sky and plead, "Lord have mercy"? If she were from New York, would she call upon the devil instead and curse, "Well, damn me to hell"? Whatever your choice, find words so true to your character, they wouldn't quite fit in anyone else's mouth.

We'll examine character-specific language in depth in Part Three.

OSTENTATIOUS LANGUAGE

In a dialogue scene near the end of James Joyce's *A Portrait of the Artist as a Young Man*, the novel's protagonist, Stephen Dedalus, and Lynch, his friend, debate aesthetics. To clinch his argument, Stephen describes the ideal relationship between an author and his finished work in these words: "The artist, like the God of creation, remains within or behind or beyond or above his handiwork, invisible, refined out of existence, indifferent, paring his fingernails."

Joyce's analogy advocates a writing method that so harmonizes characters and events, the telling seems authorless. Applied to dialogue, the Joycean ideal becomes talk so true to the vocal personalities that any hint of string pulling vanishes. Rather, each spoken word draws us deeper and deeper into the storytelling, holding us spellbound to the end.

Ostentatiousness breaks that spell. By ostentatious dialogue, I mean self-conscious displays of literariness, lines so unnecessarily expressive, so clearly out of character that they call attention to the writing as writing. The worst of these jumps out of the scene waving pompoms in celebration of its author's victory, declaring, "Oh, what a clever line am I!"

Like stand-up comics who laugh at their own jokes, like exhibitionistic athletes who dance in the end zone, literary swagger celebrates its success. But the instant a line of dialogue makes the reader or audience aware of art as art, the bond of belief fused between them and the character snaps.

As we noted in the "as if" discussion in Chapter Five, when people open a book or sit down as an audience, they shift their mental gears from the factual to the fictional mode. They know that to take part in the ritual of story, they must willingly believe in imaginary characters as if they were real, and react to fictitious events as if they were actually happening. It's a childlike state, so a bond of trust must run through the story, that ancient contract that conjoins a reader/audience to an author.

That's the deal, and no matter how realistic or fantasied the genre, the bond will hold so long as the reader/audience finds the dialogue true to the characters who speak it. The moment technique becomes visible, dialogue rings false, the reader/audience loses trust, the bond breaks, and the scene fails. Break belief often enough, the reader/ audience tears up the contract and tosses your work in the trash.

Of all aspects of characterization—dress, gesture, age, sexuality, mood, facial expression—speech is by far the most susceptible to disbelief. Odd phrasings, eccentric word choices, even out-of-place pauses can betray the odor of bad acting—fake emotions, shallow mind, and hollow heart. That's why every line of dialogue puts the writer under pressure to maintain the bond of credibility.

As an author, you must develop taste enough to sense the shift from expressivity to exhibitionism. To do so, first test the limits of language your medium imposes. What could be said with moving conviction on page may be embarrassingly unactable onstage. Because the marker dividing veracity from falsity is set as much by tradition as by authorship, first identify your story's genre(s), and then study the conventions. Finally, bring your best judgment to bear by asking this question: If I were my character, in these circumstances, what would I say? The only curbs on garishness are your innate taste and schooled judgment. So let your inner acumen be your guide. When in doubt, tone it down.

ARID LANGUAGE

The opposite of ostentation is desert-dry, Latinate, polysyllabic language composed into long sentences strung out over long speeches. The suggestions below help avoid arid speech in favor of natural, unaffected, seemingly spontaneous dialogue. But always bear in mind that these points (like all else in this book) are guidelines, not imperatives. Every writer has to find her own way.

PREFER THE CONCRETE TO THE ABSTRACT

Would a twenty-first-century character call her home a "domicile" or her car a "vehicle"? Doubtful. On the other hand, there may be people who would. So if you have a character-specific reason for your role's formality, then by all means, give her an abstract vocabulary. Otherwise, keep it real with specific names for objects and actions.

PREFER THE FAMILIAR TO THE EXOTIC

Would your character refer to his house as his *palais* or his apartment as his *pied-à-terre*? Doubtful. Then again, he may be la-di-da by nature...or actually French.

PREFER SHORT WORDS TO LONG WORDS

Would you write a line such as "His fabrications are falsifications of factuality"? Doubtful. "He stretches the truth," or simply, "He lies," or bluntly, "He bullshits," would be more credible choices.

And you always have at least two choices. English grew out of the merger of two languages, Anglo-Saxon, a dialect of Old German, and Old French, a dialect of Latin. As a result, the vocabulary of the language that became modern English immediately doubled (see the sidebar). English has at least two words for everything. In fact, with more than a million words, the English vocabulary offers near-inexhaustible choices.

HOW ENGLISH BECAME A DOUBLE LANGUAGE

After the Romans conquered England in the first century AD, they hired German and Scandinavian mercenaries from Anglia and Saxony to help fend off pirates and put down rebellions by the native Picts and Celts. When the Roman Empire abandoned England in 410 AD, more Anglo-Saxons migrated to the island, marginalizing the Gallic-speaking Celts, wiping out the Latin of the Romans, and imposing their Germanic tongue throughout England.

But 600 years later Latin came back this roundabout way: In 911 AD Danish Vikings conquered territory along the north coast of France and named it after themselves, Normandy, land of the Norsemen. After 150 years of marriage to French women, these Danes spoke what their mothers spoke, a thousand-year-old French dialect of Latin. In 1066 King Wilhelm of Normandy (a.k.a. William the Conqueror) led his armies across the English Channel and defeated the English king. With that victory, French came to England.

Throughout history, foreign conquests usually erase native languages. But England was the exception. For some mysterious reason, the Germanic language of the Anglo-Saxons and the Latinate French of the Normans merged. As a result, the vocabulary of what became modern English doubled. English has at least two words for everything. Compare, for example, the Germanic-rooted words "fire," "hand," "tip," "ham," and "flow" to the French-derived words "flame," "palm," "point," "pork," and "fluid."

Given the massive vocabulary of English, I offer this guiding principle: Shun polysyllabic words, especially those that end in Latinate suffixes such as "-ation," "-uality," and "-icity." Instead, favor the punchy, vivid one- or two-syllable words that, more often than not, come from the ancient Anglo-Saxon heritage of English. But whether your phrasings follow from the Germanic or French traditions, consider these four observations in making word choices:

1) The more emotional people become, the shorter the words and sentences they use; the more rational people become, the longer the words and sentences they use.

2) The more active and direct people become, the shorter the words and sentences they use; the more passive and reflective people become, the longer the words and sentences they use.

3) The more intelligent the person, the more complex his sentences; the less intelligent, the briefer his sentences.

4) The more well read the person, the larger his vocabulary and the longer his words; the less read, the smaller his vocabulary and the shorter his words.

Returning to an earlier example, consider the line "His fabrications are falsifications of factuality" as opposed to "The son of a bitch lies." The former polysyllabic, alliterated, Latinized accusation might be said by a bemused wigged barrister in a litigation comedy that satirizes the formalities of royal high court. The six monosyllables of the latter, however, could be said in anger by almost anyone anywhere.

When conflict builds and risk soars, people get emotional, active, direct, monosyllabic, and dumb. As conflict peaks, people often say really stupid things they later regret. In all media and all structural shapes of story, conflict-rich scenes not only carry the telling, but as strife progresses, they also tend to shape talk in the four ways I've described above.

On the other hand, when composing a story in the past tense of prose, reflective passages with little or no conflict become fairly common. So once again, let me remind you that the guidelines in this book only describe tendencies. Somewhere, somehow, someone's behavior turns every psychological doctrine ever formulated on its head. The same is true of writing. Every principle of craft sets up its creative contradiction.

Consider, for example, Boyd Crowder, the protagonist's frenemy in the long-form series JUSTIFIED. Showrunner Graham Yost pitched the dialogue for the entire cast at a heightened timbre. But for Boyd, he reached centuries back into the show's Appalachian setting and found a speech style fit for a Confederate politician. Here's Boyd on going to bed:

```
                    BOYD
        Be that as it may, I sense within me
        a growing, nagging torpor that seeks
        a temporary hibernation in a solitary
        area for comfort and slumber.
```

Over the centuries before the final merger of Latinate French and Old German into modern English, Latin and French were the languages of power in England.[2] Like many people in public life, politicians and corporate leaders alike, Boyd Crowder's quest for power and prestige propels his life down a series-long spine of action. And like the power greedy, Boyd flaunts his polysyllabic vocabulary and puts as many words as possible between the capital letter that opens a sentence and the period that closes it, scoffing at the admonition below.

PREFER DIRECT PHRASES TO CIRCUMLOCUTION

Would you write: "When I punched the guy, I suddenly realized that it hurt me a lot more than it hurt him, because after I took my hand out of my pocket and closed it as tight as I could, making sure that my thumb was on the outside and not the inside of my fingers, and then hit him in the face as hard as I could, I felt a sharp pain and couldn't close my fist anymore"? Or: "Broke my fist on his jaw. Hurt like hell."

Wording reflects the distinct qualities of a character played out against his once-in-a-lifetime conflicts. So if, for example, your character is a scientist, theologian, diplomat, professor, an intellectual of any persuasion, or simply pretentious, then he or she may very well use elaborate, academic locutions when calm and rational circumstances allow. But as a general principle, pace scenes with direct, unaffected speeches of crisp words.

This principle holds true on page and stage, but particularly onscreen. The theatre audience listens intensely. The reader can reread a novel's sentence if she doesn't get it on the first pass. Television viewers can record and rewind, if necessary, to listen to dialogue a second time. Big-screen dialogue, however, is spoken, then gone. The cinema audience concentrates through its eyes, not its ears. If moviegoers don't instantly understand, they turn to each other asking, "What did he say?"

But no matter the medium, misunderstood dialogue annoys. What difference does it make how eloquent your language is if the reader/audience misses its meaning? Therefore, expressive inversions aside, let line structure flow from noun to verb to complement in that order. Clarity above all.

PREFER AN ACTIVE TO A PASSIVE VOICE

Passive dialogue uses linking verbs such as "am," "is," "are," "was," "were," "be," and "been" to express static states (for example, "He isn't very smart"); active dialogue uses action verbs to express dynamic change (for example, "He'll figure it out for himself").

When humans enter into conflicts, their minds become energized, their views of themselves and the world around them become active, and therefore, their language becomes charged with action verbs. When situations calm, human beings become more passive, their view of life more reflective, and their language tends to fill with state-of-being verbs. Again, this pattern is only a tendency, not a rule of human behavior. Nonetheless, in a storm of conflict, state-of-being verbs slow headway like a ship dragging anchor.

The passivity that's most difficult to spot hides inside gerund phrases. In these cases, a state-of-being verb connects to an "-ing" ending verb in phrases such as "She is playing around," "They are working hard," "They were coming home yesterday." Gerunds give dialogue only slightly more energy. Before you commit to a gerund phrase, test the active case: "She plays around," "They work hard," "They came home yesterday," and see whether a single, direct verb doesn't better fit the moment.

PREFER SHORT SPEECHES TO LONG

When the pretentious wish to impress, they add syllables to words, words to sentences, sentences to paragraphs, paragraphs to speeches. They substitute quantity for quality, length for brevity, convolution for simplicity. The effect is often unintentionally comic.

For example, these three bites from the festooned language of Helen Sinclair (Dianne Wiest), the aging Broadway grande dame, in Woody Allen and Douglas McGrath's screenplay BULLETS OVER BROADWAY.

When she arrives late for a rehearsal:

> HELEN
> My pedicurist had a stroke. She fell
> forward on the orange stick and
> plunged it into my toe. It required
> bandaging.

Staring into a dark theatre auditorium:

> HELEN
> This old theatre—this church—so
> replete with memories, so full of
> ghosts, Mrs. Alving, Uncle Vanya,
> here's Ophelia, there's Cordelia...
> Clytemnestra...every performance a
> birth, each curtain, a death...

Walking through Central Park with her young playwright:

> HELEN
> Everything is meaningful in some
> unexplainable form, more primordial
> than mere language.
>   (as he tries to talk, she clamps her
>   hand over his mouth)
> Shh...shh...be silent...be
> silent...Let's just walk holding our
> thoughts...not revealing them...
> be still...let the birds have their
> song but let ours, for now, remain
> unsung.

So unless, like Woody Allen, your intention is satirical, strive to express the maximum in the fewest, truest possible words.

PREFER EXPRESSIVE LANGUAGE TO MIMICRY

Dialogue should sound like character talk, but its content must be way above normal. Fine writers listen to the world but rarely copy what they hear, word for word, to the page. If you study documentaries and listen to what real people actually say in real life, or watch so-called reality shows and listen to the improvisations of untrained actors, you'll soon realize that everyday talk on camera sounds awkward and amateurish. Fiction takes talk to a much higher level—far more economic, expressive, layered, and character-specific than back-fence chatter. Like marble carved by a Michelangelo, language is raw material chiseled by an author. Don't copy life, express it.

ELIMINATE CLUTTER

By clutter, I mean exchanges such as "Hi, how ya doing?" "Oh, I'm fine." "And the kids?" "They're fine, too." "Isn't it a beautiful day?" "Yes, finally. Last week was so rainy." In the same way people decorate empty shelves with knickknacks, inept writers dress up vapid scenes with verbal bric-a-brac, thinking that small talk adds an air of realism. But chitchat makes characters no more authentic than dressing them in sweat pants makes them athletic. Worse yet, cluttered talk not only hollows out characters and scenes; it misleads the reader/audience.

Dialogue is more than talk in the same way dance is more than movement, music more than sound, and painting more than shapes. A work of art means more than the sum of its parts, and every part of the work means more than the part itself.

Badly written dialogue tends to be literal; it means what it says and no more. Well-written dialogue, on the other hand, implies more than it says; it puts a subtext under every text. Readers and audiences schooled in the conventions of realism assume that every line has significance beyond its words or it wouldn't have been written. For that reason, story-goers seek the hidden beneath the clutter, the connotation under every denotation. If they cannot find it, confused and annoyed, they lose interest.

If your dialogue does not suggest unsaid thoughts and feelings below its surface, either enrich it or cut it.

8

CONTENT FLAWS

WRITING ON-THE-NOSE

Writing on-the-nose means putting a character's fullest thoughts and deepest emotions directly and fully into what she says out loud. Of the many varieties of inept dialogue, writing on-the-nose is by far the most common and most ruinous. It flattens characters into cardboard and trivializes scenes into melodrama and sentimentality. To understand the damaging effect of on-the-nose writing, let's study this flaw in depth.

The axiom "Nothing is what it seems" bears witness to life's duality: *What seems* is the surface of life—what strikes the eye and ear, the things people say and do...outwardly. *What is* is the actual life of thought and feeling that flows inwardly beneath the things said and done.

As we noted in Chapter Three, a person's life moves simultaneously through three levels corresponding to the said, the unsaid, and the unsayable: outwardly what people say and do, personally and socially, to get through their day (text); inwardly what they privately think and feel while they carry out these tasks (conscious subtext); and deepest yet, the massive realm of subconscious urges and primal miens that drive their inner energies (subconscious subtext).

It is, therefore, categorically impossible for a human being to say and do what she is fully thinking and feeling for the obvious reason: The vast majority of her thoughts and feelings run below her awareness. These thoughts cannot, by their nature, rise to the surface of the said. No matter how hard we may try to be absolutely open and honest, how we try to put the subtext of truth into the text of our behavior, our subconscious self haunts every word and deed. As in life, so in story: Every text condenses a subtext.

Suppose, for example, you were in mid-session with your psychiatrist, pouring out your darkest confession of the worst thing you've ever done to another human being. Tears filling your eyes, pain doubling you in two on the chaise, you choke out the words. And what's your psychiatrist doing? Taking notes. And what's in those notes? What you are *not* saying. What you cannot say.

A psychiatrist is not a stenographer, there to take down your exposés. He is trained to see through the text of you to the unsayable subtext, to those things you cannot say because you cannot consciously think them.

On-the-nose writing eliminates subtext by erasing conscious, unsaid thoughts and desires, along with subconscious, unsayable longings and energies, and leaving only spoken words, delivered in blatant, explicit, hollow-sounding speeches. Or, to put it another way, on-the-nose dialogue rewrites the subtext into a text, so that characters proclaim exactly and fully what they think and feel, and therefore, speak in ways no human being has ever spoken.

For example, this scene: Two attractive people sit across from each other in a secluded corner of a graceful restaurant. The light glints off the crystal and the dewy eyes of the lovers. Beautiful music plays in the background; gentle breezes billow the curtains. The lovers reach across the table, touch fingertips, look longingly in each other's eyes, simultaneously say, "I love you, I love you," and *actually mean it.*

This scene, if produced, would die like a squashed dog in the road. It is simply unactable.

By unactable I mean this: Actors are not marionettes hired to mouth your words and mime your actions. These artists give life to your cast by first discovering their character's true desire hidden in the subtext. They then ignite this inner energy and with it build ineffable layers of complexity from the inside out that finally surface in the character's actions, expressed in gestures, facial expressions, and words. But the scene, as I described it, is void of subtext and therefore, by definition, unactable.

The page, stage, and screen are not opaque surfaces. Each storytelling medium creates a transparency that allows us to glimpse the unsaid or unsayable in other human beings. When we watch a television series, a film, or play, or turn pages of prose, our eye does not stop at the words on the page or the actor onstage or onscreen. Our eye travels through the text to the subtext, to the deepest stirrings within the character. When you experience a quality story, don't you have the constant impression that you are reading minds, reading emotions? Don't you often think to yourself, "I know what that character's really thinking, feeling, and doing. I can see what's going on inside him better than he can, because he's blinded by his immediate problem"? The combined creativity of writer and actor gives us what we want from any story: to be a fly on the wall of life and see through the surface to the truth.

If I were an actor forced to act this candlelit cliché, my first ambition would be to protect my career. I would not let a bad writer make me look like a bad actor. I would put a subtext under that scene, even if it had nothing to do with the story.

My approach might go like this: Why has this couple gone out of their way to create a movie scene for themselves? What's with all the candlelight and soft music? Why don't they take their pasta to the TV set like normal people? What's wrong with this relationship?

Isn't that the truth? When do the candles come out in life? When things are fine? No. When things are fine, we take our pasta to the TV set like normal people. When there's a problem, that's when the candles come out.

So, taking that insight to heart, I could act the scene in such a way that the audience would see to the truth: "Yes, he says he loves her. But look, he's desperate he's losing her." That subtextual action adds substance as the scene deepens into a man's desperate attempt to rekindle the romance. Or the audience might think, "Yes, he says he loves her, but look, he's setting her up to dump her." That implied action stirs our fascination as we watch a man let a woman down gently with a last romantic dinner because, in truth, he's walking out.

With rare exceptions, a scene should never be outwardly and entirely about what it seems to be about. Dialogue should imply, not explain, its subtext. In the two variations above, the subtextual motivations and tactics are conscious but unspoken. As the audience/ reader perceives the unsaid tactic beneath the surface of behavior, the inner action gives the scene a depth that enriches the reader/audience with insight. An ever-present subtext is the guiding principle of realism.

Nonrealism, on the other hand, is the great exception. Nonrealism employs on-the-nose dialogue in all its genres and subgenres: myth and fairy tale, science fiction and time travel, animation, the musical, the supernatural, Theatre of the Absurd, action/adventure, farce, horror, allegory, magical realism, postmodernism, dieselpunk retrofuturism, and the like.

In nonrealism, characters become more archetypical and less dimensional. Stories set in imaginary or exaggerated worlds move toward allegorical event designs. Pixar's INSIDE OUT, for example. As a result, subtext tends to atrophy as dialogue becomes less complex, more explanatory, more on-the-nose. In a work such as THE LORD OF THE RINGS, no hidden or double meaning plays under lines such as "Those who venture there never return." If an actor were to layer that line with irony, it might prompt a laugh and kill the moment.

At some point during the fiction-writing process, every writer must answer that troublesome question: Exactly what kind of story am I telling? Two grand visions define the storyteller's approach to reality: the mimetic and the symbolic.

Mimetic stories reflect or imitate life as lived and sort themselves into the various genres of realism. Symbolic stories exaggerate or abstract life as lived and fall into one of the many genres of nonrealism. Neither approach has a greater claim on faithfulness to the truth.

All stories are metaphors for existence, and the degree of realism versus nonrealism is simply a writer's choice in his strategy to persuade and involve the reader/audience while he expresses his vision.

Nonetheless, one of the key differences between nonrealism and realism is subtext. Nonrealism tends to diminish or eliminate it; realism can't exist without it.

Why?

Because to clarify and purify a character's symbolic nature—virtue, villainy, love, greed, innocence, and such—nonrealistic genres eliminate the subconscious and with that, psychological complexity.

Whereas, the first premise of realism is that the majority of what a person thinks and feels is unconscious to her, and for that reason, the full content of her thoughts and feelings can never be expressed directly, literally, or completely. Therefore, to dimensionalize, complicate, and ironize the psychology of the role, mimetic genres clash desires arising from the subconscious against conscious willpower.

The psychological and social complexity of realism demands a subtext under virtually every line of dialogue. To avoid these distracting intricacies, nonrealism discourages subtext.

THE MONOLOGUE FALLACY

Every consequential moment in life pivots around a dynamic of action/reaction. In the physical realm, reactions are equal, opposite, and predictable in obedience to Newton's third law of motion; in the human sphere, the unforeseen rules. Whenever we take an important step, our world reacts—but almost never in the way we expect. From within us or around us come reactions we cannot and do not see coming. For no matter how much we rehearse life's big moments, when they finally arrive, they never seem to work out quite the way we thought, hoped, or planned. The drama of life is an endless improvisation.

For this reason, when a character sits alone staring at a wall, his flow of thought is an inner dialogue, not a monologue. This inner flux often becomes the stuff and substance of the modern novel. Prose writers can take us inside their characters' heads, bouncing inner actions back and forth between a thinking self and his doubting, applauding, criticizing, arguing, forgiving, listening, ever-reacting selves. This purpose-filled give-and-take is dialogue that takes the form of thought rather than talk.

A true monologue would provoke no response as it pours out long, uninterrupted, inactive, unreactive passages to no one in particular, turning characters into mouthpieces for their author's philosophy. Whether voiced aloud or thought from within, any speech that runs on for too long without change in value charge risks lifelessness, artificiality, and tedium.

How long is too long? The average speaking rate ranges between two to three words per second. At that pace, a two-minute speech could contain three hundred words. Onstage or onscreen, that's a lot of talk without someone or something reacting. In a novel, three hundred words is a full page. Pages of first-person musing or memory, unbroken by the crisscross of counterpointing inner reactions, would severely test the reader's patience.

On the other hand, suppose you were writing a two-character scene and feel that Character A talks throughout, while Character B sits in silence. In that case, long speeches become natural and necessary. As you write them, however, remember that even if Character A has rehearsed her confrontation with Character B, as she begins to tell him what's on her mind, the scene will not play out the way she expected.

Let's say, for example, that Character A expected Character B to defend himself against her accusations and so she memorized a long list of stinging retorts. But instead of arguing, he sits there in dead silence. His stone-faced reaction destroys her prepared speech. This unexpected turn forces her to improvise, and as we noted earlier, life is always an improvisation, always action/reaction.

On the page, therefore, insert Character A's nonverbal reactions to Character B's enigma. Into her column of talk, interlace her looks, gestures, pauses, stumbling phrases, and the like. Break her scene-long speech into beats of action/reaction within her and between her and the silent Character B.

Imagine another example: Let's say your character is reading a well-prepared sermon to her church's congregation. As her eyes move down the page, might she glance up, now and then, to check the congregation for expressions of interest or lack thereof? Suppose some people look bored, what would she do? Might not thoughts bounce through her mind, inspecting her voice, her gestures, the nervous energy in her belly, telling her to breathe, to relax, to smile, to make one adjustment after another as she performs her sermon? Her sermon may seem like a monologue, but her inner life is a dynamic dialogue.

Let's take the action/reaction principle a step further: Suppose that your character talks at length by nature. Consider Meryl Streep's Violet Weston in the film AUGUST: OSAGE COUNTY. Long speeches drive her behavior as she dominates all conversation and never reacts to what people think or feel. Such a character may bore other characters, but you can't allow her to bore the audience. Therefore, like playwright Tracy Letts, create the impression of long-windedness without actually going on and on. Watch the film and notice how Letts propels Violet's speeches, then builds each scene around the reactions of her word-weary relatives who have no choice but to suffer the talkaholic.

In 1889, playwright August Strindberg wrote *The Stronger*. The play is set in a café and dramatizes an hour-long scene that pits Mrs. X, a wife, against her husband's mistress, Miss Y. Mrs. X carries all the dialogue, but when performed, the silent Miss Y becomes the star role.

THE DUELOGUE

Think of the thousands of hours of bad film, television, and theatre you have suffered through. I suspect that more often than not, the shallow, tinny acting was not the fault of the actors but of the unactable duelogues that writers and their directors forced them to recite. **Duelogue** is my term for face-to-face confrontations in which two characters talk directly, explicitly, and emotionally about their immediate problem. Duelogues have the resonance of a brick because every line is on-the-nose, nothing left unsaid.

For example, this scene from the film GLADIATOR. The Emperor Commodus has imprisoned his rival Maximus Decimus Meridius. That night Maximus discovers Lucilla, Commodus's sister, waiting in his cell.

```
INT. DUNGEON—NIGHT

Guards take Maximus to an empty cell and
chain him to the wall. As they leave,
Lucilla steps out of the shadows.


            LUCILLA
    Rich matrons pay well to be pleasured
    by the bravest champions.


            MAXIMUS
    I knew your brother would send assas-
    sins. I didn't think he would send
    his best.


            LUCILLA
    Maximus...he doesn't know.


            MAXIMUS
    My family was burned and crucified
    while they were still alive.


            LUCILLA
    I knew nothing—


            MAXIMUS
            (shouting)
    —Don't lie to me.
```

LUCILLA

I wept for them.

MAXIMUS

As you wept for your father?

(grabbing her by the throat)

As you wept for your father?

LUCILLA

I have been living in a prison of
fear since that day. To be unable
to mourn your father for fear of
your brother. To live in terror
every moment of every day because
your son is heir to the throne. Oh,
I've wept.

MAXIMUS

My son...was innocent.

LUCILLA

So...is...mine.

(pause)

Must my son die too before you will
trust me?

MAXIMUS

What does it matter whether I trust
you or not?

LUCILLA

The gods have spared you. Don't you
understand? Today I saw a slave

become more powerful than the
emperor of Rome.

MAXIMUS

The gods spared me? I am at their
mercy, with the power only to amuse
the mob.

LUCILLA

That is power. The mob is Rome, and
while Commodus controls them, he controls everything.
(pause)
Listen to me, my brother has enemies, most of all in the senate.
But while the people follow him,
no one would dare stand up to him
until you.

MAXIMUS

They oppose him yet they do nothing.

LUCILLA

There are some politicians who have
dedicated their lives to Rome. One
man above all. If I can arrange it,
will you meet him?

MAXIMUS

Do you not understand, I may die
in this cell tonight, or in the
arena tomorrow. I am a slave.
What possible difference can I
make?

LUCILLA
This man wants what you want.

MAXIMUS
(shouting)
Then have him kill Commodus.

LUCILLA
I knew a man once, a noble man, a man
of principle who loved my father and
my father loved him. This man served
Rome well.

MAXIMUS
That man is gone. Your brother did
his work well.

LUCILLA
Let me help you.

MAXIMUS
Yes, you can help me. Forget you ever
knew me and never come here again.
(calling out)
Guard. The lady is finished with me.

Lucilla, in tears, leaves.

In Chapter Four of *The Poetics*, Aristotle argues that the deepest
pleasure of theatregoing is learning, the sensation of seeing through
the surface of behavior to the human truth beneath. Therefore, if you
use dialogue to turn your characters' unspoken needs and emotions
into conscious pronouncements as in the scene above, if, in other
words, you write the scene about what the scene is actually about, you

block that insight and deprive the reader/audience of their rightful pleasure. Worse yet, you falsify life.

In the give-and-take of life, we circle around problems, instinctively employing pretexts and tactics that skirt the painful, unspeakable truths that lurk in our subconscious. We rarely talk face-to-face, openly and directly, about our truest needs or desires. Instead, we try to get what we want from another person by navigating our way through a third thing.

Therefore, you will find the fix for on-the-nose writing in something outside the immediate conflict, a third thing that diverts a duelogue into a trialogue.

THE TRIALOGUE

Trialogue, as I redefine the term, names the triangular relationship between two characters in conflict and the third thing through which they funnel their struggle.

Four examples:

In his novel *Legs*, William Kennedy tells the story of the gangster, Jack "Legs" Diamond. In Chapter Three, as Jack comes into his house, his wife Alice confronts him. Jack's men, Oxie and Fogarty, have told her that Jack nicknamed one of their canaries Marion because the bird reminds him of his mistress. In the scene that follows, two canaries act as the third thing. The narrator is Jack's lawyer:

> We were hardly inside the house when Alice called out to Jack, "Will you come here please?" She was on the front porch, with Oxie and Fogarty still on the sofa. They were not moving, not speaking, not looking at Alice or at Jack or at me either when we got there. They both stared out toward the road.
>
> Alice opened the canary cage and said to Jack, "Which one do you call Marion?"
>
> Jack quickly turned to Fogarty and Oxie.

"Don't look at them, they didn't tell me," Alice said. "I just heard them talking. Is it the one with the black spot on its head?"

Jack didn't answer, didn't move. Alice grabbed the bird with the black spot and held it in her fist.

"You don't have to tell me—the black spot's for her black hair. Isn't it? Isn't it?"

When Jack said nothing, Alice wrung the bird's neck and threw it back in the cage. "That's how much I love you," she said and started past Jack, toward the living room, but he grabbed her and pulled her back. He reached for the second bird and squeezed it to death with one hand, then shoved the twitching, eye-bleeding corpse down the crevice of Alice's breasts. "I love you too," he said.

That solved everything for the canaries.

When Vince Gilligan pitched his long-form series BREAKING BAD to the network, his logline was "Mr. Chips goes Scarface." The protagonist, Walter White, faces multiple conflicts on all levels of life in dozens of directions, surrounded by a large cast of antagonists. Although building a drug empire seems to be Walter's super-intention, Gilligan casts the shadow of Heisenberg, Walter's doppelgänger, over all his scenes. From the very first episode, Walter's desires and dreads, his actions and reactions, are simply manifestations of Heisenberg's struggle to take over Walter and achieve the ultimate triumph of his genius. Heisenberg is BREAKING BAD's third thing.

Salman Rushdie's *Midnight's Children* is an allegorical novel whose protagonist, Saleem Sinai, is telepathic. But the third thing that modulates the novel's conflicts is not paranormal. Rather, Rushdie runs Sinai's every conflict through the cultural gap between India and Europe. By foregrounding what would normally be a background desire and painting every scene with a shade of East versus West, Rushdie colors his novel with an all-constant third thing.

For many readers and theatregoers, Samuel Beckett was the greatest writer of the twentieth century and his masterpiece is *Waiting for Godot*. The play shuttles a massive trialogue between Estragon and Vladimir (two homeless tramps) and Godot (the eponymous character named after the French slang for God). As the title implies, the two men spend the entire play waiting, hoping, arguing about, and preparing for "he who will never appear." The waiting seems futile, but it gives the tramps a reason, as they put it, "for going on."

In other words, Godot, Beckett's third thing, symbolizes the persistent belief that life will ultimately make beautiful and meaningful sense, once we find that transcendent, mysterious something that awaits us somewhere...somehow...out there...

9

DESIGN FLAWS

REPETITION

What makes otherwise vigorous language lie lifeless on the page? What makes scenes turn antiprogressive and their dialogue fall flat? I can think of many reasons, but the most common fault is the writer's dread enemy—repetitiousness.

Two kinds of repetition may infect a scene's dialogue.

1) **Accidental echoes.** When your eye skims down a page, lines like "They're moving their car over there" may speed by unnoticed. To avoid these verbal mishaps, record your dialogue after every draft, and then play it back. When you act your dialogue aloud or hear it acted to you, accidental echoes pop out, and you'll instantly know what to cut or rewrite.

2) **Repetitious beats.** Beyond echoing words, the greater danger is repetition of feeling: the same charge of value, positive-positive-positive-positive-positive, or negative-negative-negative-negative-negative, running on, beat after beat.

Repetitious feelings can be insidiously hard to spot because they hide behind variations in wording. So although the scene reads well, it feels, for some mysterious reason, dead.

Whenever a character takes an action in the pursuit of his or her scene intention, someone or something somewhere in the scene reacts. This pattern of action/reaction in character behavior is called a **beat**. For example, Character A pleads with Character B to listen to him, but Character B rejects what he has to say. Using gerunds to express action, that beat becomes begging/rejecting. (See Chapter Twelve for the complete definition of a beat.)

Beats propel scenes by advancing the action/reaction dynamic of character behaviors, each beat topping the previous beat, until the value at stake in the scene changes its charge at the turning point. (See the scene breakdowns in Chapters Thirteen through Eighteen.) But when the same beat repeats itself, the scene flattens out and boredom sets in. Repetitious behavior is far more common than accidental alliterations, more damaging to a scene, and insidiously difficult to spot. Consider this passage:

> CHARACTER A
>
> I have to talk to you.

> CHARACTER B
>
> No, leave me alone.

> CHARACTER A
>
> It's really important you listen to me.

> CHARACTER B
>
> Just let me be.

> CHARACTER A
>
> You've got to hear what I've got to say.

> CHARACTER B
>
> Shut up and go away.

Character A begs Character B three times to listen to him, and three times over she rejects his plea in virtually the same language:

"talk, listen, hear; alone, let, go away." Some writers try to solve this problem by using synonyms or switching the action/reaction beat around in the belief that textual rephrasing changes the beat. In this rewrite, for example, rejecting becomes the action and begging the reaction.

                         CHARACTER B
          Just standing there you bother me.

                         CHARACTER A
          I'm not bothering you, I'm trying to
          talk to you.

                         CHARACTER B
          I've heard enough.

                         CHARACTER A
          You haven't heard a single word I've
          said.

                         CHARACTER B
          Because I'm fed up with your BS.

                         CHARACTER A
          Believe me, it's not BS. It's the
          truth.

And on it goes. The identical beat of rejecting/begging, whether in the same words or different words, never changes, never progresses.

Some writers defend redundancies by claiming they're lifelike. And it's true. People do repeat themselves. Monotony is lifelike... and lifeless. My aesthetic calls for life-filled tellings. Stories, after all, are metaphors, not photocopies. Verisimilitude, the so-called "telling detail," is a stylistic strategy to enhance credibility, not a substitute for creative insight.

The ultimate storytelling sin is boredom—a villainous violation of the law of diminishing returns. This law states: The more often an experience repeats, the less effect it has. The first ice cream cone tastes great; the second one loses flavor; the third makes you sick. In fact, the same cause repeated back-to-back not only loses its impact, but in time also causes an opposite effect.

Repetitiousness follows a three-step pattern: The first time an artist skillfully uses a technique, it has its intended effect. If he immediately repeats that technique, it has less than half of the intended effect. If he's foolish enough to try it a third time, it will not only lack the effect he wants, but swing around from behind and inflict the reverse effect.

Suppose, for example, you were to write three scenes in a row, all tragic, expecting the audience to cry in all three. What would be the aftereffect of that composition? In the first scene, the audience members may cry; in the second scene they might sniffle; and in the third scene they will laugh their heads off. Not because the third scene isn't sad; it may be the most tragic of all. But because you have drained them of their tears, they feel it's ludicrous and insensitive of you to think they'll cry a third time, so they flip tragedy into comedy. The law of diminishing returns (true in life as it is in art) applies to all storytelling forms and contents—desires and conflicts, moods and emotions, images and actions, words and phrases.

Repetitious beats notoriously plague first drafts. Why? Because in the early going, the writer is still searching for the succinct, character-specific language that would nail each action/reaction with a single stroke of speech/reply. Instead, he repeats the same beat in different words, thinking he can substitute quantity for quality, deceiving himself with the belief that repetition reinforces meaning. In fact, it does the opposite. Repetition trivializes meaning.

So, what to do?

Never compromise. Fine writers scour their knowledge and imagination until they find the perfect choice. They write draft after draft, constantly improvising, playing one line against another, tossing lines around in their imagination, mouthing them out, and then, writing them down.

Gazing out the window daydreaming is not creativity. Aesthetic choices only come alive on paper. No matter how banal a line may be, write it down. Write down every choice that passes through your imagination. Do not wait for the moment your genius decides to wake up and give you a gift. Make the perfect choice by continuously moving your thoughts out of your brain and into the real world of the page. That's writing.

But even the most experienced writers will hit a wall as they stare at a beat and realize that for this particular action/reaction in this particular scene, no perfect choice exists. They do what they must. They stop banging their head against the keyboard and make a decision.

They go back and look through all the imperfect choices they wrote down. They ask, "Which of all of these possible choices is the best? Could there be a combination of imperfect choices that's better than any one choice?"

The final choice may not be ideal, but it is the one that comes closest to perfection. They will live with it today and hope that in some future draft, they will find an even better choice. But for the moment, at least, they've pruned their repetitious bramble.

MISSHAPEN LINES

Ideally, every line of dialogue is so perfectly worded, it fits its character in the moment and makes the immediate sense its author intended. Misshapen lines are like trip wires strung across a scene's path. They force confused readers and audiences to reread, rewind, or ask the person in the next seat, "What did he say?" I can think of three primary reasons that the wording of a line fails to instantly express itself: blurred meaning, mistimed meaning, and mistimed cues.

Blurred Meaning

Nouns name objects; verbs name actions. The amplitude of nouns and verbs ranges from the universal to the concrete, from the generic to the specific. As a general rule, specific nouns and verbs tend to sharpen meaning, while generic nouns and verbs modified by adjectives and adverbs tend to blur meaning.

Imagine writing a scene set in a shipyard. As a deckhand struggles to repair a sailboat's mast step, a boatsmith looks over his shoulder and offers advice. Which of these two lines conveys its meaning with instant clarity: "Forcefully utilize a big nail" or "Hammer a spike"?

The second, of course. The first not only seems unnaturally formal, but it also forces the reader/audience to rethink the meaning because the word "nail" covers many dozens of sharp-pointed fasteners, the adjective "big" could be anything over a couple of inches, "utilize" is as vague a verb as any in the language, and the adverb "forcefully" seems unnecessary. As a result, the first line needs two or three mental passes to make sense.

The lesson is this: Lines of dialogue that name specific objects and actions tend to express immediate understanding in clear, vivid images. Therefore, unless you intend ambiguous or mysterious qualities, avoid generic nouns and verbs strung with adjectives and adverbs.

Mistimed Meaning

The instant a speech makes sense, its reader or audience absorbs the line's action and leaps ahead to witness the reaction from the other side of the scene. Lines that mistime their meaning disrupt this action/reaction rhythm. Break interest frequently enough, and readers will toss your book; TV viewers will change channels, theatre audiences will leave at intermission. Therefore, before you send your writing into the world, reread the dialogue carefully, act out speeches if necessary, study each line, and listen for the precise moment of meaning.

Too late: When a speech drones on word after word without getting to its point, the reader/audience has one of two reactions: Either they lose patience and skip over the point, or they guess the point long before it arrives, and then sit in boredom as the speech stumbles to an anticlimax.

Too soon: When a speech begins with its meaning and then rattles on, interest quickly wanes. Readers skim over the words that follow; audiences tune out.

To skillfully time the meaning of each line, follow the guiding principles we previously covered: economy and design. 1) Say the maximum in the fewest words. 2) Master the three basic sentence designs—cumulative, balanced, suspense—so you can place meaning wherever you think best: beginning, middle, or end.

Mistimed Cues

A scene finds its natural rhythm of action/reaction in the give-and-take of meaning. Until a character has some sense of what was just said, of what just happened, he waits in limbo. But the instant Character A senses (or thinks he senses) what Character B is saying or doing, he reacts. Although most reactions seem instinctive, spontaneous, and instantaneous, they are in fact triggered by a glimpse of meaning. Character A may completely misinterpret the moment and overreact, underreact, or react off-the-wall. Nonetheless, his reaction, indeed every reaction, needs an action to prompt it.

Therefore, ideally, the last word or phrase of each speech is the core word that seals meaning and cues a reaction from the other side of the scene. On page, mistiming the core word is a relatively minor problem, but in the theatre or on a soundstage, it can break scenic rhythm and ruin performances.

A miscue happens when a core word is placed too early in Character A's line and prompts a reaction from Character B, but because Character A has more words to recite, Actor B must swallow her response and wait while Actor A finishes performing his speech.

To make cueing technique clear, let's work with this passage adapted from Act 1, Scene 5 of John Pielmeier's play *Agnes of God*.

Sister Agnes, a young nun, has given birth inside a convent. The newborn's dead body was found in a wastepaper basket next to Agnes's blood-soaked bed. Agnes claims to be a virgin. Some weeks prior to Agnes's giving birth, a hole appeared in the palm of Agnes's hand. The convent's Mother Superior wants to believe that these events are the work of God.

The police suspect that Agnes committed neonaticide, and so the court has appointed Dr. Martha Livingston, a psychiatrist, to determine Agnes's sanity. After examining Agnes, the doctor and Mother Superior talk.

As you read this passage, notice how the line structure places the core word or phrase at or near the end of speeches. This technique creates crisp cueing and a well-paced rhythm of action/reaction:

> MOTHER SUPERIOR: Look, I know what
> you're thinking. She's an hysteric,
> pure and **simple**.
>
> DOCTOR LIVINGSTON: Not simple, **no**.
>
> MOTHER: I *saw* the hole. Clean through
> the palm of her hand. Do you think
> **hysteria** did that?
>
> DOCTOR: It's been doing it for
> centuries—she's not unique, you know.
> She's just another **victim**.
>
> MOTHER: Yes, God's victim. That's her
> innocence. She belongs to **God**.
>
> DOCTOR: And I mean to take her away
> from Him. Isn't that what you **fear**?
>
> MOTHER: You bet I **do**.
>
> DOCTOR: Well, I prefer to look upon
> it as opening her mind, so she can
> begin to **heal**.
>
> MOTHER: But that's not your job, is
> it? You're here to diagnose, **not to
> heal**.

DOCTOR: I'm here to help her in whatever way I see fit. That's my duty as
a **doctor.**

MOTHER: But not as an employee of the
court. You're here to make a decision
on her sanity as quickly **as possible.**

DOCTOR: Not as possible. As quickly
as *I see fit.*

MOTHER: The kindest thing you can do
for Agnes is to make that decision
and let her **go.**

DOCTOR: And what then? If I say
she's crazy, she goes to an institution. If I say she's sane, she goes to
prison.

Now, I'll rephrase the lines and move their core words back into
the middle of each speech. Notice how the overall meanings stay
more or less the same, but the cueing stumbles, the actions/reactions
seem to spasm, and the scene staggers along.

MOTHER: Look, she's an hysteric,
pure and **simple.** I know what you're
thinking.

DOCTOR: **No,** not simple.

MOTHER: Clean through the palm of her
hand. Do you think **hysteria** did that?
I *saw* the hole.

DOCTOR: It's been doing it for centuries. She's just another victim. She's
not unique, you know.

MOTHER: Yes, she belongs to **God.**
God's victim. That's her innocence.

DOCTOR: Is that what you **fear**? That I
mean to take her away from Him?

MOTHER: I **do,** you bet.

DOCTOR: Well, opening her mind, so
she can begin to **heal,** is how I prefer to look upon it.

MOTHER: You're not here to **heal** but to
diagnose. That's your job, isn't it?

DOCTOR: My duty as a **doctor** is to
help her in whatever way I see fit.

MOTHER: You're here to make a decision on her sanity as quickly **as possible** as an employee of the court.

DOCTOR: As quickly as *I see fit.* Not
as possible.

MOTHER: Make that decision and let
her **go.** That's the kindest thing you
can do for Agnes.

DOCTOR: And what then? She goes to
prison if I say she's sane. She goes
to an institution if I say she's
crazy.

When actors encounter scenes of this kind, one of three things
will happen: Actors will cut off each other's lines, talk over each other,
or phony up their performance by politely and unnaturally waiting
for each speech to end. None of these options solves the problem of
mistimed cues.

Generally, speeches that end with cumulative sentences cause miscues. Before your scenes reach performance, act them aloud into a recorder and listen for the core words. Then go through the lines again, this time with a highlighter, and mark the core words, paying special attention to the last sentence of each speech. You will see that some phrases, especially prepositional phrases, tend to float to the ends of lines (just as they did in my last sentence). If so, cut or rephrase so that each speech ends on its cue.

MISSHAPEN SCENES

Faulty designs may also infect scenes. Like a misshapen line that mistimes its core word, a misshapen scene can mistime its turning point, bringing it in too soon or too late or not at all. A well-shaped scene pivots around its turning point in just the right way at just the right moment. From story to story, the "right" moment for any scene's turning point is unpredictable and idiosyncratic. Nonetheless, when timing misfires, the reader/audience feels it.

Too soon:

The first beat powerfully jolts the scene around its turning point. But from that moment on, the scene runs anticlimactically downhill as characters pour out exposition.

Example: A scene we'll call "The Lovers Break Up."

Version 1: In the first beat one lover declares the relationship over; the other agrees. The action/reaction of this immediate turning point swings the value charge of love from positive to negative. A beat of resolution may need to follow, but if the scene goes on and on as the lovers pour out their history, reminiscing about the good times and lamenting the bad, the reader/audience may turn against the scene and its characters, thinking, "You guys are done. Get over it."

Too late:

Repetitious beats of dialogue prattle on far too long until, sometime after the audience has lost interest, the turning point finally arrives.

Version 2: Lovers whose relationship has run its course reminisce about the good times and lament the bad until the audience sees the turning point coming long before it arrives. When the lovers finally agree to break up, the unsurprised audience sits there, thinking, "I saw this coming ten minutes ago."

Not at all:

Version 3: A couple floating in the doldrums of their relationship reminisce about the good times and lament the bad. They never take an action to either break up or recommit. The value of love is at the same tepid temperature it was when the scene opened. None of the scene's beats executes a turning point. The beats may zigzag in conflict, but the scene still has no shape, no arc, because the charge of its core value at the end of the scene is exactly what it was at the beginning of the scene. If nothing changes, nothing happens. The scene is a repetitious nonevent, leaving the audience to sit in wonder, asking, "What was the point of all that talk?"

As you compose beats of dialogue, give thought to the scene's shape. Build it beat by beat, line by line, progressively to and around the turning point, timing that pivotal beat for the perfect moment. You must decide how sharply or gradually a scene progresses. Your judgment guides what's too soon or too late. Every scene has a life of its own, and you have to feel your way to its ideal shape.

SPLINTERED SCENES

Scenes flow with life when the reader/audience senses a unity between the characters' inner motivations and outer tactics. No matter how subtle, indirect, or disguised their maneuvers may be, somehow what the characters say and do links back to their underlying desires. Scenes splinter and die for the converse reason: We sense a breakdown between what drives the scene from the subtext and what is said and done on the text, a disconnect between inner intentions and outer behaviors. As a result, the scene strikes us as false.

I can think of four reasons that an otherwise promising scene rambles out of joint, and the dialogue seems phony or lifeless: 1) The inner desires are fully motivated, but the dialogue is too bland, and so the scene falls flat. 2) The inner wishes are weakly motivated, but the dialogue is overwrought, and so the scene feels melodramatic. 3) The inner intentions and outer actions seem irrelevant to one another, and so the scene makes no sense and dialogue ricochets into non sequitur. 4) The characters' desires run side by side, never crossing in conflict. Without conflict, the scene has no turning point and so nothing changes; without change, dialogue thickens with exposition, the scene flattens into a nonevent, and we sit bored at best, confused at worst.

The writers of nonevents often try to conceal their ineptitude behind excessive language. Profanity is the common choice. They think that by inserting expletives into tepid dialogue, they raise the dramatic temperature. They would be wrong.

Not, as Seinfeld would remind us, that there's anything wrong with profanity per se. Certain settings demand profanity. In long-form crime series like DEADWOOD, THE WIRE, or THE SOPRANOS, profanity fits the characters like a silk suit. In fact, when criminals stop swearing, we know they mean business: A silent gangster is a lethal gangster.

To reshape a faulty scene, start at either level, subtext or text. You could work from the outside of it by rewriting the line and then back-tracking to create an inner action to fit. Or you could work from the inside out by going down into the inner life of your characters and layer by layer rebuild their deep psychologies and desires from the subtext outward into the scene's actions and reactions, sayings and doings. This process demands hard work and time, but because the inside-out method is more difficult, its successes are more powerful.

THE PARAPHRASING TRAP

Novice writers want to believe that writing problems are word problems, so when they sense the need to rewrite, they start by paraphrasing faulty dialogue, over and over. The more they rephrase, the more on-the-nose their language becomes, until subtext vanishes and the scene is irredeemably dull and false.

When scenes fail, the fault is rarely in the words; the solution will be found deep within event and character design. Dialogue problems are story problems.

Parts One and Two mapped out the complexities of dialogue. Part Three takes on the task of imagining and refining dialogue to serve your characters and their story.

PART 3

CREATING DIALOGUE

10

CHARACTER-SPECIFIC DIALOGUE

THE TWO TALENTS

Creative writing calls on two sources of creativity: story talent and literary talent. Story talent converts daily existence into meaningful, emotionally moving events and characters, then sculpts a work's inner design—what happens and to whom—to create metaphors for life. Literary talent converts everyday talk into expressive dialogue, then sculpts verbal designs—what's said and to whom—to create metaphors for talk. These two talents combine to shape scenes.

Drawing on both talents, fine writers employ an iceberg technique: To drive their story, they submerge the massive content of unspoken thoughts, feelings, desires, and actions out of sight in the subtext of scenes; to tell their story, they create a text of words on the visible tip of character behavior. Let's step back to the time those voices first spoke.

Homer, the earliest storyteller we know by name, recited the more than 250,000 words of description and dialogue in the *Iliad* and the *Odyssey* from memory. With the invention of the alphabet around 800 BC, his epics were written down and the first dialogue appeared on page. Homer's characters argue and accuse each other, they recount the past and predict the future, but despite the blind poet's image-rich rhyming couplets, their speeches tend toward declamations rather than conversations. As a result, although the choices and actions of his characters express their individuality, in dialogue they sound remarkably alike.

In this same period, the first onstage performances were sacred rituals in which choruses sang, danced, and chanted verse stories of gods and heroes. Religious ritual slowly evolved into theatre as the chorus leader stepped forward to become an actor with a distinguishable character. The playwright Aeschylus introduced a second actor and invented the technique of rapid face-to-face exchanges of short speeches known as stichomythia, literally line-talk (from *stikho*, meaning "line," and *muthos*, meaning "talk"). The rhythmic intensity of characters alternating single lines or phrases, combined with quick, biting language, unleashed great dramatic power, as in Aeschylus's play *Agamemnon*.

But it was the introduction of the third actor by Sophocles in plays such as *Oedipus Rex*, *Antigone*, and *Electra* that gave rise to character complexity. Sophocles transformed ancient archetypes such as king, queen, princess, warrior, and messenger into characters with personality, dimensionality, and singular voices. What these first playwrights sensed—and what writers of all story media have understood since—is that the more complex the psychology of a character, the more distinctive his dialogue must become. In other words, originality in character design finds its final expression in character-specific dialogue.

Consider, for example, this exchange between Matthew McConaughey's Detective Rustin Spencer "Rust" Cohle and Woody Harrelson's Detective Martin Eric "Marty" Hart from the television series TRUE DETECTIVE. As they watch an old-fashioned tent revival in rural Louisiana, Rust turns to Marty and says:

RUST

What do you think is the average IQ
of this group, huh?

MARTY

What do you see up there on your high
horse? What do you know about these
people?

RUST

Just observations and deduction: I
see a propensity for obesity, poverty,
a yen for fairy tales. Folks putting what few bucks they do have in
a little wicker basket that's being
passed around. I think it's safe to
say nobody here's gonna be splitting
the atom, Marty.

MARTY

You see that? Your fucking attitude.
Not everybody wants to sit alone in
an empty room beating off to murder
manuals. Some folks enjoy community,
the common good.

RUST

If the common good's got to make up
fairy tales, then it's not good for
anybody.

The scene focuses the Rust/Marty conflict through a trialogue.
In this scene the revivalist congregation becomes the third thing,
allowing word choices to distinguish Rust from Marty in two ways:
First, their conflicting attitudes toward the congregation. Rust feels
contempt, Marty compassion. Rust criticizes them; Marty forgives.
Second, Rust's logical intellectualizations versus Marty's emotional
personalizations. Rust keeps his cool; Marty loses his. As a result,
Rust's phrasings run noticeably slower and longer than Marty's.

Compare these two lines:

Rust: "Just observations and deduction: I see a propensity for obesity, poverty, a yen for fairy tales."

Marty: "Not everybody wants to sit alone in an empty room beating off to murder manuals."

Note Rust's abstract, polysyllabic terms with Latinate suffixes of "-ion" and "-ity" versus Marty's concrete images in iambs and trochees: "alone," "empty," "murder." Showrunner Nic Pizzolatto's precise word choices contrast the loner Rust and his need for justice against the gregarious Marty and his need for intimacy.

Crafting idiosyncratic speech, however, does not mean tricking up a role with vocal quirks. A self-conscious stylishness can be like bad acting, the literary equivalent of hamming it up and hogging the spotlight. Panache may impress us, but a true voice affects us. The former calls attention to itself; the latter calls us to life.

Contemporary writing workshops often stress development of an inimitable presence in language known as "a voice." To me, this talk seems pointless. A writer's style or so-called voice cannot be found or created self-consciously. Voice is not a choice; it's a result.

A distinctive writing style pays off when a creative personality embraces a broad and deep knowledge of the human condition. When talent wraps its arms around content, the tumultuous coupling that follows breeds a singular manner of expression. Voice is the instinctive, spontaneous consequence of genius working up a sweat.

In other words, as you explore your story's content of role, meaning, emotion, and action, as you do the hard work that brings life to your characters, you will write as only you would. That, for better or worse, like it or not, will be your voice. And like a painter covering canvas after canvas through decades of toil in search of his vision, your evolution toward a true voice will take time.

In writing dialogue, the same principle applies. When an original character reaches inside for expression, her voice will be the second-nature consequence of her one-of-a-kind personality, experience, knowledge, locution, and accent. Ideally, a character's language is so plausible, so seemingly natural, so idiosyncratic that every line in every scene seems to be an improvisation that no one but that specific character in that specific moment would invent.

In saying this, I am not advocating difference for the sake of difference. Quirkiness is not originality, and it takes taste to know the difference. The ability to tell a true phrase from a clever phrase does not come easy; if it's not innate, it must be learned over years of reading and rereading quality novels, while watching and rewatching exceptional television, films, and theatre. As you hone your judgment of story and character, one insight shifts into sharp focus: The foremost facet of dialogue is vocabulary.

Dramatized storytelling is not about words but characters using words as they struggle through life. All components of speech from grammar to phrasing to pace are therefore vital to dialogue. But nothing conveys or betrays personality as much as a character's choice of words, the names of the things that live within him.

VOCABULARY AND CHARACTERIZATION

As noted in previous chapters, nouns name objects and verbs name actions. A character's vocabulary names what he knows, what he sees, and what he feels. His choice of words is all-important because a character's façade of talk should be a doorway to his depths. Passive, blurry, generic phrases flatten a character and numb the audience; active, concrete, sensory language arouses insights that weave dimension and complexity into a character.

To create a brilliant surface of talk that leads the audience into a character's depths, your method must move in the reverse direction: Start within your character, and then work outward from content to form to effect.

First, draw on your sensory and visual powers to imagine content (what your character sees and feels on the inscape, the unsaid and unsayable), then craft his dialogue (the said) into a form that slips his words into the reader's or audience's ear with effect. In essence, you must transform the images in your character's inner life into the verbiage of his outer talk.

THE PRINCIPLE OF CREATIVE LIMITATION

The tougher the technique, the more brilliant the feat.

Constraint, discipline, and limitation inspire stunning creative achievement; unrestrained freedom, on the other hand, usually ends in a sprawl. If you take an easy, undisciplined path that makes little claim on your talent, the results smudge with paint-by-numbers banality. But if, contrarily, you choose an arduous technique that demands a master's proficiency, then talent builds muscle until your imagination, strained to the tearing point, explodes with power.

The great difficulties imposed by creative limitations are why a Beethoven symphony transcends whistling. Why *Whistler's Mother* surpasses a doodle. Why a high school prom is not the Bolshoi.

The strategy of surrounding yourself with aesthetic obstacles to compel creative excellence begins by pitting language against image. Language is the medium of conscious thought; image is the medium of subconscious thought. Therefore, writing the first banal phrases that pop to mind is far easier than expressing character in lucid, three-dimensional imagery found in the far reaches of your imagination. When you write off the top of your head, all characters sound alike and the sounds they make irritate like fingernails on a blackboard. Their grating voices fake life and then fill the sham with irredeemably false dialogue—out of character, out of scene, void of feeling, void of truth.

Dialogue takes work. Compare the effort to bring someone to mind with words ("my cousin Judy") to the task of first conjuring up a glowing image of your cousin—her Alice-blue eyes, and the almost Asian shape they take when she smiles—then holding her living picture before your mind while you rummage through your vocabulary, searching for the perfect words to make your vision of Judy shine in the minds of your readers. Writing vividly for the outer eye and ear of a spectator or for the inner eye and ear of a reader demands fierce concentration.

The language-bound art of writing aims its effects at the mental cortex that deciphers words. To tell a story in pure image runs contrary to writing's psycholinguistic nature. Therefore, the masters of page, stage, and screen dedicate their lives to doing exactly that. They choose the strenuous, indeed, next-to-impossible technique. To inspire excellence, to create an insightful, original telling, the dedicated writer condemns himself to chain-gang labor, a long dig down the back roads of the unconscious in search of vigorous, deep-image language.

Sensory dialogue resonates with the speaker's inner life. Specific, vivid, image-rich language leads the reader/audience to the character's subtext of hidden, unconscious thoughts and feelings. As a result, when such characters take verbal actions in pursuit of their desires, they become transparent and we can know them in depth. But when characters sound like a business report—generic, literal, Latinate, polysyllabic—their language flattens the action and diminishes the scene's inner life. The more opaque the characters become, the more we lose interest. Therefore, even if a character is in fact a bore, his dialogue must express his lifeless soul with vivid dreariness.

LOCUTION AND CHARACTERIZATION

Character-specific locutions depend on both sides of a sentence, subject and predicate. Subject (what or whom the sentence is about) and predicate (something about the subject) combine to create a line of dialogue that helps express two primary dimensions of characterization: knowledge and personality. One aspect of the line tends to convey the former, and the other, the latter.

Although characterization can be expressed through dialogue in a variety of ways, a character's knowledge tends to be expressed in the names of things, nouns and verbs, while a character's personality tends to be expressed in the modifiers that color those nouns and verbs.

Knowledge. If a character uses a vague phrase such as "a big nail," we sense that his knowledge of carpentry is limited. Generic nouns suggest ignorance. But if he names the thing—"shank," "clout," "spike," "corker," "sinker"—we sense a much fuller knowledge.

The same principle applies to verbs. Core verbs (as opposed to modal verbs) span from generic to specific. If a character remembers that someone "moved slowly across the room," we sense that his recall is dull. Generic verbs also suggest ignorance. But if his dialogue sharpens and he says that another man "sauntered," "waltzed," "padded," "slouched," "moseyed," "pranced," or "dragged himself" across the room, his choice of verb suggests a vivid memory and insight into the other man. Specific names of objects and actions convey a superior mentality.

Personality. The idiosyncratic by-products of a character's life experience—his beliefs, his attitudes, his individuality—are chiefly expressed through modifiers.

First, adjectives. Two characters look at a fireworks display. One describes it as "big" and the other as "stupendous." These are two very different personalities.

Second, adverbs. Two characters watch a motorcycle go by. One says it was going "ferociously" and the other says it was moving "quickly." Again, two very different people.

Third, voice. Core verbs also span the spectrum that runs from active to passive. In active sentences, the thing doing the action is the subject, and the thing receiving the action is the object. Passive sentences reverse this so that the object becomes the subject. As a result, someone who tends to use phrases such as "The family planned the wedding" (active) versus someone who would remember the event as "The wedding was planned by the family" (passive) have two very different feelings about how things work in life, two very different temperaments.

Fourth, modals. Modal verbs (could, can, may, might, must, ought, shall, should, will, would) attach to core verbs to add qualities of modality: ability, possibility, obligation, permission, and the like. Modal phrases convey:

1. A character's sense of self and the world around him.
2. His feelings for his place in society and the interplay of relationships.
3. His view to the past, present, and future.
4. His attitudes toward what is possible, what is permitted, and what is necessary.

Someone who says "The family could plan the wedding" versus someone who insists "All weddings must be planned by families" are probably two very different personalities.

PRINCIPLE OF CHARACTER-SPECIFIC DIALOGUE

Nouns and verbs express a character's intellectual life and range of knowledge. Modifiers (adjectives, adverbs, voice, modalities) express his emotional life and personality.

To figure out how your character's personality expresses itself, ask: "How does my character see life? Passive? Active? How does my character modify subjects and especially predicates?" Before your fingers hit the keys, constantly ask: "What words, phrases, and images would make my character's dialogue his alone? What in the psyche, life experience, and education of my character will express the content of his knowledge (names of nouns and verbs) and the one-of-a-kind mannerisms of his personality (modifiers and modalities)?"

CULTURE AND CHARACTERIZATION

To answer these questions, consider this: Through the totality of your character's living hours, awake and sleeping, his or her mind, conscious and unconscious, has absorbed an immense and character-specific volume of culture: a combination of language, family, society, art, sport, religion, and the like.

Year after year, life's events have hurt, rewarded, and influenced your character in countless ways. Into this sea of customs and encounters, the character has mixed the dispositions and physical givens he or she was handed at birth: attractive/plain, healthy/ailing, aggressive/shy, high IQ/low IQ, and so on. The result is a specific admixture of genes and life experience that makes each character unlike any other character and gives him or her a singular voice.

In the four case studies that follow, notice what their authors found when they entered into their characters' psyches: popular culture. In *The Tragedy of Julius Caesar*, Shakespeare references the Colossus of Rhodes, which was the most famous, and certainly the largest, bronze statue of the classical era, which in turn means that the well-traveled Cassius and Brutus must have sailed past it in awe. In *Out of Sight* Elmore Leonard weaves images from THREE DAYS OF THE CONDOR, a hit film in the Watergate era. His characters probably saw it in their impressionable teens. Passages from 30 ROCK feature upper-class obsessions like yachts and mergers. Fine wine, on the other hand, is no longer the province of the rich; schoolteachers are as expert as sommeliers, which plays crucially in SIDEWAYS.

To write each scene, the author has gone inside to see what his character has seen. He then discovered a cultural icon to enrich the scene as the character draws an analogy between his immediate life and a work of art or cuisine. Once again, using a third thing to create a trialogue.

Think about it: How in fact do people express themselves in words? How do they explain what they're thinking and feeling, say what needs to be said, and, most importantly, do what needs to be done? Answer: They use the bits and pieces of everything they know. And what, first and foremost, do they know? Culture. Whether popular or esoteric, whether acquired from formal education or overheard on a street corner, culture is our dominant source of knowledge. To that we add all the imagery rooted in characters' encounters with nature, cityscapes, workscapes, and religious ritual. Plus images from dreams, from fantasies about the future, from the totality of the day and night musings that weave these familiarities together. This mass of experience creates a treasure chest of images that will inspire distinctive dialogue in the mouths of your characters.

The next four case studies illustrate these principles.

FOUR CASE STUDIES

THE TRAGEDY OF JULIUS CAESAR

Consider this setup: Senator A is powerful and popular. The envious Senator B wants the respected Senator C to join forces against Senator A. So Senator B pulls Senator C aside to persuade him:

> SENATOR B
> Senator A is so popular and so pow-
> erful that compared to him, we're
> nobodies.

Senator B states the obvious in passive and opaque language. His dialogue couldn't be less persuasive, less imaginative, less interesting. The comparison he makes might irritate Senator C, but Senator B's words have no imagery to give them life; no subtext to give them depth. His complaint is so bland, Senator C could easily shrug it aside.

Here's how history's greatest dialogue artist rendered the moment in *The Tragedy of Julius Caesar*, Act 1, Scene 2:

> CASSIUS
> (to Brutus)
> Why, man, he doth bestride the narrow
> world like a Colossus, and we petty

men walk under his huge legs and peep
about to find ourselves dishonorable
graves.

Shakespeare's Cassius hugely overstates the case, which, of course, is what people do when trying to wheedle their way inside someone else's head. They use the techniques of rhetoric to distort, exaggerate, or manipulate.

The Colossus was one of the Seven Wonders of the Ancient World. More than one hundred feet tall, this bronze statue of the sun god Helios stood astride the harbor at Rhodes with ships sailing in and out of port under its legs. Cassius compares Caesar to an awesome, imaginary colossus that would have one foot in Spain, the other in Syria, and the whole Mediterranean world between its legs.

And yet, note that Shakespeare gives Cassius this phrase: "the narrow world." The instinctive, off-the-top-of-the-head phrase would be "the wide world." So, why "narrow"?

Because Shakespeare (I suspect) wrote in-character. He slipped his imagination into the mind of Cassius, so he could work from Cassius's subjective point of view. He was then able to see the world the way Cassius saw it and write imagistic dialogue for the eye: "the narrow world."

As Roman senators, Cassius and Brutus would have imperial maps spread across their desks. Every week they receive strategic reports from all corners of the empire. These men know exactly how wide the world is: the width of all things Roman. To the naive, the world may seem wide, but to these urbane politicos, it's narrow. So slender, in fact, a single man—the ambitious Caesar—could seize it and rule it alone.

While immersing himself in his characters, Shakespeare must have imagined, even researched, their childhoods, for it was in their educations that he found his inspiration for crafting the play's unique dialogue.

Aristocratic Roman schoolchildren were rigorously trained as orators, as future politicians skilled in the arts of declamation, persuasion, and rhetoric. And the guiding tenet of public speaking is, "Think as a wise man but speak as a common man." Speak, in other words, in the plain, monosyllabic manner of the street.

So note that of the twenty-eight words in Cassius's sentence, only two have more than two syllables.

Shakespeare knew that seasoned orators string short words together to create the effect of casual, artless, sincere ease while at the same time showing off their verbal ingenuity. For it takes skill to deliver monosyllables in a natural, pleasing rhythm. And Cassius is very clever. In fact, all of the play's characters have a way with simple words. The dialogue style throughout *The Tragedy of Julius Caesar* is almost exclusively monosyllabic, with some of Shakespeare's passages stringing thirty or more monosyllables in a row.[1]

What's more, as patrician senators, Cassius and Brutus have immense pride in their aristocratic heritage. The notion of seeming "petty," of "peeping about" in search of a "dishonorable" grave repels the noble Brutus. With these biting images, Cassius seduces him to assassinate Caesar.

In terms of the modal side of dialogue, because Cassius is a bold, hard-thinking man on a mission, he uses direct action verbs: bestride, walk, peep. He does not modify his predicates. If he did, it might read like this:

```
                    CASSIUS
          It seems to me as if mighty Caesar
          could bestride the narrow world like
          some kind of gigantic Colossus, so we
          poor men would have to walk carefully
          around under his huge legs, and try
          to peep about to maybe, should we get
          really lucky, someday find ourselves
          disgusting, dishonorable graves.
```

This Cassius, as I've rewritten him, becomes weak and nervous. He's so preoccupied with what's possible and not possible, what's permitted and not permitted, what's sure and unsure, that he surrounds his verbs with "could," "would," "should," and other cautious supplementary phrases.

Lastly, very importantly, consider the background desires that surround Cassius and the gentlemanly restraints that shape his behavior. He knows that Brutus is a very private man, taciturn yet perceptive. Both men have been raised in an elite society in which cultured men do not bare their souls to each other. Therefore, to write in-character, Shakespeare must have given thought and feeling to what his character would not say. For example, the refined Cassius would not speak on-the-nose:

> CASSIUS
> I loathe that power-grabbing Caesar,
> and I know you hate the bastard, too.
> So before we end up begging on our
> knees, kissing his tyrant's ass, let's
> murder the son of a bitch.

With the exception of hip-hop lyrics, the twenty-first century seems poetry-lite. Shakespearean iambic pentameter may feel out of reach; nonetheless, we want our scenes to play with an intensity that matches the emotional lives of our characters and, in turn, moves the reader/audience. To achieve this, we take inspiration from Shakespeare to enrich our dialogue with imagery. First, we visualize the scene from our character's subjective point of view, and then find language from within his nature and experience to create his character-specific dialogue.

OUT OF SIGHT

Consider this setup: During a prison break, a criminal forces a federal agent into the trunk of her car and climbs in with her. His partner takes the wheel and drives off. While sardined in the pitch-dark trunk, crook and cop are irresistibly attracted. After the getaway, neither can stop thinking about the other. Eventually she tracks him to a hotel where, despite their antagonistic roles, their mutual passion moves them to declare a truce and spend a romantic evening together.

```
INT. LUXURY HOTEL ROOM—NIGHT

Candlelight glints off the dewy eyes of the
handsome Criminal and beautiful Federal
Agent as they gaze longingly at each other.

                    FEDERAL AGENT
          I'm confused and scared.

                    CRIMINAL
          Same here, but I'm trying to be cool.

                    FEDERAL AGENT
          Me, too, but I'm afraid that you might
          rape me.

                    CRIMINAL
          Never. My only hope is to have a nice
          romantic night together.

                    FEDERAL AGENT
          Good. Because underneath your tough
          exterior I suspect there's a really
          loving guy. But still I can't be cer-
          tain. Maybe you're trying to seduce
          me so I'll help you escape the law.

                    CRIMINAL
          No, I understand you're still a fed-
          eral agent and I'm still a bank rob-
```

```
ber and you have your job to do. It's
just that you're so beautiful, I can't
stop thinking about how it was when
we met.
```

```
They sigh and take a sad sip of champagne.
```

I've written this scene in the paralytic language of people saying exactly and completely what they think and feel. The result? A flattened wreck no actor could salvage. Explicit dialogue that turns a character's inner life into words turns an actor to wood.

In contrast to the scene I sketched above, here is how Elmore Leonard, one of the finest writers of dialogue in the modern novel, rendered the cop/criminal tryst:

In Chapter Twenty of *Out of Sight*, escaped bank robber Jack Foley invites US Marshal Karen Sisco to a hotel suite overlooking the Detroit waterfront. They drink and reminisce about the prison break and their dangerous, yet erotic encounter in the trunk of her car:

She said, "Remember how talkative you were?"

He said, "I was nervous," lighting her cigarette and then his own.

"Yeah, but you didn't show it. You were a pretty cool guy. But then when you got in the trunk...I thought you'd try to tear my clothes off."

"It never entered my mind. Well, not until—remember we were talking about Faye Dunaway?...I told you I liked that movie *Three Days of the Condor*, and you said yeah, you loved the lines? Like the next morning, after they'd slept together, he says he'll need her help and she says..."

"Have I ever denied you anything?"

"I thought for a couple of seconds there, the way you said it, you were coming on to me."

"Maybe I was and didn't know it...Before they ever go to bed she accused him of getting rough. He says, 'What? Have

I raped you?' And she says, 'The night is young.' I thought,
Come on—what is she doing, giving him ideas?"

"You know you kept touching me, feeling my thigh."

"Yeah, but in a nice way."

"You called me your zoo-zoo."

"That's candy, inside, something sweet."

In this deceptively simple but complex scene, Leonard's dialogue
creates multiple layers of textual imagery over a double layer of
implied images. The first two layers are set up in the previous pages:

Layer 1. The image of the setting: For his long-fantasized rendez-
vous with Karen, Foley chooses a posh hotel suite that commands a
panorama of the city at night under a gentle snowfall. Soft lights, soft
music. They're posed like a chic couple on a Crown Royal whisky bill-
board. Leonard delights in setting up this glitzy cliché so that he can
ironize and undercut it again and again.

Layer 2. The all-too-familiar image of the situation: Their
romance is "illegal." Foley is a felon on the run; Sisco is the law. But
this has been done many times before: McQueen and Dunaway in
THE THOMAS CROWN AFFAIR, Bogie and Bacall in DARK PAS-
SAGE, Grant and Hepburn in CHARADE. It's not just any cliché; it's
a movie cliché.

And then the dialogue takes over to add more facets.

Layer 3. Escape from "reality": Over their movie scene Foley and
Sisco superimpose yet another movie—THREE DAYS OF THE CON-
DOR. They chat about their favorite moments from the film because
they're fully aware that they're living in a virtual film. As a result, the
reader blends the famous faces of Robert Redford and Faye Dunaway
with the fictional faces of Foley and Sisco, coating the whole episode
with Hollywood gloss.

Layer 4. The memory: The lovers replay their intimate adventure
in her car trunk. This takes us back to the mini-movie that ran through
our head when we read the prison break scene in the opening chapters.

Now four layers of images are superimposed on the reader's mind:
The hotel setting, the cop/criminal situation, the Hollywood ver-

sion, and the burnished nostalgia of how they met. But that's only the surface.

Beneath this, Leonard creates his characters' inner lives of unspoken needs and dreams.

Leonard uses a pair of third things: THREE DAYS OF THE CONDOR and the memory of their first adventure. These play back-to-back to create interlocking trialogues. As I laid out in Part Two, working a scene through a third thing helps keep dialogue off-the-nose.

Layer 5. The subtext: Under the lines, we sense Jack and Karen's desire to put aside their cop/criminal roles, to take time out from life, so they can indulge this rush of romance. We can well imagine their sexual fantasies clashing with the realization that their intimacy is tabooed. This in turn makes their sensual desires dangerous, even lethal, and so all the more erotic. Could either of them name what they're feeling? No. No one could and still feel it. To name a feeling is to kill it.

The present is so razor sharp, Leonard has them sidestep it by reminiscing about how they met. But as they do, everything they say about the past betrays a subtext of what they're feeling in the now.

They kid about the heart-pounding jailbreak and how they played it cool, but for all Karen knows she's sitting on a sofa with a smooth-talking rapist, and for all Jack knows there's a SWAT team with a battering ram outside the door. They tease offhandedly about the sexy tension they felt in the trunk of her car, while the heat of the moment blisters the hotel room. And, very importantly, they hide all this behind witty quotes from THREE DAYS OF THE CONDOR.

It's at this fifth layer of the unspoken that Leonard unites Karen and Jack. We realize that although they're on opposite sides of the law, at heart they're a matched pair of die-hard romantics hooked on old movies.

Layer 6. Dreams: This subtextual insight leads us to imagine the wistful daydreams of Foley and Sisco. While he hopes that she will play Faye Dunaway to his Robert Redford and somehow rescue him, he knows that in fact that will never happen. Sisco can see herself as Dunaway acting out that scenario; it's her wish, too. But like Foley, she knows it's an impossible fantasy.

Leonard must have loved dialogue or he couldn't have written it with such skill. So note that his characters also love dialogue. When he has them remember THREE DAYS OF THE CONDOR, they don't recall looks or gestures; they quote lines verbatim—lines that must have struck Leonard's ear when he saw the film.

What is the payoff to the deep insight this scene gives the reader?

Enormous suspense: Will they make love? Will she forget she's a cop and let him escape? Will she arrest him? Will she have to shoot him? Will he be forced to kill her? This seemingly casual talk between forbidden lovers expresses all of the above and more.

30 ROCK

Season 5, Episode 1, "The Fabian Strategy"

This half-hour comedy series takes place in the offices and studios of NBC in New York's Rockefeller Center.

John Francis "Jack" Donaghy (Alec Baldwin) serves as vice president of East Coast television and microwave oven programming for General Electric. Liz Lemon (Tina Fey) works for Jack as producer and head writer of a prime-time variety show. Avery (Elizabeth Banks) is Jack's fiancée.

The passages below sample Jack's verbal style. The phrases and words in bold signal his unique characterization and hint at his true character.

On his first morning back from summer vacation, Jack calls Liz on the phone:

> JACK
> Oh, Lemon, **Avery** and I just got back
> from the most amazing vacation on
> **Paul Allen's yacht. Sheer bliss.** Avery
> is the **most perfect woman ever cre-
> ated. Like a young Bo Derek stuffed
> with a Barry Goldwater.** (pause) But

it's back to reality. No more making love on the beach surrounded by
a **privacy circle** of **English-trained
butlers.**

(Note: Paul Allen co-founded Microsoft.)

In a meeting later that day with Liz and her show's producers,
Jack fears that the network's weak performance will jeopardize an
all-important merger:

> JACK
> In order for our merger to stay
> attractive to our friends at Kable-
> town, we have to **seem like a sexy,
> profitable company,** and we're **almost
> pulling it off. The Harry Potter Theme
> Park is a huge hit with both anglo-
> philes and pedophiles. The movie
> division has a James Cameron movie
> the whole world will see whether they
> like it or not.** Only NBC continues
> to be the **engorged whitehead** on the
> otherwise **flawless** face of Universal
> Media.

As their workday ends, Liz confesses that she suffers relationship
problems, so Jack gives her this advice:

> JACK
> **You can't just do the vacation part.**
> At some point **you have to** go home to
> the same house, unpack your dirty
> laundry, and have **a life together.**
> And one of you says, "We should
> redecorate." And the other says,

"Please, Avery, I'm using the **commode** right now."

                    LIZ
Oh, she wants to redecorate? She just moved in.

                    JACK
Avery has **opinions. I love her for that.** Unfortunately, she wants to repaint the upstairs hallway in a **striae faux** finish called **"Husk."** I **prefer** the color that's already there, a reddish brown shade called **"Elk Tongue."**

                    LIZ
So tell her "No." It's your house.

                    JACK
This is how I know you've never had an adult relationship. **If** I say "No," **then I will be required to say "Yes"** to something else in the future and the stakes in the future might be higher.

                    LIZ
Then say "Yes."

                    JACK
If I give in, **then** I'm no longer **the alpha in my house.** Before you know it, she'll have me **wearing jeans** and **reading fiction.**

LIZ

Yeah, well, "Yes" and "No" are kind
of your only two choices.

JACK

For most men, sure, but there is a
third option—the **Fabian Strategy**...
The Fabian Strategy **derives** its name
from **the Roman general Quintus Fabius
Maximus.** He ran away, Lemon. Rather
than engage in battle, he would
retreat and **retreat until the enemy
grew fatigued and eventually made
a mistake.** Although I **abhor** it as a
military strategy, **it is the basis
for all my personal relationships.**

Jack's handsome face, tailored suits, and $150 haircuts suggest who
he might be, but beyond his physical appearance, the writers draw on
terms such as "sheer bliss," "flawless," "Bo Derek," "a sexy, profitable
company," "privacy circle," "commode," "Husk," "Elk Tongue," "prefer," and "abhor" to nail his characterization. Modal phrases such as
"no more," "like it or not," "you can't," "you have to," and "if/then"
signal Jack's sense of power over others. The word and phrase choices
in these speeches attest to Jack's command of popular culture, his
excellent education, his identification with the upper class, his capitalist ethos, his controlling executive leadership style, and, most of
all, his supercilious, egoistic snobbery. Together, these traits etch the
outer self he shows the world—his characterization.

But vocabulary and syntax also throw light on character dimension.

A dimension is a contradiction that underpins a character's nature.
These psychological stanchions come in two kinds: 1) Contradictions
that play characterization against true character. Namely, conflicts
between a character's outer traits and his inner truths, between the
persona of his visible behavior and the person he hides behind the

mask. 2) Contradictions that play self against self. These dimensions link the warring forces within true, deep character—most often desires from the conscious self at odds with opposite impulses from the subconscious self.[2]

Jack's speech style reveals seven such dimensions: He's 1) socially sophisticated (Paul Allen's yacht/English-trained butlers) yet privately primal (the alpha in my house/engorged whitehead), 2) unscrupulous (The movie division has a James Cameron movie the whole world will see whether they like it or not) yet guilt-ridden (I will be required to say "Yes"), 3) fiscally conservative (Barry Goldwater) yet risk taking (The Harry Potter Theme Park is a huge hit with both anglophiles and pedophiles), 4) well educated (General Quintus Fabius Maximus invented his guerrilla strategy during the Second Punic War in 218 BC) yet self-deceived (the basis for all my personal relationships), and 5) intellectually pompous (a striae faux finish) yet factually informed (a striae faux finish). Jack 6) uses devious tactics to navigate his personal life (retreat until the enemy grows fatigued and eventually makes a mistake), yet idealizes his relationships with women (most perfect woman ever created). He 7) is a realist (You can't just do the vacation part), yet a dreamer (a life together). The show's directors constantly posed Jack in a close-up, staring into space, imagining his idealized future.

Multidimensional as he is, Jack Donaghy is not, however, a dramatic character; he is, at heart, a comic character, driven by a blind obsession.

Both dramatic and comic characters seek an object of desire. In that they are the same. Their core difference, however, is awareness. As a dramatic character pursues his quest, he has sense enough to step back and realize that his struggle could get him killed. Not the comic character: His core desire blinds him. His self-deluded mind fixates on his desire and pursues it, wildly unaware. This lifelong mania influences, if not controls, his every choice.[3]

Jack Donaghy blithely obsesses on an aristocratic lifestyle more suited to the 1920s than today. "Made love on a beach surrounded by a privacy circle of English-trained butlers" sounds like a diary entry by

Wallis Simpson before she became Duchess of Windsor. Vacationing on yachts recalls scenes from F. Scott Fitzgerald novels. The love of his life, a fellow aristocrat named Avery, graduated from Choate and Yale. Jack, like the Princeton alumnus he is, disdains jeans and only reads nonfiction.

His syntactically balanced sentences roll out rounded with relative clauses: "In order for our merger to stay attractive to our friends at Kabletown, we have to seem like a sexy, profitable company, and we're almost pulling it off," and "If I say 'No,' then I will be required to say 'Yes' to something else in the future, and the stakes in the future might be higher." His dialogue sounds like a tuxedoed businessman talking shop in a penthouse cocktail party. The tuxedo, in fact, is Jack's eveningwear of choice. In Season 1, Liz asks him why he's wearing a tux in his office and he explains, "It's after six. What am I, a farmer?"

Like the clothes they wear, vocabulary and syntax dress characters inside and out.

SIDEWAYS

Rex Pickett writes both novels and films. In addition to his first novel *Sideways*, and a second novel, *La Purisima*, he wrote the screenplay for the 2000 Oscar-winning short film MY MOTHER DREAMS THE SATAN'S DISCIPLES IN NEW YORK.

Screenwriters Jim Taylor and Alexander Payne earned writers' credit on the best-written episode of the Jurassic Park franchise, JURASSIC PARK III. In addition, they have collaborated with great success on CITIZEN RUTH, ELECTION, ABOUT SCHMIDT, and SIDEWAYS. More recently, Payne wrote and directed THE DESCENDANTS (2011) and directed NEBRASKA (2013).

SIDEWAYS, which Payne directed from their adaptation of Pickett's novel, has won a long list of international nominations and awards, including an Oscar for Best Adapted Screenplay. As their choice of subject matter suggests, these writers are attracted to life's losers and their futile, often comic struggles to win.

SIDEWAYS is, by genre, an education plot. Four simple conventions define this very difficult genre:

1. The protagonist begins the story with a life-denying mindset. He finds no meaning in the world around him or himself in it.
2. The story will arc the protagonist's downbeat point of view to a positive, life-affirming stance.
3. A "teacher" character will help guide the protagonist's revolution in attitude.
4. The story's greatest source of conflict will come from the protagonist's beliefs, emotions, habits, and attitudes—in other words, from an inner conflict with his own self-destructive nature.

The education plot is a natural genre for a novel because prose allows the writer to directly invade a character's deepest thoughts and feelings. In Pickett's first-person novel, for example, his protagonist whispers his secret fears and doubts directly into the reader's ear. Onscreen, however, this literary form becomes extremely difficult, requiring superb dialogue to imply within a character what the novelist can explicitly state on page.

The screenplay's protagonist, Miles, is a pudgy, divorced, failed novelist who teaches junior high school English. Although no one makes the accusation onscreen, he's clearly an alcoholic who hides his dependency behind the mask of (in Miles's words from the novel) a wine cognoscente. The title SIDEWAYS is never explained in the film, but in the novel "sideways" is slang for drunk. To "go sideways" means to get very, very drunk.

The "teacher" role is filled by the intelligent and beautiful Maya, who's also divorced, also a wine lover. Midway through the film, Miles and Maya spend an evening with Miles's pal, Jack, and Maya's friend, Stephanie. They all end up at Stephanie's house. When Jack and Stephanie retire to the bedroom, Miles and Maya sit in the living room sipping a wine from Stephanie's excellent collection. At first they chat about how they met (he was a customer in a restaurant where she waits tables), then the subject turns first to Miles (his novel), then to Maya (her MA in agrology), and, finally, to their mutual love of wine.

MAYA
Why are you so obsessed with Pinot?
That's all you ever order.

Miles smiles wistfully at the question. He
searches for the answer in his glass and
begins slowly.

MILES
I don't know. It's a hard grape to
grow. As you know. It's thin-skinned,
temperamental. It's not a survi-
vor like Cabernet that can grow and
thrive anywhere...and withstand
neglect. Pinot's only happy in specific little corners of the world,
and it needs a lot of doting. Only
the patient and faithful and caring
growers can do it, can access Pinot's
fragile, achingly beautiful qualities. It doesn't come to you. You have
to come to it, see? It takes the
right combination of soil and sun...
and love to coax it into its fullest expression. Then, and only then,
its flavors are the most thrilling and
brilliant and haunting on the planet.

Maya has found this answer revealing and
moving.

MILES
(CONT'D)
I mean, Cabernets can be powerful and
exalting, but they seem prosaic to me

for some reason. By comparison. How
about you, why do you like wine so
much?

                    MAYA
I suppose I got really into wine
originally through my ex-husband. He
had a big, kind of show-off cellar.
But then I found out that I have a
really sharp palate, and the more I
drank, the more I liked what it made
me think about.

                    MILES
Yeah? Like what?

                    MAYA
I started to appreciate the life of
wine, that it's a living thing, that
it connects you more to life. I like
to think about what was going on the
year the grapes were growing. I like
to think about how the sun was shining that summer and what the weather
was like. I think about all those
people who tended and picked the
grapes. And if it's an old wine, how
many of them must be dead by now. I
love how wine continues to evolve,
how every time I open a bottle the
wine will taste different than if I
had uncorked it on any other day,
or at any other moment. A bottle of
wine is like life itself—it grows up,

evolves and gains complexity. Then it
peaks—like your '61—and begins its
steady, inexorable decline. And it
tastes so fucking good.

Now it's Miles's turn to be swept away.
Maya's face tells us the moment is right,
but Miles remains frozen. He needs another
sign, and Maya is bold enough to offer it:
she reaches out and places one hand atop
his.

                    MILES
    But I like a lot of wines besides
    Pinot too. Lately I've really
    been into Rieslings. Do you like
    Rieslings?

She nods, a Mona Lisa smile on her lips.

                    MILES
                  (pointing)
    Bathroom over there?

                    MAYA
    Yeah.

Miles gets up and walks out. Maya sighs and
gets an American Spirit out of her purse.

Like the scene from Leonard's *Out of Sight*, this is a seduction, but in
this case between two very sensitive people—the sage earth mother,
Maya, and the emotional wallflower, Miles. Like the scene from LOST
IN TRANSLATION below, it's an exchange of revelations. But they

are not confessing personal failures; rather, the underlying actions of
both characters are bragging and promising. Miles and Maya try hard
to sell their virtues to each other.

In the subtext of Miles's big speech, he invites Maya to come to
him, and in the subtext of her reply she does, and brilliantly. So that
she leaves no doubt about her desire for him, she even touches his
hand and smiles a "Mona Lisa" come-on. But Miles chickens out, bolts
for the toilet, and leaves her in frustration.

Once again, note how the scene is designed around a trialogue.
Wine becomes the third thing under which the subtext pulses.

Now I'll rewrite their speeches on-the-nose, pulling the bragging
and promising from the subtext and putting it directly into the text by
eliminating the third thing.

> MILES
>
> I'm a hard guy to get to know. I'm
> thin-skinned and temperamental. I'm
> not tough, not a hard-hearted survi-
> vor. I need a cozy, safe little world
> and a woman who will dote on me. But
> if you are patient and faithful and
> caring, you will bring out my beauti-
> ful qualities. I cannot come to you.
> You must come to me. Do you under-
> stand? With the right kind of coax-
> ing love I will turn into the most
> thrilling and brilliant man you could
> ever have the luck to know.

> MAYA
>
> I am a woman with a passion for life.
> Hour after hour, day after day, sea-
> son after season, I thrive in the
> golden light of time, savoring its
> every precious spell. I am in my

```
prime—old enough to have learned
from mistakes, young enough to grow
and evolve, so that with every pass-
ing day I will become ever more com-
plex, ever more amazing. When I peak,
and believe me, I am peaking at this
very moment with you, I will taste
good, oh so very, very good. Please
fuck me.
```

A person might feel such feelings, might even think such thoughts in some vague way, but no one would ever say these embarrassingly painful things aloud. This bald language becomes impossibly corny when put directly into a living room chat about ideas and yearnings. Fine actors would choke on it.

Yet these are exactly the actions that Taylor and Payne want their characters to take: To put themselves in the very best light and to promise the moon in an effort to win the love of the other with seductive boasts and promises. So, how to write these beats of action into dialogue? Let them converse.

How do people converse? By using what they know as a third thing. And what do these characters know? Miles and Maya are experts on two subjects: wine and themselves. They have extensive, practical knowledge of the former and romanticized, idealized knowledge of the latter. So using the nature of wine and its cultivation as metaphor for their own natures, they each campaign to win the esteem of the other.

As I laid out in the beginning of this section, the key is vocabulary. Character-specific dialogue originates in a character's unspoken desires and the actions he takes to satisfy those desires. Actions become talk that translates the character's implicit thoughts and feelings into explicit words—the precise words that only that specific character would use at that specific moment taking that specific action.

Drawing on Pickett's novel, Payne and Taylor have added their knowledge and insight to Miles and Maya and given each a character-specific voice and vocabulary. In order to seduce, Miles and Maya describe themselves in the language of wine. Compare, for example, Miles's modal language, his sensitive adjectives and adverbs, to Maya's bold naming, her nouns and verbs.

Miles: "Thin-skinned," "temperamental," "doting," "faithful," "caring," "fragile," "have to come to," "achingly beautiful," "thrilling," "brilliant," "haunting," "really been into..."

Maya: "Life," "living thing," "connects to life," "life itself," "sun," "shining," "summer," "evolves," "gains," "peaks," "tastes so fucking good..."

These writers have an ear for their characters.

PART 4

DIALOGUE DESIGN

12

STORY/SCENE/
DIALOGUE

Now and then, we experience a flawed story that squandered surprisingly good dialogue. We have all waded through badly told stories with dreadful dialogue, but we rarely encounter a superbly told story ruined by lousy dialogue. And the reason is simple: Quality storytelling inspires quality dialogue.

Like a hectic fever, bad dialogue warns of a festering infection deep within a story. But because struggling writers often mistake the symptom for the disease, they try to bandage scenes by obsessively rewriting their dialogue, thinking that once the talk is right, the telling will heal. But maladies of character and event cannot be cured by scratching dialogue raw with draft after draft of paraphrases.

To put it as clearly as I can: Until you know what you are talking about, you cannot know how your characters go about talking. The order in which you create your story's components and how you bring all these pieces together is unique to you. But no matter how helter-skelter the process, an author ultimately gathers godlike knowledge of form (event and cast design) and content (cultural, historical, and psychological substance) to support the telling from the bottom up, to create dialogue from the inside out. Dialogue is the final step, the frosting of text atop layers and layers of subtext.

So, before we examine dialogue design, let's review the basic components of story design.

INCITING INCIDENT

At the opening of a story, the central character's life rests in a state of relative balance. She has her ups and downs. Who doesn't? Nonetheless, the protagonist holds reasonable sovereignty over her existence— until something happens that radically upsets that equilibrium. We call this event the **inciting incident**.

To incite means to start; "incident" means "event." This first major event starts the story by throwing the protagonist's life out of kilter. The inciting incident could happen by decision (she decides to quit her job and open her own business) or by coincidence (lightning strikes her store and she loses her business). The inciting incident could move her life powerfully to the positive (she invents a brilliant new product) or to the negative (a business rival steals her invention). The inciting incident could be a massive social event (her corporation goes bankrupt) or a quiet inner event (she comes to realize in her heart of hearts that she hates her career).[1]

STORY VALUES

The impact of the inciting incident decisively changes the charge of the value at stake in the character's life. **Story values** are binaries of positive/negative charge such as life/death, courage/cowardice, truth/lie, meaningfulness/meaninglessness, maturity/immaturity, hope/despair, justice/injustice, to name but a few. A story may incorporate any number, variety, and possible combinations of story values, but it anchors its content in an irreplaceable core value.

A core value is irreplaceable because it determines the story's fundamental nature. Change core value, change the genre. For example, if a writer were to extract love/hate from her characters' lives and substitute morality/immorality, this switch in core values would pivot her genre from love story to redemption plot.

The values in scenes can be very complex, but at minimum, every scene contains at least one story value at stake in the character's life. This value either relates to or matches the story's core value. Scenes dramatize change in the charge of this value. A scene may begin with its value(s) at either a purely positive charge, purely negative charge, or an admixture of both. Through conflicts and/or revelations, the opening charge of value(s) changes. It could reverse (positive to negative, negative to positive), intensify (positive to doubly positive, negative to doubly negative), or wane (purely positive to a weaker positive, purely negative to a weaker negative). The precise moment in which the charge of one or more values changes is a scene's turning point. Therefore, a story event occurs the instant a value at stake in a scene changes charge.[2]

THE COMPLEX OF DESIRE

Everyone wants reasonable sovereignty over existence. By throwing life out of balance, the inciting incident arouses the natural human desire to restore balance. Essentially, therefore, all stories dramatize the human struggle to move life from chaos to order, from imbalance to equilibrium.

Characters act because needs demand deeds, but the complexity of life swirls through a labyrinth of desires. Ultimately the art of storytelling merges and organizes many streams of desire into a flow of events. The storyteller picks and chooses only those desires he wishes to express in the specific scenes that progress his story from beginning to end. To understand this process, we need to examine the components of desire and how they propel storytelling.

Desire is a figure in five dimensions:

1. **Object of desire**
2. **Super-intention**

3. Motivation
4. Scene intention
5. Background desires

1. Object of Desire

In the wake of the inciting incident, the protagonist conceives of an object of desire, that which he feels he must have in order to put his life back on an even keel. This object could be something physical, like a stash of money; or situational, like revenge for an injustice; or ideational, like a faith to live by. Example: A humiliation on the job (inciting incident) has damaged the protagonist's reputation, radically upsetting the balance of his life, so he seeks a victory in the workplace (object of desire) to restore balance.

2. Super-Intention

The super-intention motivates a character to pursue the object of desire. This phrase restates the protagonist's conscious desire in terms of his deepest need. For example, the object of desire above (victory in the workplace) rephrased as the super-intention becomes: to gain inner peace through a public triumph.

In other words, the object of desire is objective, whereas the super-intention is subjective: what the protagonist wants versus the emotional hunger that drives him. The former term gives the writer a clear view of the crisis scene that waits at the end of the story when the protagonist will get or fail to get his object of desire. The latter term connects the writer to the feelings within the protagonist, the inner need that drives the telling.

In every story, the protagonist's super-intention is somewhat generic (for example, to win justice through revenge, to find happiness in intimate love, to live a meaningful life), but the exact object of desire (for example, a dead villain, the ideal mate, a reason not to commit suicide) gives a story originality. Whatever the object of desire may be, the protagonist wants it because he must satisfy his super-intention, his profound longing for a life in balance.

3. Motivation

Do not confuse either object of desire or super-intention with motivation. The first two answer "what" questions: What does the character consciously want? What does he subconsciously need? Motivation answers "why." Why does a character need what he feels he needs? Why does he want his particular object of desire? And if he gets what he wants, will this success actually satisfy his need?

The roots of motivation reach deep into childhood and, for that reason, are often irrational. How much you understand the whys of your character's needs and wants is up to you. Some writers, like Tennessee Williams, obsess on motivation; some writers, like Shakespeare, ignore it. Either way, what's essential to the writing of scenes and their dialogue is an understanding of the characters' conscious and subconscious desires.[3]

4. Scene Intention

A scene shapes a character's moment-by-moment struggle toward his ultimate life goal. **Scene intention** names what a character immediately wants as a step in the long-term effort of the super-intention. As a result, the actions he takes and the reactions he gets in each scene will either take him closer to or bend him farther away from his object of desire.

If the writer were to grant the character his scene intention, the scene would stop. For example, in a police interrogation scene, Character A wants Character B to stop questioning him. A's scene intention is to stop the interrogation. If B were to give up and leave the room, the scene would end. B, on the other hand, wants A to reveal a secret. From B's point of view, his scene intention is to discover the secret. If A were to confess, that too would end the scene. Scene intention names the character's imminent, conscious desire—what he wants right now.[4]

5. Background Desires

A character's **background desires** limit his choices of action. Each of us is constantly aware of the state of the relationship between ourselves and every person and every object we encounter in life—our safety in traffic, which table the maître d' gives us, our place in the hierarchy of coworkers, to name only three public examples. We are acutely aware of our private rapport with friends, family, and lovers. We're also attuned to our innermost self, our relative state of physical, mental, emotional, and moral well-being. What's more, we're aware of our place in the flow of time, of our experiences in the past, the knife-edge of the present, and what we hope for the future. These complex interwoven relationships create our background desires.

Relationships become desires in this way: Once created, relationships form the foundation of our existence; they create the system that gives us our sense of identity and security in life. Our well-being depends on them. We try to eliminate relationships of negative value, while at the same time maintaining, if not improving, positive relationships. At the very least, we want relationships of either kind kept within reasonable control.

Background desires, therefore, not only cement the status quo of a character's life; they temper his behavior. Background desires form the web of restraints that follows every character into every scene. These fixed desires for stability limit and temper the character's actions. They influence what the character will or will not say to get what he wants.

In principle, the more relationships of positive value a character accumulates in life, the more restrained, the more "civilized" his behavior. The reverse is also true: When a character has nothing to lose... he's capable of anything.

In some cultures, because of social mores, you can speak your mind; in other cultures, for the same reason, you must obey unspoken codes of address and keep your thoughts to yourself. Humanity's enormous range of cultures creates a spectrum of polar extremes that spans from cultures that are all subtext with hardly any text versus cultures that are all text and very little subtext. In the social sciences, these polar extremes are known as high-context versus low-context cultures.[5] In fiction, they determine the relative quantity of text versus subtext.

High-context cultures have a strong sense of tradition and history. They change very slowly over time, and so from generation to generation their members hold many beliefs and experiences in common. A high-context culture will be relational, collectivistic, intuitive, and contemplative. It places high value on interpersonal relationships within a close-knit community (Native Americans, for example).

As a result, within these in-groups many things can be left unsaid because their members can easily draw inferences from their shared culture and experiences. The Italian Mafia is such an in-group. In THE GODFATHER, when Michael Corleone says, "My father made him an offer he couldn't refuse," an entire episode of extortion becomes violently clear. Michael then goes on to make the event explicit to Kay Adams because she's not in the in-group.

High-context cultures, such as those in the Middle East and Asia, have low ethnic and social diversity. They value community over the individual. In-group members rely on their common background, rather than words, to explain situations. Consequently, dialogue within high-context cultures calls for extreme economy and precise word choices because within such settings a few subtle words can implicitly express a complex message.

Conversely, characters in low-context cultures, such as North America, tend to explain things at greater length because the people around them come from a wide variety of racial, religious, class, and nationalistic backgrounds. Even within the same general cultures these differences appear. Compare, for example, two American stereotypes: a Louisianan (a high-context culture) and a New Yorker (a low-context culture). The former uses a few tacit words and prolonged silences, while the latter talks frankly and at length.

What's more, in low-context cultures, shared experiences change constantly and drastically, thus creating communication gaps from one generation to the next. In immigrant societies, such as the United

States, parents and children have notoriously difficult communication problems that result in long, loud arguments. Characters become more verbose and explicit as subtext shallows out.

FORCES OF ANTAGONISM

As a character pursues her object of desire, she consciously or instinctively designs actions that she hopes will cause helpful, enabling reactions from her world, reactions that she expects will move her closer to a balanced life. But instead of getting cooperation, her actions arouse forces of antagonism that thwart her efforts. Her world reacts differently, more powerfully, in contrast or contradiction to what she reckoned. This surprising violation of expectation may move her further from or closer to her object of desire, but whether positive or negative, the turn will not happen in the way she imagined.

The term **forces of antagonism** does not necessarily refer to an antagonist or villain. Villains inhabit certain genres, and in his proper place an arch-villain, such as the Terminator, can be a fascinating antagonist. But by forces of antagonism I mean opposing forces from any or all of the four levels of conflict:

1. **Physical conflict:** The titanic forces of time, space, and every object in the manmade and natural universe. Not enough time to get something done, too far to go to get something, nature's tumult from tornadoes to viruses. To these natural forces, fantasy genres add supernatural and magical forces of amazing variety and unlimited imaginings.

2. **Social conflict:** The powerful forces of institutions and the people who run them. All levels of government and the legal systems they enforce, all religions, the military, corporations, schools, hospitals, even charities. Every institution shapes itself into a pyramid of power. How do you gain it? Lose it? How do you move up and down the power pyramid?

3. **Personal conflict:** The problematic relationships of intimacy

between friends, family, and lovers that range from infidelity to divorce to petty squabbles over money.

4. Inner conflict: Contradictory forces within a character's mind, body, and emotions. How to cope when your memory betrays you, your body breaks down, or your feelings overwhelm your common sense?

Over the progressive dynamics of a story, forces from these various levels build in power and focus, deepening and widening the story. As these complications build, the protagonist reacts by digging deeper and deeper into her willpower as well as her mental, emotional, and physical capacities in an ever-escalating effort to restore life's balance.[6]

SPINE OF ACTION

A story's **spine of action** traces the protagonist's constant quest for his object of desire. His persistent pursuit, driven by his super-intention, struggling against the story's forces of antagonism, propels the entire telling from the inciting incident through the story's progressions to the protagonist's eventual crisis decision and climactic action, ending in a moment of resolution.

What the protagonist (or any character) does from scene to scene or says from line to line is simply a behavioral tactic. For no matter what happens on the surface, no matter what outer activity catches our eye and ear, the protagonist's grand, unrelenting spine of action runs under every scene.

Because other people are the most common source of life's complications, the most common activity taken along the spine of action is talk. And like the five major movements of story (inciting incident, progressive complications, crisis, climax, resolution), talk has its own five stages—desire, sense of antagonism, choice of action, action/reaction, expression.

Of these stages, expression is the activity that carries the character's action into his world. It's most often speech, but it may be clenching a fist or planting a kiss, hurling a plate across a room or smiling deceitfully—all the nonverbal activities that may accompany or substitute for dialogue.

Imagine this story: You are a first-time writer trying to break into the profession. In that secret place where you hide from the world, you feel incomplete as you teeter through life. You dream of a creative triumph that would give you wholeness and balance: a novel, play, or script of surpassing quality (object of desire). Your need to achieve artistic success (super-intention) drives your writing life (spine of action).

You sit down (scene) and pursue your desire by attempting to write a page of dialogue (choice of action) because you hope it will unlock insight into your characters and story events to come (scene intention). But before you begin, you know that a pernicious horde of forces will oppose your efforts—your mother will call, the baby will wake up, fears of failure will churn your belly, the temptation to quit will whisper in your ear (sources of antagonism). In the face of these forces, you choose to stay at your desk and persevere (choice of action). And so you write and rewrite the same passage over and over (action). But with each pass your dialogue stumbles, sputters, and only gets worse (force of antagonism). You spew a chain of hyphenated profanity, "Stupid damn...mother...son of a..." (expression). Suddenly, from out of nowhere, a new angle of attack springs to mind (reaction). You pound out dialogue that reshapes the scene with surprising power (action). You lean back and mutter, "Wow, where did that come from?" (expression).

Every immediate desire and action, no matter how seemingly trivial, even a thing as infinitesimal as taking a thought-filled sip of coffee, is somehow affixed to your future desire and your pursuit of literary achievement. Moment by moment, your life moves along a spine of action from desire to sense of antagonism to choice of action to action/reaction to expression.

As for you, so for your characters. As for your life, so for your stories.[7]

STORY PROGRESSION

The scenes along the spine of action not only move dynamically across the positive/negative charges of the story's values, but they arc along a progression of conflict. As a character struggles toward his object of desire, the forces of antagonism build, calling on greater and greater capacities from within him, generating greater and greater jeopardy in his life, demanding greater and greater willpower to make more and more risk-taking decisions.

Finally, there comes a moment when the protagonist has exhausted all possible actions, save one. Faced with the most powerful and focused conflict of his life, the protagonist must choose one final action in a last effort to put his life back in balance. He makes his crisis decision, chooses a climactic action, and takes it. Out of the climax he either gets what he wants or fails to get it. End of story. A last resolution scene may be needed to tie up any loose ends and let the reader/audience gather their thoughts and recoup their emotions.[8]

TURNING POINTS

Ideally, every scene contains a turning point. A turning point pivots the instant the value at stake in the scene dynamically changes from positive to negative or negative to positive. This change moves the character either farther from (negative) or closer to (positive) his object of desire than the previous scene's turning point. Turning points progress the story along its spine of action toward the final satisfaction or dissatisfaction of the protagonist's desire at story climax.

A turning point can be created in only one of two ways: by action or revelation. An event turns either by an immediate, direct action, or by the disclosure or discovery of a secret or previously unknown fact. Because dialogue can express both deeds ("I'm leaving for good") and information ("I married you for your money"), it can turn a scene's value charge by action, revelation, or both at once. If a scene has no turning point, if the value charge does not change in any kind or degree, then the scene is merely an exposition-filled nonevent. Too many nonevents in a row and a story collapses into tedium.[9]

SCENE PROGRESSION

"Progression" means the continuous topping of previous actions or events. A scene creates a turning point that progresses the storyline by topping the turning point in the previous scene. Each sequence of events causes a moderate change that surpasses the previous in terms of its impact, for better or worse, on the lives of the characters. Each act climax delivers a major impact.

But no matter whether a scene creates a minor, moderate, or major change in the story, the scene progresses within itself by building beats of behavior, so that each action/reaction tops the previous beat to and around the scene's turning point.[10]

THE BEAT

Like the physical objects governed by Newton's third law of motion, every verbal action causes a reaction. The **beat** is a unit of scene design that contains both an action and a reaction from someone or something somewhere in the setting. Generally, the response comes from another character, but it could come from within the acting character himself.

Suppose Character A were to insult Character B. Character B could react in myriad ways, perhaps with an insult of his own or by laughing at Character A. Or Character A could react to his own action and apologize. Or Character A could regret what he said, feel remorse, but say nothing. Or Character B, who doesn't speak English, greets the insult with a smile. These moment-to-moment exchanges of action/reaction build a scene. Ideally, each beat tops the previous beat and leads to the next. This continuous surpassing of previous beats within a scene generates dialogue progression, shaping the scene's beats to and around its turning point.[11]

Beats are best identified by gerunds. A gerund is a noun that names an action by adding "-ing" to a verb. The four possible beats above, for example, could be labeled insulting/ridiculing, insulting/apologizing, insulting/regretting, insulting/greeting. The use of gerunds to name the actions beneath exchanges of dialogue is the best way I know to stop yourself from writing on-the-nose.

FIVE STEPS OF BEHAVIOR

When characters use what they say to pursue what they want, the rambling activity of conversation turns into the focused action of dialogue. Verbal action, indeed all behavior, moves through five distinct steps from desire to antagonism to choice to action to expression. Because people often act and react in a flash, these steps seem fused together because they fly from first to last in a blur. But that's life, not writing. No matter how quickly and instinctively things might happen, the five steps are always there. To make the flow of character behavior as clear as possible, let's examine these five steps in slow-motion detail:

1. **Desire:** The moment a character's life is thrown out of balance (inciting incident), he, in reaction, conceives of (or at least senses) what he must achieve in order to restore life's balance (object of desire). His overarching purpose to reach the object of desire (super-intention) motivates his active pursuit (spine of action). As he moves along the story's spine, at each specific moment (scene) he must satisfy an immediate want (scene intention) in order to progress toward his object of desire. The foreground desire of scene intention and underlying pull of the super-intention influence each choice of action he makes and takes. But his background desires limit his choices because they influence what he cannot or will not do.

2. **Sense of Antagonism:** Before the character can act, however, he must sense or recognize the immediate forces of antagonism that block his way. How much of his understanding is conscious or subconscious,

realistic or mistaken, depends on the psychology of the character, the nature of his situation, and the story the author is telling.

3. Choice of Action: The character then chooses to take a specific action in an effort to cause a reaction from his world that will move him toward his scene intention. Again, how deliberate or instantaneous this choice may be is relative to the nature of the character and his situation.

4. Action: The activity the character chooses to carry out his action may be physical or verbal or both. Desire is the source of action, and action is the source of dialogue.

5. Expression: To the extent that the character's action needs words to carry it out, the writer composes dialogue.

To create a scene, an author must separate the links in this chain of behavior and give consideration to each. (How conscious or subconscious this "consideration" may be varies from writer to writer. Oscar Wilde once noted that an author spends a whole morning putting in a comma and a whole afternoon taking it out. But that's Wilde. For some writers, commas just get in the way.) Finally, in however long it may take to pen one perfect speech, the writer pieces the links back together so they happen in the breath of time it takes an actor to act or a reader to read.

It is impossible to know exactly what a character will say in this fifth step until we answer these questions: What does the character want? What stops him from getting it? What will he choose to do in an effort to achieve it?

A scene lives, not in the activity of talking, but in the action the character takes by talking. So before we write dialogue, we must ask questions and find answers that guide us down the stream from desire to antagonism to choice to action, ending in expression—the dialogue that helps shape and turn the scene.

INTRODUCTION TO SEVEN CASE STUDIES

The five stages of character behavior blend in concert to create a progressive subtext that ultimately finds expression in dialogue. To demonstrate how this works, we'll examine five dramatized scenes—two from teleplays, one each from a play, a novel, a screenplay—plus two passages of narratized dialogue in prose. Each author employs a distinctively different balance, type, and intensity of conflict. The quality of conflict determines the quality of action, and the quality of action determines the quality of talk. As a result, the behaviors of characters, the dynamic of beats, and, above all, the tonality of each scene's dialogue play out in seven distinctively different ways over the next six chapters.

Balanced conflict: In the "Two Tonys" episode from THE SOPRANOS, series creator David Chase and cowriter Terence Winter turn their characters loose in a hard-fought duelogue of equals.

Comic conflict: The "Author, Author" episode from FRASIER, written by Don Seigel and Jerry Perzigian, exaggerates balanced conflict to its lunatic limits.

Asymmetric conflict: In *A Raisin in the Sun*, playwright Lorraine Hansberry sets one character's aggressive verbal action against another's quiet resistance.

Indirect conflict: In *The Great Gatsby*, F. Scott Fitzgerald's characters manipulate each other with words of covert antagonism.

Reflexive conflict: Chapter Seventeen compares the uses of narratized dialogue in two novels: In *Fräulein Else*, Arthur Schnitzler uses this technique to wage inner conflict within his protagonist, self against self; whereas in *The Museum of Innocence*, Orhan Pamuk's protagonist confesses his inner wars directly to the reader.

Implied conflict: In LOST IN TRANSLATION, screenwriter Sofia Coppola suspends her characters in depths of inner tension, self versus self, played out in the shadows of conflicts from the past.

The following chapters demonstrate a working method for scene analysis that separates a scene into its components, pulls out their subtextual actions, labels them with gerunds, and then discovers how these actions express themselves in dialogue. The technique begins with breaking a scene into its beats.

Over the decades, writers have evolved three different meanings for the term "beat." In the outlining stages of a screenplay, some filmmakers use the word to name a story's key turning points: "In the story's first beat they meet; in the second beat they fall in love."

Playwrights and screenwriters often place the term between paren-
theses in a column of dialogue, e.g., (beat), to signal a short pause. But
for the purposes of exploring how a scene's inner life inspires its dialogue, I use "beat" in its original sense: a unit of action/reaction. An
action starts a beat; a corresponding reaction ends it.

When scenes feel lifeless or false, the cause is rarely found in the
language of the dialogue. Rather, flaws fester in the subtext. For that
reason, we break a scene into its beats in order to uncover the misshapen subtextual actions and reactions that cause these faults. A skillful analysis then guides the redesign of the scene's beats and, with
that, the re-creation of its dialogue.

No matter how many times a pattern of action/reaction repeats,
it constitutes one, and only one, beat. A scene cannot progress unless
its beats change, and beats cannot change until the characters change
their tactics. Indeed, the most common early warning sign of an ail-
ing scene is repetitious beats—characters using the same tactic to take
essentially the same action, again and again, but using different words,
speech after speech, to do it. These duplicating beats hide beneath a
scene's verbiage, and it often takes an insightful, beat-by-beat analysis
to bring this flaw to light.

Before we move on, however, a note of caution: No one can teach
you how to write. I can only define the shape and function of a scene, lay
out its components, and demonstrate their inner workings. Although
the principles of scene design illuminate creativity, they are not the creative process itself. The following six chapters are logical, after-the-fact
analyses of finished work. My breakdowns do not presume to know
the artist's process or follow his or her actual writing experience.

Of this, however, I am certain: Writing rarely flows in a straight
line. Creativity likes to zigzag—trial/error, elation/depression, this
way and that, draft after draft after draft. Knowledge of story and scene
design strengthens the work, provokes ideas, and guides rewrites, but
an author must discover through her personal creative process exactly
how to use her talent and expertise to move from inspiration to last
draft.

13

BALANCED CONFLICT

THE SOPRANOS

THE SOPRANOS ran on HBO from January 1999 to June 2007. Its eighty-six episodes tell the story of Tony Soprano, a New Jersey Mafia don, portrayed by James Gandolfini. David Chase, the series creator, built this complex, multidimensional character around a core contradiction: On one hand, Tony commits violent, tyrannical, murderous acts; on the other, he falls victim to paralyzing nightmares and sudden, unexplained panic attacks.

Realizing that his panic disorder could cost him his life, Tony seeks the help of a psychiatrist, Dr. Jennifer Melfi (Lorraine Bracco). Over the next four seasons, their therapy sessions struggle through moral dilemmas, sexual tensions, and bouts of Tony's raging temper, until Tony finally breaks off his therapy.

In Episode 1 of Season 5, he convinces himself that he's deeply in love with Melfi and goes on a romantic quest. He has often flirted with her, but now he puts on his best courting behavior and asks her out for dinner twice. Twice she declines, but he persists until he finally confronts her in her office.

I will work through their confrontation with an eye to the scene's four essential modes: 1) how the five steps of behavior (desire, antagonism, choice, action, expression) translate into the characters' scene intentions and tactics, 2) how their beats of action/reaction shape progression, 3) how the values at stake arc their changing charges, and 4) how these foundational layers impel and inspire the scene's character-specific dialogue.

I will take you through this inside-out analysis to remind you once again that character talk is the final result of everything that went before, a surface manifestation of the layers of life beneath the words. The stronger the inner scene, the more powerful the dialogue.

To begin: If we were to ask Tony what he wants (desire) and what's stopping him from getting it (antagonism), he would tell us that he wants to win Jennifer Melfi's love, but she resists because she doesn't see the other Tony, the nice-guy Tony. Tony's scene intention is to seduce Melfi, and his tactic (action) is to prove that he's a nice guy.

If we were to ask Dr. Melfi the same questions, she would tell us that she wants to help Tony overcome his emotional problems (desire), but his impulse to take their relationship from professional to personal makes that impossible (antagonism). Melfi's scene intention is to help Tony change for the better, and her tactic (action) is to confront him with the truth.

However, if we look past Tony's romantic gestures, we sense that the ruling value of his life is power. His Romeo persona masks his subconscious lust, not for sex, but for ownership. He needs to dominate the only person who has ever wielded power over him—Dr. Melfi.

But Melfi packs double-fisted punches of truth and morality. She knows the truth of Tony's immature, sociopathic nature. In the face of her high moral standards and courage (antagonism), Tony flinches and withers. So his dark self, hungry to regain the upper hand, silently urges him to get her into bed and give her the orgasmic thrill of a lifetime. With that, he thinks, her moral shell will crack and she will fall into his arms, enthralled and subservient. His subconscious desire (super-intention), therefore, is to subjugate Melfi.

Dr. Melfi tells Tony she wants to help him, therapeutically; and consciously, of course, she means what she says. But if we look beneath her prudent, professional personality, we sense the very opposite of discretion and objectivity. We see a high-risk adventurer.

Consider this: During her university years, Melfi could have taken any number of career paths, but she chose clinical psychiatry. Now, picture a psychiatrist's day.

Imagine the enormous mental stamina and emotional courage it must take to burrow into the dark unknown of life-wrecked souls. Think of the damage done to the therapist as she listens with empathy to the wretched, tortured, heartbreaking confessions of neurotic after psychotic, hour by hour, day by day. Almost no one, it seems to me, would devote herself to that profession unless, deep inside, she found exploring the danger-filled jungles of other people's minds fascinating, even exhilarating.

Dr. Melfi's core dimension sends her risk-averse characterization up against her risk-enticed true character. To express her contradictory nature, the writers propel her through a series-long, dynamic, on-again, off-again relationship with Tony Soprano.

Soon after Dr. Melfi takes Tony Soprano as a patient, she discovers he's a murderous Mafia don. At first, ending the relationship seems her only option, but in time she overcomes her disgust and continues treating him. Her probing questions about his parents often provoke his rage and a break in therapy. But once time quiets his rage, she always takes Tony back, even though she knows that someday he may turn his violence against her.

Near the end of Season 1, Tony tells her that rival mobsters plan to kill her because they fear he may have revealed Mafia secrets during therapy. Melfi goes into hiding while Tony hunts down and kills the assassins. Once the danger lifts, Melfi resumes Tony's sessions.

Dr. Melfi's pattern of on-again, off-again psychotherapy raises this question: Why would a psychiatrist put her life at risk to treat a manifestly impulsive, sociopathic criminal? One possible answer:

While her conscious concern for a secure doctor/patient relationship masks her true desire, subconsciously she actually wants the very contradiction of security; she longs for risk, life-and-death risk. Her super-intention seeks the heart-pounding rush that can only be found along the fuse burning of danger.

Three values arc over the course of the scene: together/apart in the doctor/patient relationship; self-deception/self-awareness in Tony's mind; and the core value, jeopardy/security for Dr. Melfi's life. As the scene opens, these values begin with the two characters together on speaking terms (positive), Tony blind to his moral identity (negative), and, most importantly, Dr. Melfi in life-and-death jeopardy as she confronts her dangerous patient (negative).

The scene matches two powerful personalities in a balanced conflict, told over thirteen beats. The first twelve beats match Tony's actions against Dr. Melfi's reactions, but the last beat reverses that pattern and sends Tony out the door.

A transcription of the scene as televised follows, printed in bold. First read the bold passages straight through, skipping over my analysis. As you do, listen to the dialogue in your mind, or better yet, act it out aloud and feel what it would be like emotionally to live through this conflict, first from Tony's point of view, and then from Dr. Melfi's.

Once you have a sense for how the scene arcs, reread it against my analysis of the beats, their subtext, and the shaping of the action.

INT. DR. MELFI'S OFFICE—EARLY EVENING

As PATIENTS from a group session file out, Tony enters like a lost little boy.

BEAT 1

Dr. Melfi looks up, surprised to see him.

> **MELFI**
>
> **Anthony.**

As Tony glances down, embarrassed, Dr. Melfi strides up to him.

> ### MELFI
> Hello.

> ### TONY
> (with a shy smile)
> Hi.

ACTION: Tony turning on the charm.
REACTION: Melfi gearing up for trouble.
SUBTEXT: Twice that day Tony asked Dr. Melfi out for dinner, and twice she turned him down. Tony senses he's out on a limb, so as he enters, he plays sensitive and shy, hoping to win her sympathy. Beneath her cheerful welcome, she puzzles over why he's back yet again and readies herself for a third confrontation.

BEAT 2

> ### TONY
> (handing her an envelope)
> A friend of mine had these and
> couldn't use them. And I figure, well,
> maybe we could.
> (explaining)
> Tickets...Bermuda...
>
> (doing a little dance)
> ...lodging at the Elbow Beach Hotel.
> ### MELFI
> (amazed)
> I turn down a wonderful dinner invi-
> tation and you think I'll go away
> with you?

ACTION: Tony propositioning her.
REACTION: Melfi calling him an idiot.

SUBTEXT: Tony bought the tickets himself. He not only lies about that, but far worse, his underlying action treats Dr. Melfi like a whore. Dinner for two might cost $200; a weekend at the five-star Elbow Beach Hotel would run into the thousands. Tony ups the ante, thinking she turned down his previous offers because they were too cheap.

Tony's disrespect and delusions offend Dr. Melfi, but because she knows he's prone to violence, she avoids direct confrontation by repaying his insult with a rhetorical question. This ancient verbal tactic asks a question but not to get an answer; it assumes the answer in the question. So if we were to rewrite Melfi's dialogue on-the-nose, it might read: "What kind of man thinks I'll sleep with him just because he takes me to Bermuda? An idiot."

BEAT 3

> TONY
>
> Well, the guy couldn't use 'em and,
> you know, he gave 'em to me and
> what'd you want me to do, throw 'em
> away?

Dr. Melfi stands in silence.

ACTION: Tony claiming his innocence.
REACTION: Melfi avoiding conflict.
SUBTEXT: Tony tries to shrug off her criticism by pretending his proposition wasn't manipulative, just practical—he's the innocent victim of a friend's generosity.

Dr. Melfi knows he bought the tickets as a sexual bribe, but rather than call out his canard, she turns silence into a weapon. In the right context, refusing to speak can be more powerful than anything said.

BEAT 4

                    TONY
                 (continuing)
Come on, Doc. I'm breaking out the
big guns here. You're turning me into
half a stalker.

                    MELFI
Listen, Anthony. I'm not going to
go out with you, okay, and it's not
because you're unattractive or I don't
think I would have a good time. It's
just something I'm not going to do.
I would like you to respect my decision and just try to feel that I know
what's right for me. Okay?

Long pause.

ACTION: Tony playing for pity.

REACTION: Melfi blaming him.

SUBTEXT: By accusing her of demeaning him, he plays the victim again and adds guilt-tripping to his tactics, all in the hope that she'll feel sorry for him.

Instead, she begins with the "It's not you, it's me" tactic, seeming to put the blame on herself. But the phrase "I know what's right for me" alerts Tony. Despite her opening ploy, it implies that he is not right for her because there's something wrong, something broken inside him.

Tony came to her in hopes of getting laid, but when she hints at his flawed nature, the subconscious need that has driven Tony through the entire series takes hold. He desperately longs for an answer to the core question of his life, a question only his psychiatrist can answer: What is wrong with me?

BEAT 5

> **TONY**
>
> But it's not just the psychiatric eth-
> ics stuff, is it?

> **MELFI**
>
> I want to preserve the option for you
> that you could always come back to
> our work, if you wish, and that we
> could pick up where we've left off.

ACTION: Tony looking for a way out.
REACTION: Melfi giving him a way out.
SUBTEXT: On the conscious level, however, Tony would rather not confront the truth about himself, so if she had said, "Yes, it's a matter of medical ethics," he would have been relieved and the scene would be over. Instead, she offers him the hard, painful work of self-awareness through therapy.

BEAT 6

> **TONY**
>
> I don't think you get this. I want
> you!

> **MELFI**
>
> That's very flattering to me.

> **TONY**
>
> I'm not interested in flattering you.

> **MELFI**
>
> I know you're not.

ACTION: Tony laying it on the line.

REACTION: Melfi buying time.

SUBTEXT: Tony evades the big question to make a brutal pass, hoping that the offer of sex for sex's sake will excite and distract her. It doesn't, of course. Instead, she uses non-answer responses to buy time while deciding just how truthful she dares to be.

BEAT 7

> **TONY**
> Then, what is it, okay? What is it?
> (pause, quieter)
> Just...help me understand it, okay?

> **MELFI**
> You know, Anthony, during our work I
> never judged you, or your behavior.
> It's not the place of a therapist to
> do so.

> **TONY**
> All right, I get all this. Go, go.

> **MELFI**
> In a personal relationship, I don't
> think I could sit silent.

ACTION: Tony asking for trouble.

REACTION: Melfi crossing the line.

SUBTEXT: Tony begs for the truth, but Dr. Melfi knows the furious effect truth can have on him, so she stalls. Still, he insists, so after sidestepping for six beats, she finally crosses the line from professional to personal, and by doing so, she puts herself in grave danger.

BEAT 8

                                    TONY
            About what?

                                    MELFI
            Our values are...just very different.

ACTION: Tony cornering her.
REACTION: Melfi belittling him.
SUBTEXT: When he pressures her for an answer, she insults him and
hints for the second time that she knows his hidden weakness.

Tony can read subtext with the best. When she says that the values separating them are "just very different," he knows that that's
PC for "My values are clearly better than yours, but let's not fight
about it."

The word "values" startles Tony, and its insinuations anger him,
but he manages to hold his rage in check.

BEAT 9

                                    TONY
            You don't like my values?

                                    MELFI
            Honestly?

                                    TONY
            Yeah.

            A tense pause.

                                    MELFI
            No.

ACTION: Tony daring her to cross him.

REACTION: Melfi denying his worth.

SUBTEXT: We measure a person's worth in the quality of his values and the actions they motivate. By rejecting Tony's personal values, she rejects his value as a person.

When Tony confronts Dr. Melfi, she does not flinch. Instead, she states her disdain for him with such sudden, unexpected power that he drops his bullying tone.

BEAT 10

> **TONY**
> Okay.
> > (pause)
> Like what?

> **MELFI**
> > (glancing at her watch)
> It's getting late.

ACTION: Tony asking nice.

REACTION: Melfi giving him a last way out.

SUBTEXT: Feeling vulnerable and dreading the worst, Tony softens his tone. Dr. Melfi, knowing that her insights will wound Tony and perhaps enrage him, offers him an excuse not to know.

BEAT 11

> **TONY**
> No, no, no, no. Come on. It's okay.
> It's okay.

> **MELFI**
> Well...you're not a truthful
> person. You're not respectful of
> women. You're not really respectful
> of people.

ACTION: Tony inviting the worst.

REACTION: Melfi pulling her punch.

SUBTEXT: At some level, Tony realizes that the answer to "What is wrong with me?" will scald his sense of self, but he pursues it to the blistered end.

Notice that when Dr. Melfi hits Tony with the bitter facts, her language softens the blow. She could have called him a liar, abuser, or worse. Instead, she keeps her cool control—"not a truthful person," "not really respectful."

BEAT 12

>   TONY
>
>   I don't love people?

>   MELFI
>
>   Maybe you love them, I don't know.
>   You take what you want from them by
>   force, or the threat of force.

ACTION: Tony doubting himself.

REACTION: Melfi firing the first barrel.

SUBTEXT: Tony has never for a moment doubted his love for his family, friends, and lovers. But the instant Dr. Melfi shows him his essential tyrannical nature, he cannot argue back. Instead, he phrases his denial as a question, a question he seems to ask himself as much as her.

Line by line, fact by fact, Dr. Melfi has destroyed Tony's self-worth. She knows full well that, humiliated and emasculated, he might lash out in violence. She faces a dilemma between speaking the final full truth and the violence it might bring versus keeping silent and staying secure. She makes her choice of action and dares to launch the final beat.

BEAT 13

> MELFI
> (continuing)
> I couldn't live like that. I couldn't
> bear witness to violence or—

> TONY
> —Fuck you . . .

Tony runs out, slams the door, and shouts
from the lobby:

> TONY
> . . . you fucking cunt.

ACTION: Melfi firing the second barrel.

REACTION: Tony killing her with words.

SUBTEXT: In Beat 12 she impugns Tony's morals, but in Beat 13 she denigrates the whole gangster life and, with that, everyone close to him.

He could kill her for those insults; he has killed others for as much. But he runs out instead because of the way the writers staged the opening. As Tony entered Dr. Melfi's office, a dozen members of a group session filed out past him. She saw Tony standing in the crowd and called out to him. In other words, there were witnesses. If he were to attack her now, those people could put him at the scene by name. Tony's too savvy to make that mistake, so he fires off the most lethal words he knows.

This final beat turns with a sharp irony. Dr. Melfi tells Tony that she cannot witness violence, but we suspect that subconsciously she relishes face-to-face brushes with violence and the adrenaline rush they bring.

So even though Tony starts every beat but the last, it's Dr. Melfi's passive aggression that carries the scene to its climax. At first, she deflects his sexual moves, then in Beat 4 she provokes his desire to know why, and finally, she leads him to the self-discovery he dreads. On balance, Dr. Melfi owns the more powerful personality; she controls the conflict from open to close.

Subtextual Progression

Scan the list of subtextual actions below. Note how they progress the scene: Conflict builds through the first four beats, backs off for a moment in Beat 5, then progresses to the climax of Beat 13. Next note how this progression arcs the three values at stake in the scene: 1) Friendship/hatred in the doctor/patient relationship swings from positive to negative. 2) Tony's comfortable self-deception (positive irony) turns to painful self-awareness (negative irony). 3) Peril/survival for Dr. Melfi pivots from negative to positive.

BEAT 1: Turning on the charm/Gearing up for trouble.

BEAT 2: Propositioning her/Calling him an idiot.

BEAT 3: Claiming his innocence/Avoiding conflict.

BEAT 4: Playing for pity/Blaming him.

BEAT 5: Looking for a way out/Giving him a way out.

BEAT 6: Laying it on the line/Buying time.

BEAT 7: Asking for trouble/Crossing the line.

BEAT 8: Cornering her/Belittling him.

BEAT 9: Daring her to cross him/Denying his worth.

BEAT 10: Asking nice/Giving him a last way out.

BEAT 11: Inviting the worst/Pulling her punch.

BEAT 12: Doubting himself/Firing her first barrel.

BEAT 13: Firing her second barrel/Killing her with words.

To see how inner actions manifest in outer speech, let's compare the dialogue for these two characters on three points: content, length, and pace.

CONTENT: Tony comes into the scene feeling unloved and empty, suffering from an existential crisis. The reasons he used to give himself for living his high-risk life no longer make sense. In such a state, people naturally ask questions, the two biggest being: "Who am I?" and "What's the point?"

Note that half of Tony's lines are questions. The rest are either lies or pleas, told and asked in the hope that Dr. Melfi will give him the insight into himself he craves. The only line in which he does not beg for an answer is the last, and it may be his weakest, most desperate call for help.

Dr. Melfi enters the scene at the height of her profession, sated with confident knowledge. Her therapeutic skill gives her what she wants: the power to lighten the darkness in her patients' psyches. As a result, her lines make statements, the answers to Tony's questions that she slowly, at times evasively, doles out.

LENGTH: As noted in Chapter Seven, when people lose control of their emotions, their words, phrases, and sentences tend to shorten. Conversely, people in control often lengthen all three.

Tony talks in monosyllables, and his longest sentence is ten words; Dr. Melfi frequently uses three- and four-syllable terms, and her sentences run as long as twenty-five words. Each of Dr. Melfi's sentences includes a noun, verb, and object; Tony often abbreviates meaning into phrases such as "tickets," "Bermuda," "Go, go."

PACE: In an athletic event, the player who controls the pace of the game tends to win. Much the same is true in life. First note how Tony's staccato cadence and Dr. Melfi's languid rhythms mirror their contradictory emotional states. Then compare Tony's frantic phrases ("Then, what is it, okay? What is it?) to Dr. Melfi's long, slow sentences. Tony tries to bulldoze through the opening beats, but ultimately, her moral power controls the pace of the scene. She takes her time; he stumbles from moment to moment, lurching out in defeat.

Lastly, Chapter Nine argued that repetitiousness is the enemy of fine writing, and generally that's true, but, as always, the antithesis has its uses, too. Like waves pounding a shore, the writers use repetition to swell Tony's rising tide of anger and frustration. He repeats, for example, the word "okay" five times, the last two as a promise not to hurt her—which, by climax, if he could, he would ("Fuck you, you fucking cunt").

If you haven't already, watch the scene online to study how the dialogue's contrasting qualities of content, length, and pace help channel the actors' performances.

In life, emotions seem to surge from the belly and then spread through the body. For this reason, acting coaches teach their students to think, not in their heads, but in their guts. Bad actors tend to be self-puppeteers who work from the head down to pull their own strings; fine actors let conflict hit below the waist as they surrender to their character.

An instinct-driven performance is only possible if the writing, text and subtext, allows the actor to feel the meaning of the words in his guts, so that idea and emotion merge into immediate, vivid, seemingly spontaneous dialogue. Because the writing of THE SOPRANOS was the best of its day, James Gandolfini could create the from-the-guts tour de force that carried him to multiple Emmy, Screen Actors Guild, and Golden Globe Awards.

14

COMIC CONFLICT

All characters pursue secondary desires per scene (scene intention) in pursuit of a primary, overall desire per story (super-intention). If, however, we were to place all stories ever told along a spectrum ranging from tragedy to farce, we would see that dramatic characters and comic characters go about these pursuits with distinctively different dialogue styles.

The reason is simple: These two basic character types possess two fundamentally different mentalities. They do not think the same, and so they do not speak the same. Writing dialogue for one versus the other, therefore, demands two decidedly different techniques.

The dramatic character pursues what life demands with some degree of awareness. He has a mental flexibility that lets him step back from the fray and think the thought, "Wow, this could get me killed." This realization doesn't necessarily stop his quest, but he's aware of its irony and risk. Tony Soprano, for instance, in the midst of rage, has enough mindfulness not to commit murder in public.

What makes a comic character comic is mental rigidity. He pursues his all-absorbing desire as if myopic to any choice beyond it. In the scene I'll analyze below, for example, two psychiatrists (e.g., professionals who ought to know better) are so consumed by sibling rivalry they regress to infanticide.

In centuries past, the monomania of the comic character was

known as his "humor." In 1612, playwright Ben Jonson wrote a verse prologue to his comedy *Every Man out of His Humour*. In it, he drew upon theories from medieval physiology that allege that every person's body has a unique balance of four humors (fluids)—blood, phlegm, yellow bile, and black bile—and their one-of-a-kind concoction determines each person's specific temperament. (Why the ancients didn't add sexual fluids to their list of humors, I cannot say, but they sure seem influential to me.)

Jonson seized upon this theory as a metaphor for the comic character. In his definition, a humor arises

> *. . . when some one peculiar quality*
> *Doth so possesse a man, that it doth draw*
> *All his affects, his spirits, and his powers*
> *In their confluctions, all to runne one way.*[1]

In my comedy lectures, I call Jonson's "one peculiar quality" the blind obsession. As noted in Chapter Eleven, desire intensifies in the comic character to the point of obsession. This fixation holds the character so tightly in its grip he cannot deviate from it. All aspects of his identity are bound to it; without it, he is no longer comic. What's more, this obsession blinds him. He is driven to pursue it but cannot see the mania in himself. To us, he's a crazed neurotic; to him, his obsession is normalcy.

Consider, for example, Inspector Jacques Clouseau (Peter Sellers and others), the protagonist of no less than eleven Pink Panther films. Deaf, dumb, and blind to his incompetence, Clouseau obsesses on perfection. He devotes every compulsive waking hour to becoming the world's ultimate detective.

A few comic protagonists, such as Woody Allen's Alvy Singer in ANNIE HALL and Larry David's Larry David in CURB YOUR ENTHUSIASM, constantly dissect their obsession, phobically alert to any sign of neuroses. But what they do not grasp is that addictive self-analysis is itself a blind obsession. The more seriously and persistently these two guys self-psychoanalyze, the more hysterical they become—in both senses of the word.

The comic protagonist's blind obsession usually comes nested inside otherwise normal traits that anoint him with believability, dimensionalize his personality, and make him one of a kind. The art of comedy, however, imposes certain limitations on dimensionality, for this reason: Jokes require objectivity. Laughter explodes the moment two incongruous ideas suddenly clash in the mind. If their illogicality is not instantly recognized, the gag sputters in confusion. Therefore, the mind of the reader/audience must be kept sharply focused and uncluttered by compassion.

In Chapter Eleven's 30 ROCK case study, I defined a dimension as a consistent contradiction within a character's nature: either a contradiction between an outer trait of characterization versus an inner quality of true character (e.g., Jack Foley's romantic charm versus his bank robber's ethics in *Out of Sight*), or a deep contradiction within the inner self (e.g., Macbeth's blood-soaked ambition to be king versus his guilt-ridden conscience over the actions he takes to be king).

A profound self-contradiction (such as those we saw previously within Dr. Melfi and Tony Soprano) draws a reader/audience into an empathic identification with a fellow human being and a compassionate concern for that character's well-being. We welcome feelings in drama, but in comedy, empathy and compassion kill the laughs.

For this reason, comic protagonists, almost without exception, have fewer dimensions than their dramatic counterparts and virtually none at the subconscious level of conflicted inner selves. Instead, comic dimensions pit appearance against reality, the man the character thinks he is versus the fool we know him in fact to be.

Bit parts in comedy—geek, diva, jock, valley girl, fop, braggart, nag, nerd, etc.—chase their blind obsession with glaring clarity because monomania is their only trait. As you might imagine, writing fresh, innovative dialogue for these nondimensional roles can break your brain. Indeed, many comedies fail at this. Too often, when supporting characters speak, their blind obsession funnels what they say into trite lingo and clichéd reactions.

FRASIER

Peter Casey, David Lee, and David Angell spun FRASIER off from the sitcom CHEERS and filled it with a cast of unique obsessives. The show ran on NBC from 1993 to 2004, winning a record thirty-seven Emmy Awards. It tells the story of radio talk show psychiatrist Frasier Crane (Kelsey Grammer), his brother Niles (David Hyde Pierce), and the people in their lives.

Frasier and Niles share a number of blind obsessions. These become super-intentions that weave in and out of storylines, arcing through 264 episodes in eleven seasons, unifying the series: Both Frasier and Niles have a mortal fear of embarrassment; both crave social, intellectual, and cultural status—all leading to their supreme, often snobbish, pretentiousness; and, like all self-respecting comic characters, they obsess on sex.

In a first season episode entitled "Author, Author," Frasier and Niles have contracted with a publisher to write a book on the psychology of sibling rivalry. As fellow psychiatrists and siblings, this book, they feel, should be a snap. Unfortunately, they procrastinate the actual writing to the last day before the contract's deadline.

Desperate, they isolate themselves in a hotel room where they manage, after great difficulty, to compose a lead sentence. But then the fear of embarrassment grabs them by the throat: "What will people say if we fail as writers?" This fear paralyzes them with writer's block, and they spend the rest of the day and the whole of the night eating and drinking their way through the minibar, writing nothing.

The opening four beats turn on the value of humiliation/pride, but that dread quickly segues into yet another grand, series-long obsession: their mutual envy and constant competition, a.k.a. sibling rivalry, the very subject of the book they struggle to write. Onscreen, the scene runs for three minutes and fourteen seconds, igniting direct conflict between Frasier and Niles, two equally imbalanced personalities.

As in the previous chapter, I will work with the scene from two angles: Viewing it from the outside in, I will look at the beats of action/reaction that shape the scene's progression as well as the changing charge of its values. Reversing the angle to the inside out, I will trace the steps of behavior—desire, antagonism, choice, action—that translate the intentions and tactics of Frasier and Niles into comically expressive dialogue.

Once again, the scene is printed in bold. Read it through without break and then review it in light of my notes.

INT. HOTEL ROOM—EARLY MORNING

As Niles nods off in front of the computer keyboard, Frasier pulls open the drapes.

BEAT 1

FRASIER
(looking out at the day)
Oh, dear God! It's dawn! It's Friday!
(turning to his brother)
Niles, why don't we just admit it? We can't work together. There's never going to be any book.

NILES
No, not with that attitude, there isn't.

ACTION: Frasier urging Niles to accept failure.
REACTION: Niles blaming their failure on Frasier.
SUBTEXT: Niles and Frasier begin with the same scene intention: the desire to fix blame. To Frasier's credit, he's willing to share blame, but Niles, to preserve his pride, places the fault squarely on his brother.

They instantly become each other's antagonist, and for the next four beats choose name-calling as their underlying tactic. At first, their spiraling insults masquerade as accusations, but by Beat 6 the masks fall. TECHNIQUE: Comedy writing calls for artful exaggeration. Over-the-top distortion itself often prompts laughs, but its primary work is to promote enough distance between the characters and the reader/audience that we can judge behaviors against what society considers normal and find them ridiculously out of step.

Note Frasier's first line: He could have simply said, "It's morning." Instead, he calls upon the deity. Comic dialogue thrives on overstatement (although understatement is also an exaggeration).

BEAT 2

> ### FRASIER
> Will you get off it? Come on. The fat lady has sung. The curtain has been rung down. Let's just go home.

> ### NILES
> Well, I guess I shouldn't be surprised you'd give up so easily. It's not your dream after all. Why should it be, mister big shot radio host.

ACTION: Frasier calling Niles an idiot.
REACTION: Niles calling Frasier a snob.
SUBTEXT: Frasier accuses Niles of being oblivious to the obvious. We have a name for those people: idiots. Niles, in turn, accuses Frasier of being arrogantly self-important and looking down on lesser souls. We have a name for those people: snobs. Their accusations become humiliations with a literary touch.

Both Niles and Frasier are culture vultures, so notice that when Frasier declares that their work is done, he references opera and theatre.

BEAT 3

> **FRASIER**
> Is that what this little tantrum is all about, huh? You're jealous of my celebrity?

> **NILES**
> It's not a tantrum and I'm not jealous. I'm just FED UP! I'm fed up with being second all the time. You know, I wanted to be a psychiatrist, just like mom, way before you did, but because you were older, you got there first. You were first to get married; you were first to give Dad the grandchild he always wanted. By the time I get around to doing anything, it's all chewed meat.

ACTION: Frasier calling Niles a petulant child.

REACTION: Niles calling Frasier an upstaging ham.

SUBTEXT: Frasier's accusation is on point. Niles lapses into an adolescent snit as he accuses Frasier of deliberately hogging life's spotlight and thus ruining his dreams. To save his pride Niles conflates coincidence with malevolence—a massive exaggeration.

TECHNIQUE: Note the phrase "chewed meat." Its incongruity pops a smart laugh, but more to the point, the allusion fits hand and glove with the rest of the scene. Mothers around the world pre-chew meat so their infants can swallow it. The whole scene plays as an elaborate Benjamin Button–like metaphor, regressing the brothers to their diapered days, so that at climax Frasier can reenact his failed infanticide of Niles.

BEAT 4

FRASIER

You're crying about something we
can't change.

NILES

You wouldn't change it if you could.
You love it.

ACTION: Frasier calling Niles a masochist.

REACTION: Niles calling Frasier a sadist.

SUBTEXT: Frasier accuses Niles of crying for no reason. We have a name for people who indulge needless suffering: masochists. Niles, in turn, accuses Frasier of reveling in his misery. We have a name for people who enjoy watching others suffer: sadists. These brothers are psychiatrists; they punch the secret places below the belt.

TECHNIQUE: A joke is a design in two parts: setup/payoff. The setup arouses energy; the payoff explodes it into laughter. Comic energy comes from three primary sources: defensive emotions, aggressive emotions, and sex. For this reason, when we look deeply into comic subtext, things can get scary, angry, and wild. But then, the more powerful the setup, the bigger the laugh.

You may or may not agree with the darkness of my interpretation, but when we reach the climax, look back and ask if it doesn't fit.

BEAT 5

FRASIER

Oh, let it go, Niles.

NILES

I can't let it go. My nose is rubbed
in it every day. I'M the one on the
board of the Psychiatric Association;

> MY research is well respected in aca-
> demic circles; four of MY patients
> have been elected to political office,
> but it's YOUR big fat face they put on
> the side of buses.

ACTION: Frasier calling Niles a crybaby.

REACTION: Niles calling Frasier a show-off.

TECHNIQUE: Note how the writers build the joke in Beat 5. They use a technique known as trivializing the exalted.

Niles's anger over injustice infuses his setup, but he contains the energy inside a list of institutions of respect: "Psychiatric Association," "academic circles," and "political office." Then his punch line throws a bomb of banality: "big fat face they put on the side of buses."

SUBTEXT: Niles immediately senses that Frasier actually takes pride in his public transportation portrait. With that, he suffers his final humiliation. The value of humiliation/pride has run its course, and now a deeper value rooted in sibling rivalry comes to the fore: winning/losing.

BEAT 6

> **FRASIER**
> (indignant)
> I do not have a fat face.

> **NILES**
> Oh, please, I keep wondering how long
> you're going to store those nuts for
> winter.

ACTION: Frasier defending his face.

REACTION: Niles attacking his face.

SUBTEXT: By Beat 6 their subtext has risen to the text, and so the beats that follow are all more or less on-the-nose.

BEAT 7

> FRASIER
>
> Well, at least I'm not spindly.

> NILES
>
> Who are you calling spindly, fat
> face?

> FRASIER
>
> You, spindly!

> NILES
>
> Fat face!

> FRASIER
>
> Spindly!

> NILES
>
> Fat face!

> FRASIER
>
> Spindly!

> NILES
>
> Fat face!

ACTION: Frasier calling Niles ugly.

REACTION: Niles calling Frasier ugly.

TECHNIQUE: "Spindly," a unique vocabulary choice, character-izes Frasier perfectly. Nonetheless, he loses the name-calling contest because he is in fact more fat-faced than Niles is spindly. Back to the wall, he escalates from verbal to physical.

BEAT 8

> FRASIER
>
> You take that back!

> NILES
>
> You make me!

ACTION: Frasier making a fist.
REACTION: Niles making a fist.
SUBTEXT: By "making a fist," I mean they take a moment to mentally and emotionally prepare for a fight.

BEAT 9

> FRASIER
>
> I will make you.

> NILES
>
> I don't see you making me.

ACTION: Frasier deciding where to punch.
REACTION: Niles daring him to punch.
SUBTEXT: Under this brief beat, the brothers make decisions about how far to take the fight. Frasier chooses to start light.

BEAT 10

> FRASIER
>
> Oh yeah, well...
>> (ripping hairs out of his
>> brother's chest)
>
> ...here's making you.

Niles winces in pain.

ACTION: Frasier attacking Niles.

REACTION: Niles gathering his counterattack.

SUBTEXT: Under his wince and yelp, Niles chooses all-out war.

TECHNIQUE: After all of their threatening bluster, pulling out chest hairs makes a superb comic understatement. Note how the repetition of make/make/making/making gives the actors staccato, pace-building rhythm.

BEAT 11

> Frasier turns to leave, but Niles races
> across the room, jumps on Frasier's back,
> and wrestles him into a violent headlock.

>   FRASIER
>   (shouting)
>   Ow! Ow! Niles, stop it! We're psychia-
>   trists, not pugilists!

ACTION: Niles attacking Frasier.

REACTION: Frasier deceiving Niles.

SUBTEXT: Frasier could have used simpler language: "We're doctors, not fighters." Instead, to dupe Niles with vanity, he names their prestigious medical specialty and the Latinate for "boxer." The trick works.

BEAT 12

> Niles lets Frasier go.

>   FRASIER
>   I can't believe you fell for that.

> Frasier spins around and clamps Niles into
> a fierce headlock.

ACTION: Niles surrendering to Frasier.

REACTION: Frasier attacking Niles.

SUBTEXT: As they regress to childhood, Frasier's ploy suggests that they have pulled these tricks on each other many times.

BEAT 13

> Frasier throws Niles on the bed, jumps on
> top on him, grabs him by the throat, and
> starts strangling him.

> NILES
> My God, my God, I'm having a flash-
> back. You're climbing in my crib and
> jumping on me.

ACTION: Frasier going for the kill.

REACTION: Niles recoiling in terror.

SUBTEXT: Their roughhouse releases a wild, archaic instinct in Frasier.

Niles, in terror, flashes back to his babyhood and remembers the day when Frasier actually tried to kill him.

BEAT 14

> FRASIER
> (roaring as he throttles his brother)
> You stole my mommy!!

> Shocked by his murderous actions, Fra-
> sier jumps off the bed and rushes out the
> door.

ACTION: Frasier strangling his brother.

REACTION: Frasier fleeing the scene of the crime.

SUBTEXT: This hugely exaggerated beat explodes laughter because it draws energy from a primal impulse. The Cain and Abel story is a foundational archetype in Western culture. Sibling rivalry leads to violence more often than we like to believe. Ask any parent. In a drama, this last beat would be tragic. But comedy bundles catastrophe in laughter. "You stole my mommy!", delivered with Kelsey Grammer's frenzy, takes the beat delightfully over the top.

Subtextual Progression

This scene doesn't arc so much as it drills down. Scan the following list of subtextual actions to sense the spiral.

BEAT 1: Urging Niles to accept failure/Blaming their failure on Frasier.

BEAT 2: Calling Niles an idiot/Calling Frasier a snob.

BEAT 3: Calling Niles a petulant child/Calling Frasier an upstaging ham.

BEAT 4: Calling Niles a masochist/Calling Frasier a sadist.

BEAT 5: Calling Niles a crybaby/Calling Frasier a show-off.

BEAT 6: Defending his face/Attacking Frasier's face.

BEAT 7: Calling Niles ugly/Calling Frasier ugly.

BEAT 8: Making a fist/Making a fist.

BEAT 9: Deciding where to punch/Daring him to punch.

BEAT 10: Attacking Niles/Gathering his counterattack.

BEAT 11: Attacking Frasier/Deceiving Niles.

BEAT 12: Surrendering to Frasier/Attacking Niles.

BEAT 13: Going for the kill/Recoiling in terror.

BEAT 14: Strangling his brother/Fleeing the scene of the crime.

The brothers begin by attacking each other's personalities, then descend into sneering at each other's physical defects, followed by emotional assaults, bottoming out with near-lethal violence: fourteen beats of fraternal ferocity made hysterically funny.

COMEDY DIALOGUE TECHNIQUE

Laughter inspired by brutality is made possible by an eons-old convention. Since the dawn of storytelling, artists have maintained a bright line between drama and comedy by controlling the audience's perception of pain: In true drama, everybody gets hurt; in true comedy, nobody gets hurt. Not really.

Comic characters may writhe, scream, bounce off walls, and tear their hair out, but they do it with a wild spirit that allows readers and audiences to sit back, laugh, and safely feel that it doesn't really hurt. For without a clear comic style, readers and audiences would naturally feel sorry for suffering characters. To the comic writer, empathy spells death. Compassion kills laughs. Therefore, comic technique must keep the reader/audience cool, critical, unempathetic—on the safe side of pain.

Here's a short list of four techniques designed to keep emotional distance and trigger laughs.

1) **Clarity:** Not only does empathy kill laughs, but so does ambiguity, perplexity, and all forms of confusion. To keep the laughs rolling, everything must be clear, starting in the subtext. If a character is up to no good, the audience or reader may not know exactly what that no good is, but it should be crystal that what he's up to is no good.

Language, too. Piles of blurry, verbose dialogue suffocate laughter. If you wish to write comedy, go back and review the principles of style covered in Chapters Five, Six, and Seven. Their every point applies absolutely to comedy writing. Focus in particular on the fundamentals of economy and clarity. The best jokes always use the fewest and clearest possible words.

2) **Exaggeration:** Comic dialogue thrives in the gap between cause and effect. The two most common techniques of exaggeration either bloat a minor cause into a major overstatement—"You stole my mommy!"—or shrink a major cause into a minor understatement—"The Harry Potter Theme Park is a hit with both anglophiles and pedophiles." Comic exaggerations come in a variety of modes: dialects, non

sequiturs, malapropisms, impersonations, pretense, sarcasm—all the way down the line to babble and nonsense.

3) **Timing:** As I noted above, jokes pivot around a two-part design: setup and payoff, a.k.a. punch. The setup arouses aggressive, defensive, and/or sexual emotions in the reader/audience; the punch explodes that energy into laughter. The punch, therefore, must arrive at the exact moment the setup's emotional charge peaks. Too soon and you get a weak laugh; too late and you get a groan. Moreover, nothing must follow the punch that would stifle the laughter.

These two examples from 30 ROCK:

"Avery is the most perfect woman ever created. Like a young Bo Derek stuffed with a Barry Goldwater." Avery (Elizabeth Banks) and Bo Derek inspire sexual energy (setup); the antithesis of sex, Barry Goldwater, a right-wing politician from the sixties, explodes it (punch).

"If I give in, I'm no longer the alpha in my house. Before you know it, she'll have me wearing jeans and reading fiction." Here the energy of aggressive masculine dominance (setup) is undercut by a feminine act (from Jack's POV), "reading fiction" (punch).

Note that both jokes use periodic sentences. Their punch words end the gag and nothing immediately follows, giving the audience room to laugh before the next beat takes their attention. As the old vaudeville saying goes: Don't step on your own laughs.

In the FRASIER scene, notice that periodic sentences deliver all the punch words and phrases: "mister big shot radio host," "chewed meat," "the side of buses," "fat face," "spindly," "pugilists," and "my mommy."

The only line that sets its punch word back from the last is Niles's in Beat 6: "Oh, please, I keep wondering how long you're going to store those nuts for winter." The punch word is "nuts." I suspect that the phrasing "Oh, please, winter's coming and I keep wondering how long you're going to store those nuts" would have gotten a bigger laugh, but I couldn't be certain until I could see the actor deliver the line.

4) **Incongruity:** To build a joke, the relationship between setup and punch must strike a spark of incongruity; two things that don't belong together suddenly collide. The underlying incongruity in the

FRASIER scene pits civilized adults against their feral childhood selves. Psychiatrists who should be able to see their obsessions do not, and so cannot control them. In fact, they do the opposite; they let them loose. The steps they take to achieve their desires become the very things they must do to make sure they never achieve them. As a result, they act out the very book they cannot write.

15

ASYMMETRIC CONFLICT

A RAISIN IN THE SUN

Lorraine Hansberry's play opened in New York on March 11, 1959, starring Sidney Poitier, Claudia McNeil, Ruby Dee, and Louis Gossett Jr. It was the first play written by a black woman to reach Broadway and won the New York Drama Critics' Circle Award. Two years later Hansberry adapted it to the screen.

The play tells the story of a black family living in a tiny apartment on Chicago's South Side in the 1950s. The Youngers recently buried the family patriarch, Walter, who literally worked himself to death. Walter left his wife, Lena, ten thousand dollars in life insurance. Lena wants to use a third of the money for a down payment on a house; a third to help her daughter, Bennie, through medical school; and the rest for her son, Walter Lee.

Walter Lee and two of his buddies have a plan to open a liquor store, but they need cash. Walter's scene intention drives the scene below: to persuade his wife, Ruth, to help him get the whole ten thousand dollars. Ruth doesn't trust her husband's business venture and knows Lena will never give him all her money for any purpose, let alone a liquor store. Her scene intention contradicts his: to evade Walter's scheme.

As husband and wife block each other's conscious desires (force of antagonism), the scene shapes an asymmetrical conflict. Walter compels the action and the turning points happen to him. Ruth does her best to avoid conflict.

That's the surface conflict, but taking the scene deeper, what do these characters really want? Walter Lee is a chauffeur, a dead-end job if there ever was one. The liquor store, he feels, will give him money and with that will come pride, independence, and the admiration of his wife and their son, Travis. Walter Lee wants: to gain self-respect (super-intention).

What Walter Lee does not know, however, is that his wife is two months pregnant with a second child. Because they live in poverty, she secretly contemplates an abortion. Like her husband, she also works for rich white people, as a domestic. She dreams of a decent life with a regular income in a home of their own. Ruth desperately needs: to find security (super-intention).

Once again, the scene is printed in bold, interspaced with my notes on its beats and writing techniques. First read the bold passages straight through as Hansberry wrote the scene. Listen to the language in your mind, or better yet, read it aloud to yourself. Note the vocabulary with its short, punchy words; note the stripped-down grammar, and in particular, note the cadence of Hansberry's language and how the rhythm of her phrasings matches the rhythms of her characters' emotions. Once you have a feeling for how the scene plays, reread it against my analysis.

A RAISIN IN THE SUN

Act 1, Scene 1

The Younger apartment kitchen. As Ruth makes breakfast, her husband, Walter Lee, enters.

It's useful, I believe, to think of scenes as mini-dramas, often triggered by a mini–inciting incident of their own. In this case, Walter throws the morning out of balance by bringing up his liquor store plans. He knows Ruth scorns the idea, so as she makes breakfast in a sour mood, he opens the scene with a smile.

> WALTER: You know what I was thinking 'bout in the bathroom this morning?
>
> RUTH: (She looks at him in disgust and turns back to her work) No.

BEAT 1

ACTION: Walter inviting her to talk.
REACTION: Ruth snubbing his offer.
    Notice that as the scene below builds, Hansberry never repeats a beat.

> WALTER: How come you always try to be so pleasant!
>
> RUTH: What is there to be pleasant 'bout!

BEAT 2

ACTION: Walter calling her a killjoy.
REACTION: Ruth calling their life a misery.

> WALTER: You want to know what I was thinking 'bout in the bathroom or not?
>
> RUTH: I know what you thinking 'bout.

BEAT 3

ACTION: Walter insisting she listen.
REACTION: Ruth dismissing his idea.
    In the first three beats, Hansberry quickly establishes that after years of struggle to make ends meet, they're experts in hurting each other.

> WALTER: (Ignoring her) 'Bout what me and Willy
> Harris was talking about last night.
>
> RUTH: (Immediately—a refrain) Willy Harris is
> a good-for-nothing loudmouth.

BEAT 4

ACTION: Walter ignoring her.
REACTION: Ruth ridiculing him.

> WALTER: Anybody who talks to me has to be a
> good-for-nothing loudmouth, ain't he? And what
> you know about who is just a good-for-nothing
> loudmouth? Charlie Atkins was just a
> "good-for-nothing loudmouth" too, wasn't he!
> When he wanted me to go in the dry-cleaning
> business with him. And now—he's grossing a
> hundred thousand dollars a year. A hundred
> thousand dollars a year! You still call him a
> loudmouth!
>
> RUTH: (Bitterly) Oh, Walter Lee...(She sits
> at the table and drops her head on her folded
> arms)

BEAT 5

ACTION: Walter blaming her.
REACTION: Ruth hiding her guilt.

Note Hansberry's skill: This is a superb example of how to set
up a future payoff. At this point neither the audience nor any other
character knows that Ruth is pregnant and contemplating an abortion. As the scene plays, the audience's first impression may be that
there's some truth in Walter's complaint, that Ruth's pessimism is a
drag on his life. But that's Hansberry's deft setup for a forthcoming

payoff. When Ruth's pregnancy is revealed, we'll suddenly grasp the real reason she's in a tetchy, sullen mood. We'll see her character, this scene, and its subtext with a rush of deep, unexpected but retrospectively logical perception.

Therefore, the actor playing Ruth must create the pain and dread of her secret without giving it away and spoiling the audience's discovery when the Act 1 climax pays off this scene's setup.

For example, Hansberry calls for Ruth to drop her head on her arms at the table. It looks like frustration over Walter's badgering, but it could actually be that she's suppressing morning sickness. The actor might play this secretly to herself, but she wouldn't, for instance, clutch her stomach and tip off the audience.

> WALTER: (Rising and standing over her) You tired, ain't you? Tired of everything. Me, the boy, the way we live—this beat-up hole, everything. Ain't you? (She doesn't look up, doesn't answer) So tired—moaning and groaning all the time, but you wouldn't do nothing to help, would you? You couldn't be on my side that long for nothing, could you?
>
> RUTH: Walter, please leave me alone.
>
> WALTER: A man needs for a woman to back him up . . .
>
> RUTH: Walter . . .

BEAT 6

ACTION: Walter calling her selfish.
REACTION: Ruth giving in.

Ruth submits to listen, or at least pretends to listen. It's easier than battling the relentless Walter. He sees it as a sign he's getting somewhere, so he changes his manner to sweet talk.

WALTER: Mama would listen to you. You know she listen to you more than she do me and Bennie. She think more of you. All you have to do is just sit down with her when you drinking your coffee one morning and talking 'bout things like you do and—(He sits down beside her and demonstrates graphically what he thinks her methods and tone should be)—you just sip your coffee, see, and say easy like that you been thinking 'bout that deal Walter Lee is so interested in, 'bout the store and all, and sip some more coffee, like what you saying ain't really that important to you— and the next thing you know, she be listening good and asking you questions and when I come home—I can tell her the details. This ain't no fly-by-night proposition, baby. I mean we figured it out, me and Willy and Bobo.

RUTH: (With a frown) Bobo?

BEAT 7

ACTION: Walter seducing her.
REACTION: Ruth smelling a rat.

It doesn't occur to Walter that the coffee klatch scene he acts out ridicules women. In fact, the audience wouldn't have noticed and might even have found it amusing because in 1959, offhanded sexism was commonplace and virtually invisible. But not to Hansberry. This is another of her excellent setups. She's planting Walter's sexism here so she can harvest it at the end of the scene when he attacks all black women for their alleged betrayal of black men.

WALTER: Yeah. You see, this little liquor store we got in mind cost seventy-five thousand and we figured the initial investment on

the place be 'bout thirty thousand, see. That
be ten thousand each. Course, there's a couple
of hundred you got to pay so's you don't spend
you life just waiting for them clowns to let
your license get approved—

RUTH: You mean graft?

BEAT 8

ACTION: Walter playing the businessman.
REACTION: Ruth foreseeing disaster.

WALTER: (Frowning impatiently) Don't call it
that. See there, that just goes to show you
what women understand about the world. Baby,
don't nothing happen for you in this world
'less you pay somebody off!

RUTH: Walter, leave me alone!

BEAT 9

ACTION: Walter proving his worldliness.
REACTION: Ruth rejecting his folly.

Ruth is a deeply moral woman. The thought of an abortion, which was a felony in the 1950s, eats at her. She must be desperate to talk about it, but note how Hansberry wisely keeps it in the subtext.

RUTH: (She raises her head, stares at him vig-
orously, then says quietly) Eat your eggs,
they gonna be cold.

WALTER: (Straightening up from her and looking
off) That's it. There you are. Man say to his

woman: I got me a dream. His woman say: Eat
your eggs. (Sadly, but gaining in power) Man
say: I got to take hold of this here world,
baby! And a woman say: Eat your eggs and go
to work. (Passionately now) Man say: I got to
change my life, I'm choking to death, baby.
And his woman say—(In utter anguish as he
brings his fists down on his thighs)—your eggs
is getting cold!

BEAT 10

ACTION: Ruth placating him.
REACTION: Walter accusing her of disloyalty.

RUTH: (Softly) Walter, that ain't none of our
money.

Walter falls silent and turns away from her.

BEAT 11

ACTION: Ruth swinging a moral hammer.
REACTION: Walter coping with defeat.
FIRST TURNING POINT: This scene plays in not one but two movements. The first movement begins at the positive as Walter has hope
that he can convince Ruth to help him get his mother's money. He runs
a guilt-tripping argument, claiming that because Ruth ruined his prior
chance at business success, she owes him her help now. What's more,
as his wife, she is morally obligated to support her husband's venture.
Of course he undermines his "moral" position with his willingness to
pay bribes. Ruth finally explodes his argument by pointing out that
they have no right to the money. His dead father earned that money
with decades of sweat and pain. It's Lena's money, not theirs. It would

be immoral to seduce her out of it. Beat 11 creates a negative turning point that shatters Walter's scene intention. He knows he cannot argue against that truth, so he goes silent for a moment to gather himself for an attack in a new direction with a new scene intention: to escape his overwhelming sense of failure.

> WALTER: (Not listening at all or even look-
> ing at her) This morning, I was lookin'
> in the mirror and thinking about it. I'm
> thirty-five years old; I been married eleven
> years and I got a boy who sleeps in the liv-
> ing room—(very, very quietly)—and all I got
> to give him is stories about how rich white
> people live . . .
>
> RUTH: Eat your eggs, Walter.
>
> WALTER: Damn my eggs . . . damn all the eggs
> that ever was!
>
> RUTH: Then go to work.

BEAT 12

ACTION: Walter begging for sympathy.
REACTION: Ruth ignoring his plea.

> WALTER: (Looking up at her) See—I'm trying
> to talk to you 'bout myself—(shaking his head
> with the repetition)—and all you can say is
> eat them eggs and go to work.
>
> RUTH: (Wearily) Honey, you never say nothing
> new. I listen to you every day, every night
> and every morning, and you never say noth-
> ing new. (Shrugging) So you would rather be

Mr. Arnold than be his chauffeur. So—I would
rather be living in Buckingham Palace.

BEAT 13

ACTION: Walter accusing her of not loving him.
REACTION: Ruth accusing him of living in a fantasy.

> WALTER: That is just what is wrong with the
> colored woman in this world...don't under-
> stand about building their men up and making
> 'em feel like they somebody. Like they can do
> something.

> RUTH: (dryly, but to hurt) There are colored
> men who do things.

BEAT 14

ACTION: Walter blaming her for his failure.
REACTION: Ruth blaming him for his failure.
SECOND TURNING POINT: After his self-pity and guilt trips fall on
deaf ears, Walter tries this logic: All black women make all black men
failures. Ruth is black. Therefore, she's to blame for his failure. But
again she destroys his argument, this time with a fact and its implication: Some black men succeed. He is responsible for his failed life.
She's right and he knows it. Her bitter truth turns the scene to a double negative.

> WALTER: No thanks to the colored woman.

> RUTH: Well, being a colored woman, I guess I
> can't help myself none.

BEAT 15

ACTION: Walter clinging to his lame excuse.
REACTION: Ruth sneering at his self-deception.

> **WALTER:** (Mumbling) We one group of men tied
> to a race of women with small minds.
>
> Ruth looks away in silence.

BEAT 16

ACTION: Walter soothing his wounded ego.
REACTION: Ruth retreating into her fears.

Let's look at Hansberry's sequence of beats and how she designed their progression. She starts with a mini–inciting incident: Walter's cheerful invitation to talk, followed by Ruth's hostile, one-word answer, "No." From Beat 1 to Beat 6, Hansberry builds the beats to the negative. Each exchange tops the previous beat as Ruth and Walter add pain on pain, humiliation on humiliation, putting their love and hope in greater and greater jeopardy.

BEAT 1: Inviting her to talk/Refusing his invitation.
BEAT 2: Calling her a killjoy/Calling their life a misery.
BEAT 3: Insisting she listen/Dismissing his idea.
BEAT 4: Ignoring her/Ridiculing his idea.
BEAT 5: Blaming her/Hiding her guilt.
BEAT 6: Calling her selfish/Giving in.

Ruth surrenders for a moment to listen to what he has to say.

As Walter acts out the "coffee klatch" in Beat 7, the scene takes on a lighter, almost amusing tone. The mood rises toward the positive, and we begin to feel that Ruth might take his side. But when he mentions Bobo, she reacts with suspicion, and the scene swings back toward a deeper negative, building to the turning point at Beat 11.

BEAT 7: Seducing her/Smelling a rat.

BEAT 8: Playing the businessman/Foreseeing disaster.

BEAT 9: Proving his worldliness/Rejecting his folly.

BEAT 10: Placating him/Accusing her of disloyalty.

BEAT 11: Swinging a moral hammer/Coping with defeat.

Beat 11 climaxes Walter's scene intention. He realizes that Ruth will never help him get his mother's money. Walter has failed again. This blow silences him for a moment, and the scene takes a breath while Walter gathers his anger and unleashes the scene's second movement.

First he must somehow bandage his wounded ego. So in Beat 12 he tries pleading for Ruth's understanding, but then in Beats 13 and 14 he turns on her to blame her and all black women for his failure. Finally she nails him with the truth.

BEAT 12: Begging for sympathy/Ignoring his plea.

BEAT 13: Accusing her of not loving him/Accusing him of living in a fantasy.

BEAT 14: Blaming her for his failure/Blaming him for his failure.

Beat 14 climaxes both the second movement and the scene as Ruth forces Walter to confront his responsibility for his own miserable life.

BEAT 15: Clinging to his lame excuse/Sneering at his self-deception.

BEAT 16: Soothing his wounded ego/Retreating into her fears.

The last two beats are a resolution movement that eases the tension as Walter retreats into self-pity and Ruth retreats into her secret fears about her pregnancy.

A sampling of the gerunds used to name the actions and reactions of husband and wife lays out the scene's asymmetrical conflict:

Walter's actions: inviting, insisting, blaming, seducing, proving, accusing, versus Ruth's reactions: dismissing, hiding, giving in, placating, ignoring, retreating.

A sampling of lines reveals the word choices and modals used to carry out those actions.

Walter's aggressive accusations:
You still call him a loudmouth?
You wouldn't do nothing to help, would you?
A man needs a woman to back him up.
I'm choking to death, baby!
Ruth's passive reactions:
Oh, Walter Lee . . .
Please leave me alone.
That ain't none of our money.
I guess I can't help myself none.

The scene arcs its primary values from positive to negative: hope to despair, security to danger, success to failure, self-respect to self-hatred. As the scene opens, Walter has hope to gain success and with that, self-respect. Ruth clings to her hope for security. But the scene's ever-escalating beats of action/reaction push Ruth further and further from a secure future, while driving Walter further and further from his immediate goal of financial success, and even further from his life-fulfilling desire for self-respect. What's more, because we sense that underneath the arguing these two people love each other, the climax of the scene puts their marriage in jeopardy. The scene ends on the deeply negative: Walter's hope turns to despair; Ruth's security turns to danger.

To fully appreciate Hansberry's genius, notice that as she executes her immediate task of arcing the scene around its value changes, she also uses its second movement to set up Walter's long-term character arc.

A character arc is a profound change, for better or worse, in a character's moral, psychological, or emotional nature, expressed in values such as optimism/pessimism, maturity/immaturity, criminality/redemption, and the like. The character's inner nature may arc from the positive (caring) to the negative (cruel), as does Michael in THE GODFATHER PART II, or from the negative (egoist) to the positive (loving), as does Phil in GROUNDHOG DAY.

Therefore, the writer must clearly establish the character at the positive or negative of a value early in the story, so that the audience can understand and feel the arc of change. Walter is the only character in the play that undergoes moral change, and so Hansberry ingeniously uses Beats 12 to 16 to set up his nature and need for change.

In five progressive beats of dialogue, Hansberry expresses Walter's desperate desire for self-respect and the respect of his family and dramatizes that he has neither. After turning Walter's super-intention to the negative (wounded pride) in Act 1, Hansberry takes Walter down to an even deeper hell of self-loathing and familial disgust at the Act 2 climax. At last she resurrects Walter when he makes a choice and takes an action that wins him self-respect as well as the love and admiration of his wife and family at the story climax. Walter's character arc from self-hatred to self-respect lifts *A Raisin in the Sun* well above conventional social dramas about racial prejudice.

Now let's take this excellent scene and ruin it. I'll demonstrate how the same dialogue beats could have been anti-progressive:

Suppose Hansberry had started the scene with its turning points: Walter asks Ruth whether she'd like to know what he's thinking about and she says, "I already know. Your father's life insurance. Walter, that is not our money! It's your mother's. So forget it. And what's more, I'm tired of listening to your whining about your misery and blaming me for your failed life. You, Walter, are responsible for every mistake you've ever made."

In reaction Walter could still go on about Ruth's lack of support, the glories of the liquor store business, how easy it would be to persuade his mother, how he hates his life and blames Ruth's typical black woman's attitude for it all. The necessary exposition about the money, his plans, his life, and his feelings about his wife would get out. The audience would learn what it needs to know but be bored stiff because it realizes that Walter's arguments are pointless. Ruth has said "No!" and means it. So, with zero tension and zero suspense, the scene would bump and crumble into a rubble of exposition.

Or I could ruin it another way by bringing in the turning points too late, elongating the scene by repeating its beats. Walter could expand on all the money he could have made in the dry-cleaning business; he could sing the praises of those extraordinary businessmen, Willy and Bobo; he could glorify the liquor store scheme and describe the furs, jewelry, and new home he would buy for Ruth and their son with the fortune he would make.

When she finally nails him with the fact that his mother's money is not his, Walter could then launch a century-long history of the black woman as the black man's burden—on and on until Ruth shuts him up. Again the audience loses interest as fact after fact is hammered home over and over. When the turning points finally arrive, they'd have less than half their full impact because the exposition has worn down the audience. Notice that when Hansberry does use repetition, such as Walter's "egg" speech (Beat 7), it's to give the actor three drumbeats to build to an emotional peak—but no more.

Or worse yet, she could have written the scene with no turning points at all. She could have poured out three pages of breakfast table talk about business plans, Mother's money, their lousy marriage, and the fate of black men and women. But she didn't. She wrote a revealing, moving, progressive scene that beat by beat hits two turning points that in turn set up her whole play.

Like the scene we just studied, every scene, ideally, works as both payoff and setup. Something has changed since the last confrontation between a scene's characters. Therefore, what is said now pays off things that happened in the past. As these payoffs reverberate through the dialogue, what is said now will in turn set up effects in future scenes.

And like the examples from THE SOPRANOS and FRASIER, Hansberry's skilled creation of Walter Lee carried Sidney Poitier into nominations for a Tony Award, a Golden Globe, and a BAFTA, the British Academy of Film and Television Award.

In the three previous chapters, dramatized scenes called for actors to strike major chords of heated emotion around wrenching turning points. Let's now look at a prose scene with cool tones and muted action.

16

INDIRECT CONFLICT

THE GREAT GATSBY

Chapter One of F. Scott Fitzgerald's novel introduces the reader to the story's narrator, Nick Carraway. Nick has come to New York to begin his Wall Street career. He has rented a house in West Egg, Long Island. His neighbor is Jay Gatsby, a fabulously wealthy young man who has made a fortune as a bootlegger. West Egg is home to the well-to-do, but it is far less fashionable than its very exclusive counterpart across the bay, East Egg. Nick's cousin, the beautiful Daisy, lives in an East Egg mansion with her wealthy husband, Tom Buchanan, a powerfully built former Ivy League athlete. The Buchanans invite Nick for dinner, and there he meets Miss Jordan Baker, a female tennis star who, like the Buchanans, is also upper class.

Fitzgerald has written his novel in the first person from Nick's point of view. Below is Fitzgerald's subchapter broken into eight beats. The scene begins with the foursome sipping drinks before dinner. Miss Baker turns to Nick and says:

BEAT 1

"You live in West Egg," she remarked contemptuously. "I know somebody there."

"I don't know a single—"

"You must know Gatsby."

"Gatsby?" demanded Daisy. "What Gatsby?"

BEAT 2

Before I could reply that he was my neighbor, dinner was announced; wedging his tense arm imperatively under mine, Tom Buchanan compelled me from the room as though he were moving a checker to another square.

Slenderly, languidly, their hands set lightly on their hips, the two young women preceded us out onto a rosy-colored porch open toward the sunset where four candles flickered on the table in the diminished wind.

BEAT 3

"Why candles?" objected Daisy, frowning. She snapped them out with her fingers.

BEAT 4

"In two weeks it'll be the longest day in the year." She looked at us all radiantly. "Do you always watch for the longest day of the year and then miss it? I always watch for the longest day in the year and miss it."

BEAT 5

"We ought to plan something," yawned Miss Baker, sitting down at the table as if she were getting into bed.

"All right," said Daisy. "What'll we plan?" She turned to me helplessly.

"What do people plan?"

Before I could answer her eyes fastened with an awed expression on her little finger.

"Look!" she complained. "I hurt it."

We all looked—the knuckle was black and blue.

BEAT 6

"You did it, Tom," she said accusingly. "I know you didn't mean to do it but you did do it."

BEAT 7

"That's what I get for marrying a brute of a man, a great big hulking physical specimen of a—"

"I hate that word 'hulking'," objected Tom crossly, "even in kidding."

BEAT 8

"Hulking," insisted Daisy.

That ends the scene.

Before I begin my analysis, a few words on point of view.

First, a definition: **Point of view** is that place in the global space of a story's world that the writer or director places us so we can witness the scene. By global space, I mean the 360 degrees of horizontal angles that surround a subject, combined with the 360 vertical degrees of angle above and below the subject.

In the theatre, we look at the onstage life from that fixed POV of the seat we purchased. All of the characters' actions and reactions are in front of us at all times. We are more or less free to glance from one character to another at any moment, but that's our only POV choice, and that choice will be greatly influenced by the director's staging as well as the voices and movements of the actors.

In television and film, we see what the camera sees. As it moves through the global storytelling space, it controls but does not rigidly limit our POV. For as we gather in the establishing shots, supplemented with group shots, two-shots, or close-ups, and the like, we become aware of life offscreen as well as onscreen. As a result, we often imagine actions and reactions we do not in fact see.

Prose offers the writer the greatest freedom in point of view choices, and yet at the same time, for the reader, prose is the most controlling storytelling medium. Like other media, prose can view scenes from anywhere in the physical world, but it also adds subjective angles within a character's mental world. Once the prose writer makes a choice of person (first, third, or the eccentric second), her eye moves from that angle like a spotlight. The author holds our perception in her fist.

As we follow her sentences, she takes us where she wishes: through the places, times, and societies of her world; or into a single character's thought-filled depths, there to witness rationalizations, self-deceptions, and dreams; or deeper yet, into the character's subconscious to reveal her raw appetites, nightmarish terrors, and lost memories.

When skillfully executed, POV has such power that unless we deliberately stop, pull out of the telling, and put our imaginations to work, we are drawn through the tale, seeing and hearing only what the storyteller wants us to, and no more.

Therefore, in the following analysis, when I describe Tom Buchanan's reaction to Daisy's abrupt snuffing out of the candles, I am imagining the scene the way Fitzgerald might have imagined it before he wrote the final draft. Like all fine writers, Fitzgerald no doubt worked through the scene draft after draft, adding, cutting, reordering, phrasing, and rephrasing until he had a sense of its totality. And as he reworked the scene, he likely imagined it from each and every character's viewpoint, even though he knew that he would ultimately control his prose through Nick's point of view.

Now to the scene: Suppose you prepared a romantic candlelit dinner and your spouse abruptly snuffed out the candles without a word or look to you. What would you feel? How would you react? Tom must have been offended. So to analyze the full life of Fitzgerald's mini-drama, I must re-create the scene as he envisioned it before he wrote it and include the reactions that Fitzgerald chose to imply but not describe.

Inciting Incident

As the scene opens, Daisy's and Tom's life seems contented and in balance. The value of marriage/divorce is at its positive charge. But secretly, Daisy finds married life very tedious. Her inner charge of excitement/boredom sits at the nadir.

BEAT 1

ACTION: Jordan revealing that Gatsby lives in West Egg.
REACTION: Daisy concealing her surprise.

Beat 1 triggers the novel's inciting incident: Daisy discovers that Jay Gatsby has moved nearby. What's more, Jordan and Nick know him. This revelation immediately throws her life out of balance. The positive charge of marriage/divorce begins to erode toward the negative, while her excitement for Gatsby resurfaces.

In her late teens Daisy fell passionately in love with Jay Gatsby. Their rich girl/poor boy affair ended when Gatsby left to fight in World War I. Soon after their breakup, the socially ambitious Daisy married the wealthy Tom Buchanan. In recent years Gatsby has become scandalously rich and famous. Daisy has no doubt read or heard about his exploits. She may also have learned that he purchased a huge estate across the bay. In fact, Gatsby bought the home so he could look across the narrow waters to the lit windows of her home.

When Daisy asks, "What Gatsby?" she knows full well it's Jay Gatsby, but she cleverly uses the question to conceal her genuine surprise to learn that her former lover is now a virtual neighbor and, furthermore, that her friend knows him and her cousin lives near him.

The realization that Gatsby has moved close to her, undoubtedly drawn to West Egg because of her, upsets the balance of Daisy's life and arouses in her the desire to see him. To renew their love? Have an affair? Leave her husband? Who can say how far she intends to go? Daisy's fluidly fickle nature makes her incapable of decisive plans into the future, but this much is clear: Her super-intention is, at the very least: to see Jay Gatsby. Gatsby becomes her object of desire.

This puts two core values into play: marriage/divorce and boredom/passion—the security of her marriage versus her passion for Gatsby. She must risk the former to gain the latter.

Daisy's choice: To keep marital peace or go to war? At the top of the scene, the value charges are positive for Daisy's marriage (before dinner, husband and wife are amiable) but negative for Daisy's passion (Gatsby is out of reach).

Beyond seeing Gatsby, exactly what Daisy wants from him, Fitzgerald deliberately hides in the subtext. But note Daisy's choice: She risks her marriage and goes to war with her husband.

BEAT 2

ACTION: All walking to the dinner table.
REACTION: Daisy planning to humiliate Tom.

Daisy's problem is that she cannot just pick up a telephone and call Gatsby. Her pride and vanity won't allow her. What's more, if her husband and the rigid, snobbish society she moves in were to discover that she pursued the notorious Gatsby, the scandal would ruin her.

Instantly, instinctively, she decides to put on a show in front of Nick and Jordan so that one or both will carry a message to Gatsby, a message that says the Buchanan marriage is in trouble. Daisy takes command of the scene and drives it to its turning point. Her scene intention becomes: to humiliate her husband in public. Tom's scene intention, it's fair to assume, is: to avoid public humiliation. These directly opposed desires set the scene's terms of antagonism.

Tom Buchanan has had his household staff set the dinner table with candles. He may have done it for Daisy's sake, or perhaps he intended this romantic touch to encourage Nick and Jordan. Indeed, in time those two will have a summer affair.

BEAT 3

ACTION: Daisy destroying her husband's romantic gesture.
REACTION: Tom concealing his annoyance.

But whatever Tom's reason, as they step up to the table, the "frowning" Daisy objects to the candles and snuffs them out with her fingers. Tom reacts by concealing the hurt she causes him and saying nothing. The positive charge of marriage declines further as Daisy's boredom changes into excitement.

BEAT 4

ACTION: Daisy opening a conversational subject.
REACTION: Daisy turning the subject back to herself.

In this beat Daisy starts a conversation about the summer solstice, but before anyone can respond to her strange question, she reacts to her own action and ends the topic by referring it back to herself. The value charges of marriage/divorce and excitement/boredom are unaffected and remain the same as they were in Beat 3.

BEAT 5

ACTION: Jordan and Daisy wondering aloud to the others.
REACTION: Daisy calling attention to her finger.

The summer season has just begun, so Jordan starts the next beat by suggesting that they plan something to do. Daisy simply continues that action by repeating the question twice, not to her husband, but to Nick. But before Nick can answer, she instantly and literally wraps the conversation around her little finger. The value charges of marriage/divorce and excitement/boredom continue on pause.

BEAT 6

ACTION: Daisy accusing Tom of injuring her.
REACTION: Tom hiding his reaction in silence.

Daisy faces a crisis dilemma: She could insult her husband (negative), which might send a message to Gatsby (positive), or she could protect her marriage (positive) but not win Gatsby's attention (negative). Daisy chooses to accuse her husband of bruising her finger. Again, Fitzgerald gives Tom no visible reaction, not a word of protest. The value charge of marriage/divorce turns dark, while excitement/boredom shines.

BEAT 7

ACTION: Daisy insulting her husband in public.
REACTION: Tom ordering her not to insult him again.

Daisy, then, with cool irony, insults her husband with a special emphasis on a word that she knows he hates: hulking. Finally, Tom objects.

Bear in mind that these are educated, upper-class characters, so when I use the verb "ordering" to name Tom's reaction, it's because that's what he's doing in the subtext. Tom is too well behaved to say, "Damn it, Daisy, never use the word 'hulking' again!" But under the phrase "I hate that word..." is an indirect command.

Daisy's insult throws marriage/divorce sharply to the negative, while in the subtext, excitement for Gatsby conquers her boredom.

BEAT 8

ACTION: Daisy attacking him a second time.

REACTION: Tom retreating in silence.

Daisy climaxes the scene by defying her husband's order and repeating the hated word with emphasis. In reaction, Tom once more falls silent.

Daisy wins her marital power struggle in six beats and humiliates Tom. This duel between husband and wife, Tom's defeat and Daisy's victory, would not be lost on her audience of the very sensitive, observant Nick and the gossipy Jordan Baker. Daisy knows this. Now she hopes that they'll carry the news to Gatsby. Daisy has embarrassed her husband, and it has had the effect she wants.

As Daisy chooses Gatsby over Tom, her marriage ends in all but name while her excitement about the future peaks.

DIALOGUE VERSUS DESCRIPTION IN PROSE

As mentioned previously, prose writers (with exceptions) tend to keep their dramatized dialogue economical, simple, and plainspoken. Of the scene's 123 spoken words, 107 are of one syllable, 14 of two syllables, and just 2 of three syllables. None of the scene's characters uses metaphors or similes when they speak.

Fitzgerald, on the other hand, enriches his descriptions with figurative language such as "Tom Buchanan compelled me from the room as though he were moving a checker to another square" and "... Miss Baker, sitting down at the table as if she were getting into bed." When he uses polysyllabic words, they tend to be adverbs that describe tones of voice (contemptuously, accusingly, crossly) and actions (slenderly, languidly, radiantly).

The scene's power comes from Daisy's actions in the subtext, actions that Nick, limited by his first-person point of view, cannot know. Instead, Fitzgerald encourages the reader to see through Daisy's veil of innocence by dropping hints along the way such as Daisy's "demand" to know "What Gatsby?"

TURNING POINT/SCENE CLIMAX

The scene arcs the Buchanan marriage dynamically from positive to negative in eight beats. In the first beat, their marriage seems respectful and faithful. By the last beat, Daisy's actions reveal a marriage filled with hatred and disrespect as she plots her path back to Gatsby. At the same time, each negative action against the marriage becomes a positive beat for Daisy's desire for the adventure that Gatsby brings to her life. Daisy's tactic works: She wins the war against her husband and gives Jordan and Nick the message they will carry to Gatsby.

The eight beat progression takes this shape:

BEAT 1: Revealing/Concealing

BEAT 2: Walking/Planning

BEAT 3: Destroying/Concealing

BEAT 4: Opening a subject/Turning the subject to herself

BEAT 5: Wondering aloud/Turning attention to herself

BEAT 6: Accusing/Hiding

BEAT 7: Insulting/Ordering

BEAT 8: Attacking/Retreating

Each beat tops the previous beat, progressing to the turning point when Daisy defies her husband's order and humiliates him—each beat, that is, except Beats 4 and 5. They seem to be a hole in the dialogue's progression because they are not aimed at Daisy's scene intention. Indeed they're not, because Fitzgerald uses them for another, larger purpose related to the novel's spine of action.

Notice the pattern in Beats 4 and 5: Daisy asks a question that opens up a general topic for the others, but then without pause, before anyone can answer, she instantly draws their interest back to her. Fitzgerald repeats this pattern in Daisy's dialogue throughout the book. In ways that are amusing, sympathetic, or mysterious, Daisy constantly steers all talk back to herself. In other words, Fitzgerald wants us to understand that Daisy is a very beautiful, very charming narcissist.

What is the real reason she creates this scene? Why can't she defy her husband, break social convention, and visit Gatsby herself? Why must she send a veiled message through Jordan and Nick? Because narcissists call attention to themselves, never others. For Daisy, it is critical that Gatsby seek her out. Gatsby must come to her. Fitzgerald uses those beats and many others elsewhere to express the dueling spines of action that drive *The Great Gatsby*: Gatsby's obsession with Daisy and Daisy's obsession with Daisy.

17

REFLEXIVE CONFLICT

INTRODUCTION TO THE SELF

Chapter One defined dialogue as any words said by any character to anyone. This traffic of talk runs along three distinct avenues: said to others, said to a reader or audience, and said to oneself. The chapter that follows focuses on the latter two tracks: direct address to the reader and inner dialogue between selves. Although the stage and screen limit the use of these two modes, for the novelist and short-story writer, they are the stuff of first-person prose.

When characters talk directly to the reader, the topic tends to be past events and their impact on themselves (e.g., *The Museum of Innocence*), whereas when characters talk to themselves, their inner dialogue acts out intra-dynamic events in the now. These dramatizations of self versus self carry psychological nuance into the depths of the unsayable (e.g., *Fräulein Else*). Once again, it's the difference between telling and showing.

In the former, a character with less than perfect self-awareness tells us about past inner conflicts and describes their effects; in the latter, a character puts her deep psychology into action in front of us and unknowingly dramatizes inner complexities she could never describe. Needless to say, telling and showing call upon two very different dialogue techniques.

An ancient literary convention grants us the godlike power to overhear a character's thoughts, all the while knowing that she is not talking to us. If so, then to whom is she speaking? Dialogue, by definition, is a two-sided exchange between a speaker and a listener. Who besides us is listening to her? If she's talking to another self within herself, her mind must be dual. If dual or even multiple, how does her mind divide itself into selves? Exactly how many are there? Who are they? How do they link?

These questions are neither new nor unique to storytelling. Twenty-five hundred years ago, the Buddha taught his followers to ignore all such wonderings because they flow from the false premise that the self exists, when in fact it does not. The sense of "me," he believed, is an illusionary side effect of uncountable, ever-shifting physical and sensory forces.

About the same time, Socrates argued the opposite view. He taught his students that the self not only exists, but you cannot live a meaningful, civilized life without making every effort to know who you are. In the centuries since, this debate over the nature of intrapersonal communication has swung back and forth between these two philosophical extremes and remains unsettled at best.

Science, on the other hand, has taken a stand.[1] Like Socrates, modern science strives to know the hidden nature of consciousness, but at the same time, like Buddha, it feels misled by intuition. While our sixth sense tells us we have a core of consciousness located behind our eyes, brain scan researchers report that several different mental processes, mediated by different brain regions, collaborate to create this illusion. No single, central, physical, all-controlling self exists; "me" is indeed a side effect. On the so-called "hard question" of consciousness, neuroscience now favors Buddha over Socrates but without a clear conclusion.[2]

Although science cannot ground consciousness in the physical, and philosophy cannot locate it in the metaphysical, artists know exactly where to find the self. When art whistles, the self comes running like a bounding dog. For the storyteller, the self makes its home in the same subjective reaches where it has always lived and thrived.

Delusional or not, consciousness of self is the essence of our humanity. If, as science tells us, the self is not confined to a specific lobe of the brain but emerges out of a composite of sources, so what? It's my composite and I like it. If, as philosophy claims, the unreliable self shifts and changes from one day to the next and, therefore, cannot be known absolutely, so what? It's my changing self and I enjoy watching it evolve, hopefully into a better person.

For prose writers striving to express the inner life, philosophy's deductive logic and science's inductive logic dull aesthetic insight. Neither leverages the inside-out power of the subjective; neither creates the meaningful emotional experience of the self that every major work of story art since Homer inspires. Story doesn't answer the "hard question"; it dramatizes it.

I think the best approach to creating inner dialogue is simply this: Treat your character's mind like a setting, a world populated with a cast of characters called selves. Let the mindscape sprawl like a cityscape, landscape, or battleground, a mental mise-en-scène for the staging of a story. Then move into that world yourself and take up residence in the protagonist's center of consciousness. From this point of view, create inner dialogues that dramatize an answer to the question "What is it to be this particular human being?"

To return to the question that started this introduction: When a character talks to herself, who besides the reader is listening? To whom is she speaking? Answer: the silent self. As we listen to a character talk to herself, we instinctively know that another side, a quiet side of herself, is listening. In fact, we know this so instinctively that we never think about it. We don't have to because we know, without thinking, that we talk to our personal silent self constantly.

Inside every mind, it seems to me, a separate, silent core of being sits back, watching, listening, evaluating, storing memories. If you meditate, you know this self very well. It floats behind you, so to speak, watching you do everything you do, including meditation. If you try to meditate toward this self, it instantly swings around behind you again. You cannot face yourself within yourself, but you always know that your silent self is there and aware, listening to everything you have to say.

As inner dialogues of prose cycle between the talking self and the silent self, they generate reflexivity.

REFLEXIVE CONFLICT

In the physical sciences, reflexivity refers to a circular or bidirectional relationship between cause and effect. An action triggers a reaction that impacts the action so fast the two seem simultaneous. (Some theories of quantum physics argue that at the subatomic level cause and effect are in fact simultaneous.) Action and reaction then lock together, whirling in a gyre. The cause becomes the effect, the effect becomes the cause, and neither can be clearly identified as either.

In the social sciences, reflexivity signals a kind of codependency between individuals, or within groups, institutions, and societies. Once the reflexive spiral begins, neither the action nor its reaction can be assigned as the cause or the effect. The two so intra-influence each other, they seem to happen instantaneously, without the need for decisions or even thought.

In the art of story, **reflexive conflict** refers to those inner battles that begin when a character's effort to resolve an inherent dilemma boomerangs back on herself. By taking her impasse inward, her effort to deal with her crisis becomes a cause that only worsens the effect. Self-contradictions generate ever-more complex sources of antagonism as causes become effects and effects become causes in an ever-deepening whorl until the conflict itself becomes the reason it cannot be solved.

Reflexive conflict translates into dialogue the moment a troubled character starts talking to herself. As I pointed out in Chapter One, the mind, by its very nature, can step back within itself to observe itself as if it were an object. A person temporarily splits in two to develop a relationship, often critical, between her core self and other sides or aspects of herself. She can project images of her past self, her unattractive self, her better self, her future self. She can feel the presence of her conscience, her subconscious, and, above all, her silent, listening self.

At times these relationships may be conflictless as, for example, when we comfort ourselves with excuses, self-deceptions, or blame placed on others. But more often than not, our inner selves strike opposing sides in the struggle to make choices, do the right thing, sacrifice for another, bring a troubled self under control—any of the tumultuous contrarieties of the inner life.[3]

Reflexive conflicts can be acted out in the present tense directly or related indirectly in the past tense. Onstage and onscreen, a character can perform the former in soliloquy and the latter in either dialogue spoken to another character or in direct address to the audience. On page, the protagonist can talk to her other self and act out her inner conflicts in the present tense (*Fräulein Else*), or talk to the reader and describe previous episodes of reflexive conflict in the past tense (*The Museum of Innocence*).

FRÄULEIN ELSE

Arthur Schnitzler, the Austrian novelist and playwright, experimented with stream of consciousness throughout his career, beginning in 1901 with the short story, "Lieutenant Gustl." In the 1924 novella *Fräulein Else*, he invited readers to eavesdrop on the troubled thoughts of its eponymous protagonist by writing exclusively in first-person inner dialogue.

SETUP

Else, a beautiful nineteen-year-old Viennese debutante, on holiday with her aunt at an Austrian mountain resort, receives a letter from her mother telling her that her father, a lawyer, has been caught stealing tens of thousands from a client's account. He faces prison or suicide if he can't pay the money back in two days.

Else's mother begs her to save her father by asking Herr von Dorsday, a rich art dealer staying at the spa, for a loan to cover the theft. Else, despite her suffocating shame, asks the old man for help. He says he will telegraph the funds to cancel her father's debt the next morning, but only if she repays him in sexual currency that night.

These three events—her father's theft, her mother's scheme, Dorsday's proposition—trigger the story's inciting incident and throw Else's life radically and negatively out of balance. Two contradictory desires immediately flood her mind: to save her parents and sacrifice herself versus to save herself and sacrifice her parents. Either way she chooses, a great price must be paid, because when I say "save herself," I mean that literally. Else's identity is tied to her morality. If she saves her family, she loses her morality; if she loses her morality, she loses her identity.

Trapped by this double bind of irreconcilable goods/lesser of two evils, Else's only path of action runs between her inner selves. So for the rest of the afternoon and evening, Else wanders the resort alone, her mind in reflexive chaos: At first, she tells herself to give in, save her family, and endure the disgrace; then she contradicts herself, choosing instead to reject Dorsday, and force her family to pay for its ignominy. At one point, she tries to cheer herself up, imagining that surrendering to Dorsday could launch a luxurious career as mistress to rich men, but then her conscience urges her to defend her moral self and accept poverty with honor.

Moral dilemmas like this, played out on a protagonist's mindscape, often spiral into reflexive conflict. For example, as the moment to meet Dorsday nears, Else says to herself:

How huge the hotel is. Like a monstrous, illuminated magic castle. Everything is gigantic. The mountains, too. Terrifyingly gigantic. They've never been so black before. The moon hasn't risen yet. It will rise just in time for the performance, the great performance in the meadow, when Herr von Dorsday makes his female slave dance naked. What's Herr von Dorsday to me? Now, Mademoiselle Else, what are you making such a fuss about? You were ready to go off and be the mistress of strange men, one after the other. And you boggle at the trifle which Herr von Dorsday asks of you? You were ready to sell yourself for a pearl necklace, for beautiful clothes, for a villa by the sea? And your father's life isn't worth as much as that?"

Reflexive Dialogue

Fourteen thoughts ricochet through this passage of inner dialogue. In the first seven (from "How huge" to "hasn't risen yet") Else's imagination projects her terror and sense of frailty onto the frightening, enormous, almost unreal world around her. The word "magic" gives away her childlike state.

Then her mind grabs the last word of the seventh sentence, "yet," and free-associates to an image of her future self, naked and dancing in the moonlight. With the rhetorical question "What's Herr von Dorsday to me?" she tries to shrug off the insinuations in the word "slave" and feign indifference.

But suddenly, her mind seems to segue into another self, armed with a sharp, critical voice. For the next five lines this critical self whiplashes Else's core self with a series of "Damned if you do/damned if you don't" insults. The critical self calls her a hypocrite, "such a fuss" (damned if you don't); then a slut, "mistress of strange men" (damned if you do); then a coward, "you boggle" (damned if you don't); then a slut again, "sell yourself" (damned if you do); and finally an ingrate, "your father's life" (damned if you don't).

Else's mind spins in reflexive conflict: "Which do I want to be? A jewel-decked whore or a cowardly ingrate?" She dreads both and wants neither, but question mark after question mark paralyzes her until the passage ends in mental gridlock. Spoiler alert: At the climax of the novel, Else's impasse explodes into an act of wild exhibitionism and a drug overdose.

As we have seen in previous examples, emotions tend to shorten lines, while rationality tends to lengthen them. As fear races through

Else, her first seven thoughts average 4.1 words each. But then the critical self takes charge and the next seven lines average 14.5 words.

Writing In-Character

When Arthur Schnitzler published *Fräulein Else*, he was a sixty-two-year-old man writing in the first-person inner voice of a nineteen-year-old socialite. How is this possible? First, he wrote plays as well as prose, so his dramatist skills must have helped him find words for this character. Then, life experience. He married a twenty-one-year-old actress when he was forty-one. In fact, over a lifetime he had many affairs with young women. Each must have given him a chance to hear a fresh voice and imagine life from a new and female point of view.

But my best guess is this: In addition to talent, skill, and a practiced ear, Schnitzler could act. Maybe not in front of an audience, but at his desk and pacing his study. He became her. He wrote in-character, a technique we will explore in Chapter Nineteen.

THE MUSEUM OF INNOCENCE

Orhan Pamuk published *The Museum of Innocence* two years after winning the 2006 Nobel Prize in Literature. He worked long and hard with novelist Maureen Freely to perfect the English translation. The English edition, rather than the original Turkish, was the likely basis for further translations (sixty languages to date), and so its faithfulness was critical.

SETUP

Pamuk's novel tells a story of love at first sight and its conflict-filled aftermath. Kemal, a Turkish businessman, has converted a house in Istanbul into a repository of mementos and memories he calls *The Museum of Innocence*. Like the Taj Mahal, the museum celebrates love. In Kemal's case, nine passionate years with Füsun, his exquisitely beautiful lover and eventual wife, now deceased.

The author's unique narrative strategy places Kemal inside the museum, where he acts as docent and guide to its exhibits. Pamuk then treats the reader as a visitor to the museum, allowing Docent Kemal to speak to the reader in first person as if the reader were the museum's guest.

Nine tumultuous, love-soaked years have seasoned Docent Kemal to maturity. But living in his memory is the museum's main exhibit: Kemal's previous, immature, ultra-romantic self. Throughout Kemal's youth, this self feverously sought something he could not grasp. He told himself he was in love with Füsun and, up to a point, he was. But deep within, his true obsession was a passion for passion. He quested after that ancient and elusive absolute: the life-fulfilling, transcendent romantic experience. Füsun merely played a role in his all-consuming drama.

Obsessive romantics devour the rites of romance: quiet walks in moonlight, tireless lovemaking, candlelit dinners, champagne, classical music, poetry, sunsets, and the like. But these enthralling rituals are pointless without an exquisite creature to share them, and so the man-in-love-with-romance tragedy begins when he falls for a woman because, and only because, she is gorgeous. Young Kemal, in other words, suffered from the curse of beauty: that insatiable craving for the sublime that makes living a simple life unthinkable.

Having created these two selves, Docent Kemal and Romantic Kemal, the author needed to characterize the two voices and solve three dialogue problems: 1) In what tone and manner would the Docent Self speak to a visitor? 2) How would the Docent Self express the Romantic Self's silent inner dialogue? 3) When we hear Romantic Kemal speak, what qualities would texture his voice?

The passage below answers those questions as Docent Kemal talks to us:

I have here the clock, and these matchsticks and match-books, because the display suggests how I spent the slow ten or fifteen minutes it took me to accept that Füsun was not coming that day. As I paced the rooms, glancing out the windows, stopping in my tracks from time to time, standing motionless, I would listen to the pain sluicing within me. As the clocks in the apartment ticked away, my mind would fixate on the seconds and the minutes to distract myself from the agony. As the appointed hour neared, the sentiment "Today, yes, she's coming, now" would bloom inside me, like spring flowers. At such moments I wanted time to flow faster so that I could be reunited with my lovely at once. But those minutes would never pass. For a moment, in a fit of clarity, I would understand that I was fooling myself, that I did not want the time to flow at all, because Füsun might never come. By two o'clock I was never sure whether to be happy that the hour had arrived, or sad that with every passing minute her arrival was less likely, and the distance between me and my beloved would grow as that between a passenger on a ship leaving port and the one he had left behind. So I would try to convince myself that not so very many minutes had passed, toward this end I would make little bundles of time in my head. Instead of feeling pain every second of every minute, I resolved to feel it only once every five! In this way I would take the pain of five discrete minutes and suffer it all in the last. But this too was for naught when I could no longer deny that the first five minutes had passed— when I was forced to accept that she was not coming, the forestalled pain would sink into me like a driven nail...

Docent Kemal begins this passage in the present tense as if he were standing in front of an exhibit case filled with heirlooms and speaking to a visitor. But *The Museum of Innocence* is primarily a temporal museum; its chief artifacts are episodes from a love story, taken out of time and placed in its galleries. So Docent Kemal switches to the past tense as he puts Romantic Kemal, trapped in an archived event, on display.

Docent Kemal quotes Romantic Kemal just once with four present-tense phrases: "today," "yes," "she's coming," and "now," uttered with the staccato of excitement. Other than this exception, Docent

Kemal leaves the implied line-by-line thoughts of Romantic Kemal's inner dialogue to the reader/visitor's imagination. In the sixth sentence, a third self, Critical Kemal, appears briefly to chide Romantic Kemal for his childish self-deceptions.

Docent/guest is a ceremonial relationship, more formal than professor/student. Professors and their students engage in the excitement of ideas, but the docent and museum guest join in a solemn reverence for the past. Therefore, Docent Kemal's dialogue pours out flowing, elegiac sentences.

The passage runs 325 words long in eleven sentences that average 29.5 words each. Subordinate clauses in series build each sentence to a mini-climax: "pain sluicing within me," "distract myself from the agony," "Füsun might never come," and so on. The passage's formality and grace also suggest that Docent Kemal has relived this scene again and again, recited it to many guests many times, perfecting his wording with each rendition.

Although Docent Kemal is no longer the hopeless romantic he once was, nostalgia for romance still fills his voice. He is as much poet as docent. So to characterize his protagonist's heightened romantic imagination, Pamuk interlaces Docent Kemal's descriptions with metaphors and similes. Here and there the docent resorts, as people do, to clichés: sugar-sweet images such as thoughts blooming like spring flowers inside Romantic Kemal, and the tear-streaked B-movie scene of a passenger on a departing ship gazing back at a beloved left on shore. Docent Kemal's most personal language, however, goes dark and animates pain: Liquid pain flows through his body, then takes the form of a driven nail. In the most vivid image of all, he transforms time into the conduit for pain, complete with a mental valve, as it were, that can turn it on and off.

Of the passage's eleven sentences, the word "would" finds its way into all but the first line. "Would" is the past tense of the verb "will," but in this context the author uses it as a modal to create a soft sense of uncertainty.

Feel, for example, the difference between the hard versus the soft expression of the same ideas: "I listen to" and "my mind fixates on" as opposed to "I would listen to" and "my mind would fixate on." Instead of the phrase "pain sunk into me," the translator uses "pain would sink into me" to give the moment a sense of melancholy. Overall, the frequent repetition of "would" softens the hard edge of reality and spreads an aura of things happening as much in its characters' imaginations as in an actual room in the actual past.

The phrase "would never" intimates unknown repetitions; "would try" hints at hope and wishing. Taken together, ten "woulds" yield an air of things that may or may not happen. The word "suggests" and the phrase "ten or fifteen" further distend this shifting atmosphere, until Docent Kemal's dialogue sounds like what it is: a memory in the mind of a failed romantic.

Reflexive Conflict

Pamuk's writing draws its energy from two sources of reflexive conflict: the tyranny of love and the tyranny of time.

The tyranny of love: While engaged to another woman, Romantic Kemal met Füsun, a beautiful shop clerk. The lightning of love at first sight struck, and his life veered out of control on a trajectory aimed at the transcendent romantic experience. Romantic Kemal blames fate, but fate is the excuse we use when our subconscious pries our hands off the wheel of life.

The arch-romantic wants his beloved with him every minute of every hour of every day. Suffering her absence causes more suffering as the agony of loneliness feeds on itself, making her absence all the more acute. The more he thinks about it, the worse it gets. If and when she were to finally show up, who knows how his mood might have reversed.

The tyranny of time: The clock on the wall measures time, but our inner Big Ben has no hands. Sometimes hours vanish in a glance; sometimes a minute drags by longer than an arctic February. Romantic Kemal tries concentrating on time because he thinks it will soothe his torment: "As the clocks in the apartment ticked away, my mind would fixate on the seconds and the minutes to distract myself from

the agony." But fixating on time makes its passage all the more excru-
ciating. He tries to bring time under control by bundling it, parsing it,
speeding it, slowing it, but his battle to rein time only gives time all
the more power to torture him.

This is the nature of reflexivity: The character inflicts it on himself
and then persists in stirring its poison. Needless to say, reflexive conflict offers the storyteller soaring dialogue opportunities.

A final note: Docent Kemal portrays Romantic Kemal's passion
with a powerful and yet self-obsessed intensity. When Füsun doesn't
show up, he might have thought: "My God, did something happen to
her? Is she hurt?" But he didn't. Instead, he dissected his painful antici-
pation of pleasure to the microsecond. For the romantic, it is, as we
say, always about him.

18

MINIMAL CONFLICT

INTRODUCTION: THE BALANCE OF TEXT AND SUBTEXT

Every line of dialogue strikes a balance between the literal meaning of the words said and the unsaid meanings that the reader/audience senses resounding through the subtext.

When this balance tilts so that a minor motivation causes a massive vocal response, dialogue sounds hollow and the scene feels forged. Recall the definition of melodrama from Chapter Six: the overwrought expression of limp needs. Like chefs who use rich sauces to hide spoiled food, writers who whip up blubbery stylistics to smother stale content risk the sour odor of melodrama.

When balance levels out so that unsaid thoughts and feelings transcribe directly and fully into what is said, we call this blatancy writing on-the-nose. If a scene's implicit and explicit meanings echo each other, subtext turns into text, depth dries up, lines sound tinny, and the acting clanks.

When the balance favors content over form, when minimal words express maximal meaning, dialogue gains its greatest credibility and power. Using Robert Browning's famous phrase, "Less is more."[1] Any word that can be cut should be cut, especially if its loss adds to the line's effect. Sparseness of language gives the reader or audience a chance to peer ever more deeply into the unsaid and unsayable. With few exceptions, when understatement takes the upper hand, dialogue resonates.

What follows is a superb example of the fewest possible words used to express the maximum possible feeling and meaning.

LOST IN TRANSLATION

Sofia Coppola wrote and directed LOST IN TRANSLATION when she was thirty-two. It was her fourth script to reach the screen and her second feature to direct. The film won numerous awards around the world, including an Oscar for Best Original Screenplay.

Coppola grew up surrounded by artists, she has traveled to Japan many times, and, like all of us, she has won and lost at love. So although it's fair to assume that personal experience influenced Coppola's storytelling, it would be a mistake to treat LOST IN TRANSLATION as autobiography. Rather, her writing expresses the widely read, finely tuned mind of an artist who uses fiction to express her insights into life's secret places.

In Coppola's minimalist writing, dialogue progression does not use arguments to sling words like stones (the conjugal hostilities of *A Raisin in the Sun*) or manipulations to weave words into a trap (Daisy's malicious feigning in *The Great Gatsby*). Instead, subtle, indirect, sparse language shapes implicit, virtually invisible but deeply felt conflicts that haunt her characters out of their pasts and into the present.

In the scene below, Coppola works into the inner selves and past selves of her characters simultaneously. She reveals both in each without resorting to choices under the pressure of dilemma.

Choices between irreconcilable goods and the lesser of two evils, once poised, are profoundly revealing of true character but relatively easy to dramatize. Coppola takes another path: Her characters are not in conflict with what life imposes but with the emptiness of what life denies. This quiet scene hooks, holds, and pays off without direct, indirect, or reflexive conflict.

SETUP

The key to creating a scene of minimum dialogue and maximum impact is its setup. If, prior to a scene, the storytelling has brought characters to crisis points in their lives, the reader/audience can sense their needs swirling in the subtext. These desires may or may not be conscious, but the reader/audience knows them, feels them, and waits in high tension to see how they play out. A well-prepared reader/audience reads chapters of content implied behind a phrase or gesture.

LOST IN TRANSLATION perfects this technique. The film's opening scenes crosscut to counterpoint dual protagonists: Charlotte, a recent Yale graduate, traveling with her photographer husband, versus Bob Harris, a middle-aged Hollywood star, famous for action roles. As the two settle into the Park Hyatt Tokyo, we see their differences of age (at least thirty years), fame (everyone ignores Charlotte; everyone fawns on Bob), and marriage (she needs her husband's attention; he wishes his wife would leave him alone).

That day, they notice each other in passing twice—once in an elevator and later in the lounge. That night, neither can sleep, so they make their way to the hotel bar where they meet by chance.

Scene Intentions

As the scene opens, Charlotte and Bob seem to share a simple need: to kill time over a drink. But if all they really wanted was a drink, they could have opened their minibars. Instead, an unthought wish for someone to talk to sends them out of their rooms. Once they see each other, their scene intention becomes: to kill time with talk.

Scene Values

As Charlotte nears Bob sitting at the bar, tension rises. Earlier that day, she and he exchanged a smile, but suppose he turns out to be an arrogant bore, or he discovers that she's a lunatic fan. The question "Should I talk to this stranger or drink alone?" runs through the minds of both.

Those doubts charge the tension of comfortable isolation versus risky intimacy that opens the scene and inflects their choices.

Once they dare to converse, however, a deeper, instinctive need inspires them to move from a chat to confession. As they reveal unpleasant home truths about themselves, intimacy wins out over isolation. That step then ignites yet another value: lost in life versus found in life. Lost/found becomes the story's core value.

As the film's title suggests, Bob and Charlotte, each in their own way, feel lost. When the scene opens, lost/found sits squarely at the negative. Over the course of the scene, it never touches the positive; rather, it sinks to the bleakness of Beat 15. At the same time, however, the charge of isolation/intimacy arcs toward the light and by the capping beat, their relationship touches an immediate and natural closeness.

At the end of each beat, I have scored its value charge (+) for positive, (-) for negative, (++) for doubly positive, etc.

Read the scene (printed in bold) straight through to get a feel of the dialogue's minimalist language. Then review it against my notes on the arc of its beats, subtext, and value charges.

INT. PARK HYATT BAR—NIGHT

Bob sits alone over a drink.

BEAT 1

BOB

(to the Barman)

He got married a couple of times to some nice women, beautiful women, too, I mean you and I would be crazy for these women, but there were always rumors. I never liked his acting, so I never gave a damn whether he was straight or not.

ACTION: Bob trying to impress the Barman.

REACTION: The Barman pretending he's impressed.

Intimacy/Isolation (-)

Rather than starting with that all-too-familiar image of a solitary man sitting at a bar, staring into the back of his head, Coppola opens the scene with showbiz chitchat. A Hollywood star gossiping to a Japanese Barman makes Bob's loneliness character-specific and poignant. This first beat hits an amusing note that counterpoints the dark beat that climaxes the scene.

BEAT 2

> Charlotte steps up to the bar. The Barman
> pulls out a stool near Bob.
>
> CHARLOTTE
> (to Barman)
> Thank you.
> (to Bob)
> Hi.
>
> (to Barman as she sits)
> Thanks.

ACTION: The Barman seating her.

REACTION: Charlotte fitting in.

Intimacy/Isolation (-)

When composing a scene, ask this question before committing to any line of dialogue: At this precise moment, what are my character's choices of action? Which tactic could she take? Which does she take? Every choice of tactic suggests a quality in the character's nature and determines the words she'll use to carry it out. Once again, dialogue is the outer result of inner action.

So, what are Charlotte's reactions, choices, and tactics as she enters this all-but-deserted bar and sees a world-famous movie star sitting on a stool alone? She could be intimidated and leave, she could give him his privacy and take a table, or she could sit within talking distance.

As the Barman offers her a stool, she makes the boldest choice of the three and joins Bob. Her choice to sit, at the risk of embarrassment, expresses poise.

BEAT 3

BARMAN

What can I get you?

CHARLOTTE

Hmmm . . . I'm not sure . . . hmmm.

ACTION: The Barman attending to her.
REACTION: Charlotte testing her welcome.
Intimacy/Isolation (-)

Again, choices: Charlotte could have ordered her favorite drink immediately. But tensed by the risk she's taking, she hesitates and gives Bob a chance to react. What he does now tells her whether or not she's actually welcome.

BEAT 4

BOB

(quoting his commercial)

For relaxing times, make it—

BOB & BARMAN

(in unison)

"Suntory time!"

CHARLOTTE
I'll have a vodka tonic.

Bob glances at her, impressed.

ACTION: Bob making her feel at home.
REACTION: Charlotte joining in.
REACTION: Bob endorsing her choice.
Intimacy/Isolation (+)

Bob's choice of self-ridicule makes her feel welcome. As she orders a serious drink, he nods in approval, and their sense of intimacy versus isolation moves toward the positive. Two strangers settle in to talk.

Bob's self-ridicule announces a character dimension: Actors take their work, even in commercials, seriously, but he chooses to mock himself. This choice of action reveals an inner contradiction between his artist's pride and self-disdain.

BEAT 5

CHARLOTTE
(to Bob as the Barman leaves for her
drink)
So what are you doing here?

BOB
Couple of things...Taking a break
from my wife, forgetting my son's
birthday, and, ah, getting paid two
million dollars to endorse a whiskey when I could be doing a play
somewhere.

CHARLOTTE
(staring in disbelief)
Oh.

ACTION: Charlotte inviting a conversation.
REACTION: Bob confessing to his three chief failures in life.
REACTION: Charlotte concealing her shock.
Lost/Found (--)

Charlotte opens a door to the unexpected. If you were her, imagine your reaction as you sit next to a world-famous movie star whom you think leads an enviable lifestyle, ask him how he's doing, and, offhandedly, he tells you that his life is misery. The phrase "taking a break" doesn't tell Charlotte whether Bob blames himself, his wife, or both for his marital problems, but he clearly damns himself for forgetting his son's birthday and, most of all, for corrupting his creative life by choosing money over art.

Bob's declaration of failure not only surprises Charlotte, but it crosses a red line—that formal distance we traditionally keep between strangers and ourselves. His trespass puts Charlotte under a bit of pressure. Now that the personal value of lost/found has entered the conversation, she wonders if she should take a giant step toward intimacy and add her confession to his. She does. Bob's revelation wrenches their chat into cycles of confession.

BEAT 6

BOB

But the good news is the whiskey
works.

She laughs.

ACTION: Bob soothing her feelings.
REACTION: Charlotte sympathizing.
Intimacy/Isolation (+)

This beat of mutual empathy takes them a smidge closer to intimacy. Bob's confession in Beat 5 upset her, but he's sensitive enough to see what he has done and regret it. He quickly softens the moment with a joke. She, in return, sees that he's embarrassed, so she laughs in sympathy to ease his chagrin.

BEAT 7

> ### BOB
> What are you doing?

> ### CHARLOTTE
> Hmmm, ah, my husband's a photographer, so he's working, and, hmmm, I wasn't doing anything, so I came along. And we have some friends who live here.

ACTION: Bob inviting her confession.
REACTION: Charlotte confessing to an empty, perhaps troubled personal life.
Lost/Found (--)

From the moment their eyes met in Beat 4, they communicate openly and honestly. Cocktail chat becomes in vino veritas. In Beat 5 Bob dared an intimate confession, and now he tempts her to join him. Once again choices: She could have replied, "Oh, I'm having a wonderful time. My husband's on a photo shoot and I'm enjoying some old friends." Instead, her passive, tepid phrases imply the unflattering truth of her married life. Bob reads her troubled subtext.

BEAT 8

> Bob lights her cigarette.
> ### BOB
> How long have you been married?

> **CHARLOTTE**
> Oh, thank you.
>
> (pause)
>
> Two years.

> **BOB**
> Twenty-five long ones.

ACTION: Bob readying his pass.
REACTION: Charlotte preparing to take it.
REACTION: Bob making his pass.
Intimacy/Isolation (--)

Charlotte has just confessed that her married life is unfulfilling, so Bob cannot resist making a pass at this beautiful young woman by complaining about his unfulfilled married life.

Note how Coppola has the older man make his move: He reacts to his own action. He asks Charlotte how long she's been married, knowing that whatever number she might name, he can top it with a quarter century of dissatisfaction.

Note also Charlotte's choice. As he lights her cigarette, she sees the pass coming and could have deflected it by answering, "Two wonderful years," or more aggressively, with a question of her own, "Why do you ask?" Instead, she lets it skate.

But make no mistake. This is a sexual proposition. How serious is hard to say. Bob could be doing it out of masculine ritual, but when a middle-aged guy laments his lengthy, less-than-happy marriage to a young woman at a bar, he's hoping for more than sympathy.

Bob's pass could push Charlotte away, but instead, she moves closer:

BEAT 9

> **CHARLOTTE**
> You're probably having a midlife
> crisis.

> (pause)
>
> Did you buy a Porsche yet?

> BOB
>
> (amused)
>
> You know, I was thinking about buying
> a Porsche.

ACTION: Charlotte foiling his pass.

REACTION: Bob complimenting her wit.

Intimacy/Isolation (+)

Charlotte knows his pass is halfhearted at best, and so she teases him about his age in order to say "No" with a touch of kindness. He graciously acknowledges her wit.

BEAT 10

> CHARLOTTE
>
> Twenty-five years . . . that's, ah . . .
> well, it's impressive.

> BOB
>
> Well, you figure, you sleep one-third
> of your life. That knocks off eight
> years of marriage right there. So
> you're, you know, you're down to
> sixteen and change, and, you know,
> you're just a teenager . . . like mar-
> riage . . . you can drive it, but you
> can . . . there's still the occasional
> accident.

> CHARLOTTE
>
> (laughing)
>
> Yeah . . .

ACTION: Charlotte offering a silver lining.

REACTION: Bob confessing his rocky marriage.

REACTION: Charlotte complimenting his wit.

Lost/Found (--)

From previous scenes, we know Charlotte has doubts about her husband and her future. When she tries to compliment Bob's marriage, he reminds her of a reality she knows from her own life: Relationships rarely live up to our dreams. Bob softens that harsh truth with a deft comparison of marriage to teen driving, but his cynical answer offers no hope. Nonetheless, Charlotte laughs to compliment his insight.

Note that Beats 4, 5, 8, and 10 play in three steps, rather than the conventional two. Normally, a new action immediately follows an action/reaction. Instead, these beats run action/reaction/reaction. When a reaction triggers yet another reaction, it often signals a deeper connection between the characters, a greater sense of intimacy.

As Oscar-winning screenwriter Philip Yordan put it: "Do not drown your script with endless dialogue and long speeches. Every question does not call for a response. Whenever you can express an emotion with a silent gesture, do so. Once you pose the question, permit it to linger before you get a reply. Or better yet, perhaps the character cannot reply; he or she has no answer. This permits the unspoken response to hang in midair."

BEAT 11

BOB

What do you do?

CHARLOTTE

Hmmm, I'm not sure yet actually. I
just graduated last spring.

BOB

And what did you study?

> **CHARLOTTE**
> Philosophy.

> **BOB**
> Well, there's a good buck in that
> racket.

> **CHARLOTTE**
> (embarrassed laugh)
> Yes...well, hmmm, so far it's pro
> bono.

ACTION: Bob inviting her personal story.
REACTION: Charlotte confessing to an unpromising future.
Lost/Found (--)

 Having made his second confession in Beat 10, Bob draws Charlotte out again, and she confesses that, like her personal life, her professional life is adrift.

BEAT 12

> **BOB**
> (laughs)
> Well, I'm sure you'll figure out the
> angles.

> **CHARLOTTE**
> (laughs)
> Yeah...

ACTION: Bob offering false hope.
REACTION: Charlotte laughing it off.
Intimacy/Isolation (+)
Lost/Found (-)

The world-weary Bob offers hope encrusted with irony. Charlotte's laugh lets him know she gets it, and then she needles him with:

BEAT 13

> **CHARLOTTE**
> I hope your Porsche works out.

> **Bob nods.**

ACTION: Charlotte also offering bogus hope.
REACTION: Bob signaling that he too gets it.
Intimacy/Isolation (++)
Lost/Found (--)
They both get it: Unhappy as they are, they won't lie to themselves. Sharing this tough truth draws them closer yet.

BEAT 14

> **CHARLOTTE**
> (toasting)
> Cheers to that.

> **BOB**
> Cheers to that. Kam pai.

ACTION: Charlotte celebrating their victory over self-deception.
REACTION: Bob joining her celebration.
Intimacy/Isolation (+++)
This upbeat gesture prepares for the downbeat turning point that caps the scene.

BEAT 15

```
    A long pause.

                    CHARLOTTE
    I wish I could sleep.


                      BOB
    Me, too.

    Another long pause.
```

ACTION: Charlotte confessing she feels lost within herself.
REACTION: Bob confessing that he, too, feels lost.
Lost/Found (---)
Intimacy/Isolation (++++)

The lines "I wish I could sleep" and "Me, too" intimate a subtext of suffering as moving as any I can remember.

Sleep restores sanity. Without it, existence becomes a mad, ticking clock. When you toss and turn, unstoppable racing thoughts send worries and fears swirling and churning through the mind. Charlotte and Bob cannot sleep. Why not? Jet lag? Racing thoughts?

In my reading of the subtext, their sleeplessness has a deeper cause. As their confessions reveal, they feel cast off from their marriages, adrift in their working lives, and at sea within themselves. A hollow place has opened up inside both that neither family nor work can fill. Charlotte and Bob have lost their purpose in life.

Character and Dialogue

As the film's title suggests, the co-protagonists cannot translate their emptiness into fullness; they cannot imagine their future; they cannot interpret life's absurdity into meaning. In more romantic times, Charlotte and Bob would have been known as "lost souls."

Notice how Coppola's aesthetic avoids verbal combat and uses casual, offhanded behavior to imply private battles waged behind a smile. She then squeezes vast content into the fewest, simplest mono-syllables: "Well, I'm sure you'll figure out the angles," and "Yeah, I hope your Porsche works out." How does she do it?

First, backstory. Like the scene from *The Museum of Innocence*, Coppola could have her characters narrate past conflicts vividly and explicitly. Instead, she keeps the dramas offscreen and implicit. Bob and Charlotte narrate three stories apiece—marriage, career, and private self. They end each storyline in a loss and do it with superb economy of language. Bob: "taking a break from my wife/endorsing a whiskey when I could be doing a play." Charlotte: "he's working and I wasn't doing anything." They tell each unhappy tale with a charm, wit, and self-mockery that guides us around their world-weary facades to their ongoing inner conflicts.

Second, the pause for subtext. Notice how Bob and Charlotte enter sentences on glides such as "Well...," "Yeah...," and "Yes...," put-ting a thought-filled mini-pause before most everything they say. The actors also space their words with vocalized moments of reflec-tion such as "Oh...," "Ah...," and "Hmmm...," plus non-vocalized reactions of laughter, nods, glances, pauses with eye contact, and pauses staring into space. These hesitations, short and long, halt the words coming out of the character and invite the audience inside. A mini-pause opens space for thought.

Third, naturalistic characterizations. In many of his lines, Bob Harris, a world-famous action actor, sounds in-character. Phrases such as "I never gave a damn whether he was straight or not," "figure the angles," "a good buck in that racket," and "the whiskey works" could have been said by any of the tough-guy characters he plays. Now they infuse his personality.

Charlotte's vocabulary, in sharp contrast to Bob's, consists of pas-sive verbs and generalized nouns, absent a single adjective, adverb, or superlative that might add color: "I hope," "I wish I could," and "I'm not sure" said twice. Her tone is pleasant but her vocabulary reflects her achromatic, motionless life.

Value Progression and Dialogue

Once we separate the activity of talk from the actions the characters take, the shape of the scene shines through, as escalating value charges progress the dialogue from the first beat to the last.

Coppola designed her scene as a downward spiral that builds its negative power three times over. She progresses it through a series of tumbling confessions that take loss from bad to worse to worst.

First, Bob confesses that as a husband and a father, he's a fraud, faking his way through his personal life (bad). Charlotte confesses that she's just tagging along after a husband who loves his work more than her (bad). Bob confesses that he's a sellout. He should be working as a serious actor; instead, he's pushing booze (worse). Charlotte admits that she has no career or even the plans for one, and so her life outside of marriage has no direction and no purpose (worse). Then the last beat takes them to the basement. They each confess that they cannot sleep (the worst).

By building the scene around confessions, Coppola peels away the characters' personae, so they can see each other for who they are. These lost souls confess to expose themselves. To be seen.

Why do these confessions feel progressive and not random? To begin with, Bob and Charlotte live parallel lives: Both have failed in all of life's arenas. Coppola then composes their confessions so that they alternate in descending order. Which is worse? A personal loss in your private relationships or a professional loss in your working life?

Professional failure. Why? Because failed relationships are a mutual loss. Neither person is entirely blameless, nor entirely at fault. When a relationship fails, you can lighten your load of guilt by heaping it on your partner.

When you lose in your chosen career, however, you know the fault is yours alone. We may make excuses and blame "the system" or bad luck, but in our heart of hearts we know that if we lose in our calling, it will be due to our lack of discipline, talent, knowledge, judgment, or hard work...the usual gaps that spell professional disaster.

But still, is professional failure always worse than relationship failure? Does losing a job mean more than breaking up a marriage? The key to the bar scene is a build toward a loss of identity. So the question is not one of getting or losing a job; it's one of gaining or losing your identity.

If, for example, a woman were married and had a job clerking at Walmart, then a loss of relationship may prove worse than being fired, because the woman's likely source of identity comes more from marriage than a job.

But neither of this film's characters identifies with a marital relationship. Bob and Charlotte find their identities in themselves as artists. Therefore, for Bob and Charlotte, professional failure is far worse than relationship failure. Charlotte has made no effort to even name her ambition, let alone build a career. Later in the film, she hints at wanting to be a writer, but to date, she hasn't written anything. Who but Charlotte is to blame for that? Bob is rich, famous, and in demand, but he chooses to waste his time and talent mugging for a liquor spot. Again, who but Bob is to blame for that?

Coppola's next twist of the knife is this: Which is worse? Professional failure or loss of self? Loss of self. Why? Because if we wanted to, we could decide that careers, fame, fortune, and even creative achievement are fleeting and illusionary. We could escape the public realm. Fine, but we have to live somewhere. If we cannot find our place in personal relationships, if we cannot find self-worth in professional achievement, what's left? We must look inside and find a life of value within our being.

The dilemma at the heart of LOST IN TRANSLATION creates an existential crisis. Bob and Charlotte have no visible reason to be unhappy. They seem well educated, well off, well married, and surrounded by friends—in Bob's case, by a world of fans. No, Bob and Charlotte are not lonely; they are lost.

The difference is this: You're lonely when you have something to share but no one to share it with. You're lost when you have nothing to share, no matter with whom you live. Of course, you can be both lonely and lost, but of the two, lost inflicts the greater pain.

Below are the beat by beat gerunds of action/reaction with the value charges they cause. Overall, the positive charges of isolation/intimacy alternate with the negative charges of lost/found to pace the scene dynamically without repetition:

BEAT 1: Impressing/Pretending
Intimacy/Isolation (-)
BEAT 2: Seating her/Fitting in
Intimacy/Isolation (-)
BEAT 3: Attending/Testing
Intimacy/Isolation (-)
BEAT 4: Welcoming/Joining/Endorsing
Intimacy/Isolation (+)
BEAT 5: Inviting/Confessing/Concealing
Lost/Found Life (--)
BEAT 6: Soothing/Sympathizing
Intimacy/Isolation (+)
BEAT 7: Inviting/Confessing
Lost/Found Life (--)
BEAT 8: Readying/Preparing/Making a pass
Intimacy/Isolation (--)
BEAT 9: Foiling/Complimenting
Intimacy/Isolation (+)
BEAT 10: Offering hope/Confessing/Complimenting
Lost/Found Life (--)
BEAT 11: Inviting/Confessing
Lost/Found Life (--)
BEAT 12: Offering false hope/Laughing it off
Intimacy/Isolation (+)
Lost/Found Life (-)
BEAT 13: Offering false hope/Shrugging it off
Intimacy/Isolation (++)
Lost/Found Life (--)
BEAT 14: Celebrating/Celebrating
Intimacy/Isolation (+++)
BEAT 15: Confessing/Confessing

Lost/Found Life (---)

Intimacy/Isolation (++++)

The personal revelations of losses in Beats 5, 7, 10, 11, 12, and 13 continually top each other in terms of the damage to their lives. In Beats 10 through 12, the characters' confessions become all the more honest and all the more sad. When Charlotte and Bob toast the wreckage in Beats 13 and 14, their newfound intimacy lifts the mood for an instant, but it turns sharply into the powerful irony of Beat 15.

In the pause that follows their third and most painful confession ("I wish I could sleep"/"Me, too"), each suddenly recognizes a kindred spirit. Their immediate desire is realized in Beat 15 as their lives shift from Isolation (-) to Intimacy (++++). With irony, of course: They can't sleep (--), but they can talk (++); they're lost souls (---) who connect with a mirror soul (++++).

When you survey the gerunds that name their actions, notice how Charlotte and Bob mirror each other. When two people sit at a bar, unconsciously imitating each other's posture and gestures, then echoing each other's subtextual actions, they connect with an intimacy they themselves may not realize.

The scene climaxes on an overall positive irony and a glimmer of hope. This quiet but surprisingly dynamic scene arcs from easy rapport to bleak loss to the possibility of love. The last beat hooks strong suspense for the rest of the film: Now that Bob and Charlotte have joined forces, will they grow into lives found?

19

MASTERING THE CRAFT

LISTEN

To master the technique of saying little but expressing much, first train your eye to see into the depths of the unsaid and the unsayable inside the people around you, then train your ear to hear the said. William Goldman, perhaps the finest writer of dialogue in film history, has often been complimented for having "the best ear in Hollywood." If you think about it, however, the expression "an ear for dialogue" seems odd.

The phrase conveys an image of a writer with reportorial or stenographic gifts riding on buses and listening to the people around him talking, and then writing down what they say quickly and accurately. Well, I know William Goldman, and it has been a long time since he got around New York on buses. But wherever Goldman finds himself, he listens in a writer's way, in depth, and so he hears far more than words said.

Listen to life. From infanthood on, the future writer actively listens to real-world voices—their rhythms, tones, and jargons. No matter where you are, now and then eavesdrop on people, take mental notes, or jot down interesting turns of phrase and what they imply.

Talking is doing. So like William Goldman, listen to people on two levels: text versus subtext, what they say versus what they do. Listen to their word choices and grammar, to the way they shape their talk. Listen to the way people use words not to reveal but to conceal their actions. When you sense the unspoken, you discover the subtle tactics people take. Listen deeper yet to the unsayable, to the drives and desires that move beneath awareness and motivate actions. Listen for strategy, for talk as a social ploy. Listen to the way one person uses words to cause another person to react in a way that furthers the speaker's desires.

When you put your ear to the wall of society, you soon learn that although dialogue is far more economical than talk, it's talk that builds your vocabulary. Our Internet-driven world forges marvelous new words by the minute. Terms like "tweet," "hashtag," "selfie," and "narcisstick" (a stick to lengthen your selfie reach) are inspired by technology. But compound puns like manspreading (splaying your legs to keep other people from sitting next to you on the bus), lumbersexual (a fashionably rugged guy), budtender (a server in a pot shop), and linguisticky (a difficult word) are born out of the natural love of talk. Listen for such words around you or make them up yourself, and then put them to work in your storytelling.

Second, read the good and rewrite the bad. Working writers spend much of their non-writing time nose-deep in a book. They read novels and plays, screen and television scripts. They watch and listen to dialogue performed onstage and onscreen, big and small. They develop an ear for dialogue as a by-product of all the stories they've read and seen, colored by all the living talk that's passed through their days.

Quentin Tarantino's dialogue strikes a brilliant balance between a natural sound and high expressivity. No one in reality has ever spoken the way Tarantino's characters talk, but audiences believe the patter as if it were recorded off the street. The imagistic dialogue of Tennessee Williams flows like wine from a decanter. No one can match novelist Elmore Leonard for creating high-styled repartee between lowlife characters. The dialogue of these renowned writers fits the ear like everyday talk, yet at the same time, expresses authentic characters with unique voices.

If, on the other hand, you find yourself reading a badly written script or book, don't dismiss the writer and toss his pages aside. Go back and rewrite him. Scratch out his words and insert your own. Rewriting bad dialogue is the fastest, most efficient way I know to train your talents.

WRITE IN-CHARACTER

Scenes can be imagined from two possible angles: outside in or inside out.

When an author writes from the outside in, she sits as if in an audience of one, tenth row center of her characters' lives, observing her own imagination at work, watching scenes, overhearing dialogue. Given free rein to improvise, this technique can generate unlimited variations on every possible event. The writer sorts through these choices, testing them by trial and error until she finds an ideal sequence of beats that shapes her scene to and around its turning point.

This objective method, open-minded and elastic as it is, risks superficiality. If the writer always stays on the outside, always imagines her characters "over there," her perceptions may shallow out and lose touch with the emotional currents that run through her characters' inner lives, driving them to action, and then from action to talk. As a result, her dialogue will fall victim to the many flaws of content and form.

For this reason, a writer also works from the inside out. She places herself at the center of her character's being, that irreducible core of humanity that answers to the name "Me." From this inner angle, she sees life through her character's eyes; she experiences her imaginary events.

In other words, the writer is the character's first actor. Writers are improvisationists who enter all of their characters—man, woman, child, beast—to shape them from the inside out. She becomes her character, alive in the now, struggling to get what she wants, emotions and urges surging, taking action after action against the forces that thwart her desires. She feels what her character feels, her pulse pounding apace with her character's heart. This subjective method of creating dialogue I call **writing in-character**.

To write in-character, use the legendary acting coach Constantin

Stanislavski's concept of the "Magic If." Do not ask, "If my character were in this situation, what would my character do?" because that puts you outside the role looking in. Do not ask, "If I were in this situation, what would I do?" because you are not the character. What you might feel, do, or say in any situation may have little or nothing to do with your character's behaviors. Instead, ask: "If I were my character in this situation, what would I do?" Create out of your own being, but not as yourself, as your characters.

In fact, when we look into the background of famous playwrights from Aristophanes to Shakespeare to Molière to Harold Pinter, we discover that they all began as actors. Acting, even for prose writers, may be the best preparation for the writing of dialogue.

In her biography of her father, Mamie Dickens describes watching her father, Charles Dickens, at work:

> I was lying on the sofa endeavoring to keep perfectly quiet, while my father wrote busily and rapidly at his desk, when he suddenly jumped from his chair and rushed to a mirror which hung near, and in which I could see the reflection of some extraordinary facial contortions which he was making. He returned rapidly to his desk, wrote furiously for a few moments, and then went again to the mirror. The facial pantomime was resumed, and then turning toward, but evidently not seeing, me, he began talking rapidly in a low voice. Ceasing this soon, however, he returned once more to his desk, where he remained silently writing until luncheon time. It was a most curious experience for me, and one of which, I did not until later years, fully appreciate the purport. Then I knew that with his natural intensity he had thrown himself completely into the character that he was creating, and that for the time being he had not only lost sight of his surroundings, but had actually became in action, as in imagination, the creature of his pen.[1]

To encourage your character to speak in a manner true to her nature, do as Dickens did: act her out. Let her thoughts flood your mind, and then shape her language in all the contours of vocabulary, grammar, syntax, diction, trope, phrasing, phonetics, idiom, and pace. Pay close attention to verbal details and create a one-of-a-kind voice that catches the audience's ear and lasts in its memory.

If, after that, you still find yourself mired in clichés, I have another suggestion. Turn your computer off and go take improvisation classes. If you can invent dialogue on your feet in front of a class, you can certainly do it sitting alone at your desk.

Once you have created a scene from the inside out, reimagine it from the outside in. To fully develop your craft, alternate imagining scenes from both angles. Lastly, sit back as if you were a first-time reader or audience and let the scene go to work on you.

Develop your dialogue skill by crafting words as an inner action that becomes an outer activity, and in those hours when your work flows smoothly from imagination to page, when you sense the rightness of your words, do not pause for analysis. Just keep moving. But if your scenes war with your senses, if confusion stifles creativity, what to do? Ask questions.

KEY QUESTIONS

During the crafting of dialogue, doubts naturally stream through the mind. For which sense do I write? The eye or the ear? Too much description may stall into portraiture; too much dialogue may drone into recitations. How much is too much? Too little?

Debates over design and purpose: What does this line do for my character? For the beat? The scene? My story? Like Lady Justice, blindfolded and poised with a sword in one hand and a scale in the other, every author weighs the balance of image versus word, of word versus silence, in every scene she judges.

Creativity isn't learning the right answers but asking the strongest questions. To take your newfound knowledge of scene and dialogue design into creative practice, I've laid out a list of questions to guide your writing and rewriting into the furthest depths and breadths your talents can reach. Whenever you are stuck, get back on track by posing the questions below from each and every character's point of view. Clear answers will not only renew momentum but also liberate your talent.

The answers to the following questions create the subtext that makes powerful dialogue possible:

Background desires: What complex of background desires surrounds the character's situation in life and his relationships with other characters? How do the background desires limit and control his choices of action and his use of language? What actions can he not take, at least not yet? What words can he not use, at least not yet?

Objects of desire: What does the character tell himself he wants in order to restore life's balance? Looking into the subtext, does he also have a subconscious desire? If so, how do these two desires contradict each other?

Super-intention: What need drives the character down his spine of action? Is it conscious only, or does another desire from his subconscious mind oppose him? Is he his own worst enemy?

Scene intentions: At this moment, what is the character's scene intention? What does he seem to want? For complex, multidimensional characters, also ask: What does he really want? What is his subconscious scene intention? Is his scene intention a step in his pursuit of his super-intention? In other words, does this scene make sense in light of the overall story arc?

Motivation: Why does this character want what he wants?

Scene driver: Who drives this scene and makes it happen?

Forces of antagonism: What are the sources of conflict in the scene? Do they come from within the character? Other characters? The setting?

Scene value(s): What value(s) is at stake in the character's life in this scene? What is the opening charge of the value(s)? The closing charge of value(s)?

Subtext: Beneath what the character seems to be doing, what is he actually doing? What tactics might the character use to pursue his scene intention?

Beats: What specific action does the character take in the subtext of each line? What reactions might these actions cause? On which side of the beat does this line play? Is it an action or a reaction?

Progression: How do the beats progress my scene? Do they progressively top each other?

Tactics: With these words, said in this way, what specific tactic is the character taking? What effect is he trying to cause?

Turning point: How does the scene's value(s) move in a positive/negative dynamic? Where is the scene's turning point? In what precise beat of behavior does the value(s) change to the final charge?

Deep character: How do the choices of action in this scene reveal the truth about my characters?

Scene progression: How does this scene progress my story?

These questions guide the final step:

Text: Outwardly, what would my character say in order to get what he wants? What words and phrases might the character use to help him carry out his tactics, actions, and reactions?

Exposition: What facts of history, society, and biography does this line contain? Are they dramatized invisibly or narratized explicitly? Do they come in too soon, too late, or at just the right moment?

Characterization: Do the characters' verbal styles match their particular personalities, backgrounds, and traits of characterization?

Ask and answer these questions on every beat. When in the middle of writing the scene's dialogue, ask and answer these questions again. After you've written the scene, ask and answer these questions for a third time. The best questions create the best answers.

LAST WORDS

The technique of writing in-character may, at first, seem daunting. But instinctively you've done this all your life. After every confrontation you've ever had with another person, what have you done? You've rerun the scene through your imagination, re-creating it and rewriting it the way it should have gone down. You've put yourself inside your own head and the head of your antagonist, and then imaginatively reinvented the conflict beat by beat. And I'll bet that your rewrites of life are always vivid, always effective. To write dialogue, you essentially do the same thing you do when you rewrite life.

To create character-specific dialogue, you need to gather knowledge of human behavior through close observations of people around you and through reading both fiction and nonfiction. On the balance, however, the source of all fine character writing is rooted in self-knowledge. As Anton Chekhov said: "Everything I know about human nature I learned from me."

Ultimately, you find your characters in yourself; you find their words in your imagination. Ask the Magic If: "If I were this character in these circumstances, what would I do? What would I say?" Then listen for the honest answer, for it is always correct. You would do and say the human thing.

The more you penetrate the mysteries of your own humanity, the more you're able to understand the humanity of others and the unique ways they express it. As your self-awareness grows, you will discover you can be many people. You can create them, act them, and speak in their voices.

"Here's looking at you, kid."

NOTES

Chapter One The Full Definition of Dialogue

1. John L. Austin, *How to Do Things with Words,* ed. J. O. Urmson and Marian Sbisà (Oxford, England: Oxford University Press, 1962).
2. Hjalmar Söderberg, *Doctor Glas,* trans. Paul Britten Austin (London: The Harvill Press, 2002).
3. James E. Hirsh, *Shakespeare and the History of Soliloquies* (Madison, New Jersey: Fairleigh Dickinson University Press, 2003).
4. Jay McInerney, *Bright Lights, Big City* (New York: Random House, 1984).
5. Bruce Norris, *Clybourne Park* (New York: Faber and Faber, Inc., 2011).
6. Jonathan Franzen, *The Corrections* (New York: Farrar, Straus and Giroux, 2001).

Chapter Two The Three Functions of Dialogue

1. Edward T. Hall, *The Silent Language* (New York: Anchor Books, 1973). First published 1959.
2. Elizabeth Bowen, *Afterthought: Pieces about Writing* (London: Longmans, 1962).

Chapter Three Expressivity I: Content

1. Edward T. Hall, *Beyond Culture* (New York: Anchor Books, 1977).

Chapter Four Expressivity II: Form

1. Peter Brook, *The Empty Space* (New York: Touchstone, 1968).
2. Yasmina Reza and Christopher Hampton, *The God of Carnage* (London: Faber and Faber Limited, 2008).
3. David Means, *Assorted Fire Events: Stories* (New York: Faber and Faber, Inc., 2000).

4. Robert Penn Warren, *All the King's Men* (New York: Harcourt, Brace and Co., 1946).

5. Ken Kesey, *One Flew Over the Cuckoo's Nest* (New York: Viking Press, 1964).

6. Julian Barnes, *The Sense of an Ending* (New York: Vintage Books, 2011).

Chapter Five *Expressivity III: Technique*

1. Ezgi Akpinar and Jonah Berger, "Drivers of Cultural Success: The Case of Sensory Metaphors," *Journal of Personality and Social Psychology*, 109(1) (Jul 2015), 20–34.

2. Malcolm Gladwell, *Blink* (New York: Little, Brown and Company, 2005).

3. David Means, *Assorted Fire Events: Stories* (New York: Faber and Faber, Inc., 2000).

4. Norman Mailer, *An American Dream* (New York: The Dial Press, 1964).

5. Yasmina Reza and Christopher Hampton, *Art* in *Yasmina Reza: Plays 1* (London: Faber and Faber Limited, 2005).

6. William Strunk Jr. and E. B. White, *The Elements of Style* (London: Longman, 1997).

Chapter Six *Credibility Flaws*

1. A. H. Maslow, "A Theory of Human Motivation," *Psychological Review*, 50 (1943), 370–96.

2. Michael Burleigh, *Sacred Causes* (New York: HarperCollins, 2006).

Chapter Seven *Language Flaws*

1. Betty Kirkpatrick, *The Usual Suspects and Other Clichés* (London: A & C Black Academic and Professional, 2005).

2. George Orwell, "Politics and the English Language," *Horizon Magazine*, 13 (1946).

Chapter Eleven *Four Case Studies*

1. Mark Van Doren, *Shakespeare* (New York: Doubleday, 1965).

2. Robert McKee, *Story: Substance, Structure, Style and the Principles of Screenwriting* (New York: ReganBooks, HarperCollins, 1997).

3. McKee, *Story*.

Chapter Twelve *Story/Scene/Dialogue*

1. McKee, *Story*.

2. McKee, *Story*.

3. McKee, *Story*.

4. McKee, *Story*.

5. Hall, *Beyond Culture.*

6. McKee, *Story.*

7. McKee, *Story.*

8. McKee, *Story.*

9. McKee, *Story.*

10. McKee, *Story.*

11. McKee, *Story.*

Chapter Fourteen Comic Conflict (FRASIER)

1. Marvin Carlson, *Theories of the Theatre* (Ithaca and London: Cornell University Press, 1984).

Chapter Seventeen Reflexive Conflict (Fräulein Else and The Museum of Innocence)

1. Bruce Hood, *The Self Illusion* (New York: Oxford University Press, 2012).

2. David Eagleman, *Incognito: The Secret Lives of the Brain* (New York: Pantheon Books, 2011).

3. Jurgen Ruesch and Gregory Bateson, *Communication: The Social Matrix of Psychiatry* (New York: W. W. Norton & Co, 1987).

Chapter Eighteen Minimal Conflict (LOST IN TRANSLATION)

1. This phrase originated in the line "Well, less is more, Lucrezia: I am judged" from Robert Browning's dramatized poem "Andrea del Sarto" (1855).

Chapter Nineteen Mastering the Craft

1. Mamie Dickens, *Charles Dickens* (Charleston, South Carolina: Nabu Press, 2012).

INDEX

ABOUT THE AUTHOR

Robert McKee, a Fulbright Scholar, is the world's most sought-after lecturer in the art of story. Over the last 30 years, he has mentored screenwriters, novelists, playwrights, poets, documentary makers, producers, and directors. McKee alumni include over 60 Academy Award winners, 200 Academy Award nominees, 200 Emmy Award winners, 1000 Emmy Award nominees, 100 Writers Guild of America Award winners, and 50 Directors Guild of America Award winners.

MISSION STATEMENT

Twelve strives to publish singular books, by authors who have unique perspectives and compelling authority. Books that explain our culture; that illuminate, inspire, provoke, and entertain. Our mission is to provide a consummate publishing experience for our authors, one truly devoted to thoughtful partnership and cutting-edge promotional sophistication that reaches as many readers as possible. For readers, we aim to spark that rare reading experience—one that opens doors, transports, and possibly changes their outlook on our ever-changing world.

12 Things to Remember about TWELVE

1. Every Twelve book will enliven the national conversation.
2. Each book will be singular in voice, authority, or subject matter.
3. Each book will be carefully edited, designed, and produced.
4. Each book's publication life will begin with a month-long launch; for that month it will be the imprint's devoted focus.
5. The Twelve team will work closely with its authors to devise a publication strategy that will reach as many readers as possible.
6. Each book will have a national publicity campaign devoted to reaching as many media outlets—and readers—as possible.
7. Each book will have a unique digital strategy.
8. Twelve is dedicated to finding innovative ways to market and promote its authors and their books.
9. Twelve offers true partnership with its authors—the kind of partnership that gives a book its best chance at success.
10. Each book will get the fullest attention and distribution of the sales force of the Hachette Book Group.
11. Each book will be promoted well past its on-sale date to maximize the life of its ideas.
12. Each book will matter.